NOEL SKELTON AND THE PROPERTY-OWNING DEMOCRACY

NOEL
SKELTON

AND THE PROPERTY-OWNING
DEMOCRACY

To Nick —
I'll buy you lunch if
you actually end up
reading this!

Best wishes

David

DAVID TORRANCE

biteback ᵛᵛ

First published in Great Britain in 2010 by
Biteback Publishing Ltd
Heal House
375 Kennington Lane
London
SE11 5QY

ISBN 978-1-84954-011-7

10 9 8 7 6 5 4 3 2 1

A CIP catalogue record for this book is available from the British Library.

Set in Constantia
Printed and bound in Great Britain by xxx

CONTENTS

ACKNOWLEDGEMENTS

'For most political biographers . . . the ideal subject is an, as yet, unwritten major figure,' observed the political historian D. R. Thorpe in 2007. 'The problem, as for mountaineers, is that the number of virgin Himalayan peaks is rapidly diminishing. Often the only alternative is to explore a hitherto unknown, but lesser range.'[1]

Noel Skelton is, I think, both an 'unwritten major figure' and an occupant of the 'hitherto unknown, but lesser range' of Himalayan peaks described by Thorpe. That made researching and writing his life hugely rewarding. Although the idea was my own, Thorpe's encouragement was invaluable in making sure it actually happened. Also essential was the generous financial assistance provided by Henry Angest (kindly facilitated by Murdo Fraser MSP) and the Scottish Unionist Association Trust (cheerfully organised by Ann Hay) towards the cost of publication. I am, of course, particularly grateful to Iain Dale and all his colleagues at Biteback Publishing for agreeing to publish the result of my exploration.

Alas, occupants of the lesser ranges also leave behind fewer sources, thus illustrating certain aspects of Skelton's life proved a major challenge. This means that the initial chapter is a little thin on detail, for which I apologise in advance. Otherwise, thanks must go to Elaine Mundill, the archivist at Glenalmond College in Perth, who tracked down details of Skelton's schooldays; to Yvonne and all the staff at the A. K. Bell Library in Perth for their help and enthusiasm in helping me chart Skelton's career as the city's MP; and particularly to Lord Crathorne, who kindly granted access to letters from Skelton to his late aunt, Baroness Elliot of Harwood, which form perhaps the single most important source in this book. Papers and other sources held at the National Archives of Scotland, the National Library of Scotland, the Senate House Library at the University of London and the British Library allowed me to flesh out the remaining aspects of Skelton's political and personal life. Thanks also to the Macmillan Trustees for allowing me to quote from three letters among the Macmillan Papers at the Bodleian Library in Oxford, and to Colin Harris for taking the time to locate them.

As ever, friends, family and colleagues proved vital in proof-reading the manuscript and saving me from various errors of fact and interpretation. Nick Lee, my good friend Douglas Pattullo, D. R. Thorpe and my brother Michael all read the complete text and offered various insights and suggestions. All remaining mistakes are, of course, my own responsibility. Thanks also to my friends Philip Atkinson and Alice Foulis for their hospitality during a research trip to Yarm in North Yorkshire, and a big thank you to my friend and former housemate James Douse, who never lost faith in this project even when I did. He tirelessly tracked down source material, printed off draft manuscripts and helped make my pitch a little more exciting, for which I will be forever grateful.

It was not always easy to convince people that Noel Skelton deserved a biography but here it finally is, more than four years after I found myself becoming intrigued by the uncharted life of a long-forgotten political figure. Hopefully, if only in a small way, I have helped rescue him from the thankless obscurity of an historical footnote.

David Torrance
Edinburgh, March 2010

FOREWORD

Noel Skelton was one of the most unsung and under-rated figures of twentieth-century Conservatism. A biography has long been one of the great gaps in modern political biography, a gap now superbly filled by David Torrance, whose deep knowledge of Conservative history, and in particular Scottish Conservatism, makes him ideally qualified for the task. His book *The Scottish Secretaries* (2006), a study of those who have headed the Scottish Office from its inception, showed his flair for research and the use of telling details. These qualities are no less evident in this pioneering biography of Noel Skelton.

'Progressive conservatism', to counter the growth of socialism, was Skelton's abiding aim. His booklet *Constructive Conservatism* (1924) inspired a whole generation of emerging Conservative figures, notably two future Prime Ministers, Anthony Eden and Alec Dunglass (later Douglas-Home), who looked to him as their inspiring mentor. When I was writing the biographies of Eden and Douglas-Home this became very clear to me and I found evidence in their papers of the importance of Skelton in their political philosophy. Indeed Alec Douglas-Home told me that had Skelton not died prematurely in 1935 he could well have been a future leader of the party. This was also the opinion of Kay Elliot, Walter Elliot's widow, who kindly let me study her papers for my Douglas-Home biography, which were full of Skelton letters and some election leaflets from a vanished age. One acrostic read:

Skelton is the workers' friend;
Keeps his promise to the end;
Ever faithful, ever sure,
Longs to make our joys secure,
Tries to bring to all content,
Our 'Ideal' for Parliament,
None so fit to represent.

Noel Skelton's most famous concept was enshrined in his declaration: 'Until our educated and politically minded democracy has become a property-owning democracy, neither the national equilibrium nor the balance of the life of the individual will be restored.' After the war, when the Conservatives were rebuilding in opposition, Anthony Eden used Skelton's phrase about the 'property-owning democracy' in his famous speech to the Conservative Party conference at Blackpool on 3 October 1946. And, of course, on the Conservatives' return to office in 1951 Harold Macmillan, whose 'middle way' approach was much influenced by Skelton, made the Skelton vision reality when the team he led at the Ministry of Housing built 300,000 houses a year. On the eve of the 1964 general election, Eden, in retirement, urged Douglas-Home to remember that a 'property-owning democracy' must always remain a central aim. But there was no need for such a reminder. Alec Home had never forgotten what Skelton had done in giving the Conservatives a progressive agenda to improve the condition of the people, and those who now read this excellent book will not forget it either.

D. R. Thorpe
Brasenose College, Oxford, January 2010

A PROPERTY-OWNING DEMOCRACY

He had the ear of Stanley Baldwin, served in the National government of Ramsay MacDonald, impressed the future Prime Minister Neville Chamberlain, profoundly influenced Anthony Eden, Harold Macmillan and Sir Alec Douglas-Home, and indirectly guided Margaret Thatcher, yet today Noel Skelton is largely forgotten.

He also coined the memorable phrase 'a property-owning democracy', which remained his rallying cry throughout a short political career tragically curtailed by his death from cancer aged only fifty-five (it is also the only quote from Skelton included in the *Oxford Dictionary of Political Quotations*). As a basis for Conservative ideology, it has proved remarkably durable. In his book *Ideologies of Conservatism*, E. H. H. Green argued that Conservative thought, and studies thereof, had been completely overlooked by political academics and historians. This was symptomatic of the notion that the Conservative Party was somehow 'non-ideological', or as J. S. Mill famously described it, 'the stupidest party'. The widespread view was that Conservatives wanted to conserve national institutions and practices in spite of modern developments, and were not interested in deep reflection on the meaning of politics or articulating a set of principles. One Marxist scholar even said that 'the Tory tradition is not best understood as a tradition of ideas'. Curiously, contemporaries of Skelton seemed to concur. In the 1920s Walter Elliot noted that Conservatism was based on 'an observation of life and not a priori reasoning', while the novelist John Buchan stated that Conservatism was 'above all things a spirit not an abstract doctrine'.[1]

It is true that the Conservatives were guilty of complacency when it came to articulating their party's ideology or raison d'être, despite the efforts of Disraeli and Salisbury in the Victorian era. But then, the 1906 Liberal landslide aside, the Conservatives were the dominant party of government and probably did not see a pressing need to do so. By the early 1920s, however, it seems as if the Conservatives – faced with a new electoral structure and increasingly popular, not to mention ideologically opposed, political competition – began to reassess their priorities. Furthermore, following the economic recession of 1921 and its associated social problems, the natural party of government simply had to formulate a coherent ideological response.

Skelton was among the first to do this. Blackwoods published his influential blue-covered pamphlet, *Constructive Conservatism*, in 1924. Others followed: Robert Boothby, Harold Macmillan, John Loder and Oliver Stanley's *Industry and the State* in 1927, Walter Elliot's *Toryism and the Twentieth Century* the same year, Arthur Bryant's *The Spirit of Conservatism* in 1929 and, much later, Harold Macmillan's *The Middle Way* in 1938.

But Skelton's was the first, and introduced to the political lexicon a phrase – 'a property-owning democracy' – which is still in use today, although its meaning has changed over time. The sentiment had distinguished roots. In c. 335 BC Aristotle wrote in his *Politics* that 'it is a happy state of affairs when those who take part in the life of the state have a moderate but adequate amount of property', for the alternative was either 'extreme democracy or unmixed oligarchy'. Contemporary Conservative literature – most notably *The Landless People* and *Are You a Capitalist?*, both of which appeared in 1922 – also emphasised the importance of wider ownership. So Skelton's idea was not entirely new, but consistent with a longstanding Conservative defence of property together with ideas about the benefits and responsibilities of ownership.

The phrase was first embraced by a group of young Conservative MPs during the 1924–9 parliament. Speaking on 'The Future of Conservatism' at the 1912 Club in early 1926, Harold Macmillan said the 'only answer to socialism was to build up by every possible means a property-owning democracy',[2] while by 1931 the Conservative leader Stanley Baldwin was using the expression in his speeches. The suggestive soundbite also appealed to the writer-politician John Buchan, a longstanding friend of Skelton's. In a 1933 speech Buchan said he 'believed in a property-owning democracy. Unless a man owned a certain amount of property he could not have real freedom. The vital task before a civilised state was not to do things for a man, but to put him in a position to do things for himself.'[3] Importantly, Skelton et al. were referring to a democracy that owned land and industry rather than housing.

Skelton's phrase fell into disuse during the remainder of the 1930s and for most of the Second World War, perhaps because other, more pressing, political issues took precedence over property ownership and definitions of Conservative ideology. Anthony Eden is widely credited with having revived it at the 1946 Conservative Party conference in Blackpool, when he called for the creation of a 'nationwide property-owning democracy', this time more explicitly linked to home ownership. The politician Terence O'Neill – a future Prime Minister of Northern Ireland – even boasted in 1950 that so 'far as the country areas are concerned, Ulster is already a property-owning democracy',[4] presumably a reference to the province's mosaic of private farm holdings.

The three pregnant words first appeared in a Conservative Party manifesto that same year. *This Is the Road* stated that 'we intend to help all those who wish to own a house of their own or a smallholding. A true property-owning democracy must be based upon the wide distribution of private property, not upon its absorption in the State machine.' Clement Attlee, the Labour Prime Minister, tried to turn the meaning of the phrase on its head, arguing that 'you have much more of a property-owning democracy than when we came into power: the railways, the Bank of England, and the coal mines – and a lot more things you will own presently'.[5] Eden retorted that 'of course nationalisation does not result in a property-owning democracy; it is the exact opposite . . . For instance, in Soviet Russia there is complete state ownership of all means of production, distribution and exchange. But nobody would suggest that Soviet Russia is a property-owning democracy. On the contrary, it is a property-denying state.'[6] And the MP for North Lanarkshire, Peggy Herbison, said that although Conservatives talked of a property-owning democracy, 'they really mean buying privilege with money. We believe in a property-owning democracy in the best sense of these terms.'[7] Both left and right now claimed to be the true guardians of Skelton's ideal.

It also began to attract international attention. In 1950 the Prime Minister of New Zealand announced government plans for encouraging private building and home ownership, a policy he said was 'part of the Government programme for a property-owning democracy giving the widest spread of individual ownership to the people'.[8] But unlike his British counterparts, he actually had some practical proposals, including an increase in the maximum loan for house building and a suspensory loan of 10 per cent to help offset high building costs. By 1957 the National Party in New Zealand was still using the phrase, while in 1960 the West German government – or more specifically the Christian Democratic Union – also took it up. Further afield, in 1974 Raja Tan Sri Mohar, special economic adviser to Tun Abdul Razak, the Prime Minister of Malaysia, proclaimed: 'We want a property-owning democracy. The Government is doing everything possible.'[9]

In 1955 Anthony Eden succeeded Churchill as Conservative leader and Prime Minister, using his first speech as premier to reaffirm his belief in Skelton's maxim. 'As the people grow to feel they are part of this property-owning democracy,' he said, 'then the appeal of socialism will mean less and less to them. That is the true message we have to carry to our people.'[10] In the general election that followed Eden's elevation the phrase completed its shift across the political spectrum, appearing in both the Labour and Tory manifestos. The Labour leader, Harold Wilson, even criticised successive Conservative governments for not making enough progress towards achieving this goal in 1963, arguing that building societies were refusing to give enough people mortgages because they earned too little. 'This rules out a high proportion of manual workers, most teachers, young civil servants and very many other white-collar workers,' he said. 'This is what the property-owning democracy is meaning in practice.'[11] And early the following year, Wilson said that 'despite all their talk about a property-owning democracy, there were 60,000 fewer mortgages than in 1959'.[12]

The Conservative manifesto for the October 1974 general election, *Putting Britain First*, proclaimed: 'The Conservative ideal is a property-owning democracy.' From then on, the phrase was reclaimed not just by traditional Conservatives, but also by a new breed later known as Thatcherites. The so-called right to buy, which appeared in Margaret Thatcher's 1979 Housing Bill, was infused with Skeltonian rhetoric. In her 1981 party conference speech, Thatcher boasted that the 'fact that over 55 per cent own their own homes is a tribute to successive Conservative governments. Each one of which has helped to build the property-owning democracy.'[13] But Skelton was, by the beginning of the 1980s, forgotten by all but a few ageing statesmen like Harold Macmillan, and authorship of the phrase was regularly misattributed to better-known figures like Eden and Iain Macleod.

By 2006, for example, the 'property-owning democracy' was even credited by the new Conservative leader David Cameron to Baroness Thatcher. Although the aim was by then largely a reality, it did not necessarily bring with it Conservative voters, as Thatcher had discovered in the 1980s. The battle for a property-owning democracy had been won – now the contemporary political fight was for another media catchphrase, that of 'affordable housing'.

As Chancellor, Gordon Brown needed no convincing of Skelton's phrase as a useful slogan in this context. 'Property-owning democracy, an asset-owning democracy,' he enthused during an interview, going on to echo Harold Wilson's criticisms. 'I would say a home-owning, asset-owning, wealth-owning democracy is what would be in the interests of our country . . . The problem is that even with the great ambitions of the 1950s or the 1980s they [the Conservatives] did not succeed in widening the scope for home ownership to large numbers of people who want[ed] it.'[14]

Altogether, the story of Skelton's ideal, 'a property-owning democracy', is a narrative of modern British politics.

ONE

'THE HERO OF A DISRAELI NOVEL COME TO LIFE' (1880–1922)

The family into which Archibald Noel Skelton was born on 1 July 1880 was at the heart of Edinburgh's literary and administrative life. At its head was John Skelton, a prominent essayist, historian, advocate and civil servant. His wife, Noel's mother, was Anne, daughter of James Adair Lawrie, a professor of surgery at Glasgow University. Together they leased the Hermitage of Braid, a mansion situated near the left bank of the Braid Burn on the outskirts of the Scottish capital. This house, rich in literary associations, was to be Noel's childhood home.

A few months before Noel was born, Benjamin Disraeli, leader of the Conservative Party, had been defeated by William Gladstone at the 1880 general election. The latter's second Midlothian campaign had returned the Liberals to political dominance, including the Edinburgh constituency in which the Skelton family lived. In 1868 Disraeli, himself a literary man, had appointed John Skelton secretary of the Scottish Board of Supervision, which administered laws relating to the poor and public health, it was assumed because of his admiration for Skelton's literary work, which included essays and reviews under the pseudonym of 'Shirley' in *Fraser's Magazine*. A year after his appointment, Skelton expressed his gratitude in print, albeit anonymously, with a sympathetic sketch of his patron,

Benjamin Disraeli: The Past and the Future . . . by a Democratic Tory.

Fittingly, Disraeli would later become one of the most important influences upon Noel Skelton's political philosophy, particularly his maxim that if the Conservative Party was 'not a national party, it is nothing'. Years later, Lady Tweedsmuir would even liken Skelton to 'the hero of a Disraeli novel come to life'.[1]

Noel was the youngest of three sons, succeeding his elder brothers James and John Henry by several years. The census of 1881 also records two daughters called Evelyn Margaret (with whom Skelton would later live) and Mary Janet. The Hermitage of Braid was well equipped for the large Skelton family, with five servants (including a coachman) and extensive grounds in which its younger members could play.

In the year Noel celebrated his tenth birthday, his father published *The Handbook of Public Health* and *The Local Government (Scotland) Act in Relation to Public Health*, having administered the Public Health Act of 1867, for which he compiled a special edition of the act with notes. John Skelton also consolidated his literary reputation with a series of historical works in defending Mary, Queen of Scots. In 'his historical work', notes Skelton's entry in the *Dictionary of National Biography*, 'he characteristically displayed something of the spirit of the advocate'.[2]

Of his more purely literary works the best known were *The Essays of Shirley* (1882) and *The Table Talk of Shirley* (1895). This 'table talk' consisted chiefly of conversations with personal friends and literary contemporaries at the Hermitage of Braid. Quaint, almost eccentric, in treatment, Skelton's essays were popular with authors as disparate as William Thackeray, Leonard Huxley and Thomas Carlyle. James Froude, Carlyle's biographer and Skelton's editor at *Fraser's Magazine*, formed a particularly close intimacy with 'Shirley' and was a frequent visitor to the Hermitage. 'An evening or two with you in your beautiful glen will be better than any quantity of idle dinner-party talk,' he wrote to Skelton in March 1876, and in 1884 he was exultant at the prospect of another visit. 'I shall be delighted to see the old Hermitage again,' Froude wrote, 'and you and Mrs Skelton and your little ones, now grown into big ones. Your house, I am afraid, like every other, will be crammed.'[3]

John Skelton was clearly a profound influence on one particular 'little one', his son Noel. Speaking against the Reorganisation of Offices (Scotland) Bill – which proposed the abolition of the Scottish Board of Health on grounds of 'inefficiency' – in 1928, Skelton recalled his father's role in the administrative tapestry of the Scottish capital:

> Among the friends of my younger days there were few I valued more than Sir James Palten MacDougall, head of the Local Government Board. My father was Secretary and Chairman for thirty-one years of the predecessors of the present Board of Health. I am not going to talk about anything that happened so long ago as thirty-one years, but I mention these facts to show that, living more or less in the milieu of the Office in Edinburgh, I never heard it suggested that it was inefficient.[4]

In 1887 John Skelton was created CB (and KCB in 1897, although he died before he could be invested). He retained the post of secretary to the Board of Supervision until 1892, when he was elected chairman, and in 1894 became vice-president of its successor body, the Local Government Board for Scotland. Sir John served until his retirement in March 1897, dying just four months later at the Hermitage of Braid.[5]

More than a year earlier, in January 1896, Noel Skelton had arrived at Trinity College, Glenalmond (it later became simply, Glenalmond College) as a boarder. He was one of 152 pupils in an independent school founded by William Gladstone and J. R. Hope (later Hope-Scott of Abbotsford). Situated on the river Almond near the village of Methven, Glenalmond was about 8 miles west of Perth, the town which Skelton would later represent in the House of Commons. Although Skelton grew up, and lived for most of his life in Edinburgh, he would often refer to Perth as his spiritual home.

Skelton was placed in the higher stream of pupils – the 'Classical side' – quickly progressing from the Classical IV form under the tutelage of Mr Farquharson to Classical VI in October 1897, Queen Victoria's Diamond Jubilee year and Glenalmond's fiftieth. He appears to have been a rounded pupil, winning prizes for modern languages and mathematics while being recognised, in his final year, for his talent as a solo vocalist. Skelton was also secretary of the college's Natural History Society and a founder member of its Ornithological Society, beginning a life-long interest in nature. Sport, however, did not figure in his milieu.

Skelton also prepared for his future political career by becoming an active member of Glenalmond's Debating Society. In the *Glenalmond Chronicle* of December 1897, he is reported as having proposed the motion that 'bicycling is a public nuisance and calculated to prove injurious to the human race'. He also spoke for the motion that 'modern warfare demands less courage than warfare in the time of Caesar', and on another occasion he addressed the house against the motion that 'a Modern Side education fits one better for the world than a Classical Side education', and seconded the motion that 'free service is better than conscription'. In his final term, Skelton spoke against the motion that 'in the opinion of this House, fashion is a form of slavery'.[6]

Glenalmond's motto was *Floreat Glenalmond* ('Let Glenalmond Flourish'), a maxim Skelton also applied to himself. In 1898 he secured the double honour of being appointed a college prefect and winning an Open History Scholarship of £80 per annum to Christ's College (otherwise known as Christ Church), Oxford.[7] The money would have been welcome, as following the death of Sir John, Skelton's mother was living off her own means. Considering Skelton's classical bent, it is curious that he opted for modern history, especially given that all previous Oxford scholarships awarded to Glenalmond boys had been for the classics. Nevertheless, Skelton left 'Coll', as the school was affectionately known by pupils and staff, following two successful years.

Skelton, who as a scholar made up about one third of the undergraduates at Christ Church, went down to Oxford having been selected from among the ablest school leavers (then exclusively male) in the country. By the time he arrived in the City of Dreaming Spires, the college curriculum of classics and maths had long been expanded to include a range of other subjects, including Skelton's chosen field of modern history.

Although still a cathedral foundation, Christ Church had begun to admit non-Anglicans and, from the 1890s, more and more students arrived from abroad. Skelton – who was presumably, like his father, an Episcopalian – was probably accommodated in the Meadow Buildings, a Venetian Gothic construction designed by T. N. Deane, which was put up to accommodate more undergraduates on campus. The college's picture-lined dining hall and the 'Tom' quadrangle were among the most impressive in Oxford.

In addition to his formal studies Skelton was active in the Cardinal Club, a debating society, and was honorary secretary for a while without being active in debates. Skelton appears in the club photographs of 1900, 1901 and 1902 (and he was listed as a member for 1903), hatless but otherwise smartly dressed with a double-breasted waistcoat. Slim and rather gaunt, he had already begun slicking his dark hair straight back.

Skelton was placed in the second class in the School of Modern History at Christ Church in 1902. On returning to Scotland he studied for a second degree, this time in law, at the University of Edinburgh. There he attended another debating club, called the Speculative Society (of which Skelton's father had been a member in the mid-1850s). Skelton was introduced on 15 December 1903 and attended reasonably diligently, revealing an interest in Irish affairs by delivering essays on 'The Threshold – some considerations on the present political situation in Ireland' and 'Two great leaders of men, O'Connell and Parnell'. By March 1906 he proposed in debate that the new Liberal government (formed following the resignation of Arthur Balfour as Prime Minister in late 1905) was 'unworthy of the confidence of the country', while in November Skelton spoke in favour of establishing a standard minimum wage.

On 21 December 1906 Skelton was called to the Scottish Bar, and thus became a member of the Faculty of Advocates, as had his father half a century before. He continued to attend the Speculative Society, always rich with lawyers, and became a permanent member on 8 January 1907, although not without experiencing some youthful mischief. 'On a ballot being taken the black balls were found to exceed the white balls by a greater number than there were members present and on [a] motion . . . the ballot was declared void,' recorded the Society's minutes. 'On a second ballot being taken Mr Skelton was duly accorded extraordinary privileges.'[8]

During the January–February 1906 general election campaign, after which the Liberal government of Sir Henry Campbell-Bannerman was re-elected with a landslide majority, Skelton made several platform speeches in favour of the Unionist (or Conservative)[9] candidate for the Eastern Division of Perthshire, the Hon. A. D. Murray, and by 1907 he had become a regular speaker on the Unionist platform circuit. His legal work, meanwhile, consisted mainly of contested wills and unremarkable divorce cases.

The year 1910 saw two general elections as a result of the constitutional crisis which followed the defeat of David Lloyd George's 'People's Budget' by the House of Lords. Skelton was a candidate at the second poll, held in December 1910, which opened the last chapter in Balfour's leadership of the Unionist Party. Together with his father's patron, Disraeli, the philosopher-politician Balfour was one of Skelton's chief political influences. The December election reopened a bitter internal party feud. Joseph Chamberlain's tariff reform campaign, launched in 1903, had pitted the Unionist Party's free-traders against those who believed that some form of imperial protection was essential to integrate the British Empire's economy. Furthermore, the protectionists saw tariffs, including duties on food, as the only way to pay for the social reforms necessary to make the imperial race fit for the twentieth century. Speaking at a 'smoking concert' under the auspices of the Central Edinburgh Unionist Association in early November 1910, Skelton revealed himself as an advocate of protection and tariff reform. Next June, he said, the Colonial and Imperial Conference would meet in London and again recommend protection, but 'could only regard the possibility of a Radical [Liberal] Government being in power in June 1911 with the greatest misgiving'.[10]

A special joint meeting of the Conservative and Liberal Unionist Associations for East Perthshire (the two parties would merge formally in 1912) convened on 21 November 1910 to confirm Skelton as its candidate. He gave a short address before Colonel Smythe of Methven moved the motion that Skelton be adopted. The motion was unanimously agreed to. He opened his campaign at Bridge of Cally two days later, telling a crowded meeting that 'the cause of the Unionist party was a national and democratic one' and that its proposals 'for the reform of the Lords were more democratic and infinitely more statesmanlike than the absurd schemes of the Radicals'. 'The only change required to make the second chamber as representative as any other in the world was in its composition,' he continued, while welcoming Balfour's pledge that 'when the reconstructed Lords had disagreement with the Commons on an important measure, the government should not require to have a dissolution, but that that measure should be immediately referred to the people by means of the referendum'.[11] Thus was born one of Skelton's abiding political interests.

A 'large and very enthusiastic meeting' in the Town Hall at Alyth was also treated to the fledgling candidate's oratory, this time on the issue of tariff reform. Responding to questions, Skelton admitted 'that the present election was a referendum. The extent to which Germany had overtaken us was a clear proof of the value of tariff reform.' He admitted that the Conservative Party had had plenty of time to reform the House of Lords during the twenty years they had spent almost continuously in office, 'but the time was not then ripe'.[12]

On 29 November Balfour declared that a Unionist government would submit its tariff proposals to a referendum if the Liberals would do the same over home rule for Ireland, for the previous twenty-five years a dominant issue in British politics. But the referendum pledge simply tore the party apart, instead of uniting it as had been the intention. That same day, Skelton continued his campaign by addressing meetings at Kinloch and Blairgowrie. He was heckled on the constitutional question and tariff reform at the former by Peter Dewar, a local farmer, 'to whom he replied that if his sketch of a reformed Second Chamber was not true, he would certainly cease to be Unionist representative of this or any other constituency'. The gathering at the latter was just as busy, but more orderly. Skelton said that 'the proposed wheat tax was not to keep the comparatively small wheat-growing area of this country, but to help the limitless area of the colonies'. Of those who had left the area for a better life in the colonies, he would 'prefer to see them [on] small holdings [which] would have a chance of some success, as [in] Denmark'.[13] Thus was born another of Skelton's enduring political beliefs. More frivolously, he also pledged to support a bill for closing ice-cream shops on Sunday.

Skelton waxed lyrical on similar themes over the next few days, declaring himself 'a devoted adherent to the policy of Tariff Reform'.[14] On a very wet day in December Skelton addressed a meeting of workers and asserted that the Unionists stood for two-chamber government and the reform of the House of Lords, 'but more especially for the referendum, the direct appeal to the people. The Liberals were not to touch the reform of the House of Lords, but they are now talking of the referendum.' He praised Balfour's 'fairness' in saying that even if he were returned to power he would not accept the present vote as being in favour of tariff reform, but would put the question to the people in a referendum. He elaborated thus:

It was all very well and quite understandable when there were only two parties in the House, but when, as at present, there were at least four [including the Irish Nationalists], what would be expected to increasingly happen? A sop from the one party to the other – 'I'll give you a sop now if you give me a sop again.' Thus each party got part of its will, and they got down to the level of government by 'scratch my back and I'll scratch yours'.[15]

The result of the general election, held from 3–19 December (the last British poll to be conducted over several days), was a great blow for the Unionists. Although the party recovered many of its 1906 losses in England, it made little or no progress in Scotland. In the Eastern Division of Perthshire the count began early on 14 December and the result was announced 'in the presence of a small assembly of people'[16] at 11.30 a. m. The result was:

Young, W. (Liberal)	3,658
Skelton, A. N. (Unionist)	2,826

The Liberal majority in a straight fight was a respectable 832. Skelton, then living at 48 India Street in Edinburgh's New Town, had been defeated in his first attempt to become a member of Parliament, yet the basis for many of his lasting political beliefs had been set – an almost obsessive belief in the use of the referendum to resolve disputes between the Upper and Lower House, and the subdivision of vacant agricultural land into smaller, and therefore more productive, holdings. 'Mr Skelton proved a surprisingly sturdy candidate and worked hard from start to finish,'[17] commented the *Perthshire Advertiser* of his first electoral outing.

The Unionists had been defeated for the second time in a year. Although the party won the largest number of votes, the Liberals – led by Herbert Asquith – had 272 MPs to the Unionists' 271, and therefore formed a government with the support of seventy-four Irish Nationalists.

Some of the Unionist MPs elected to the 1910 parliament were known by contemporaries as 'young men', although many had been born as long before as 1865. They came from different, but generally affluent, backgrounds. Some were landed, others were journalists or lawyers, but all were united in their professional approach to politics. They expected more, just as their constituents expected more of them, and they complained of the aloofness of the party leadership, the inaccessibility of the whips and the lack of official encouragement or opportunities for political advancement. Had Skelton been elected in 1910 he would no doubt have been a vociferous member of this group. The 'young men' were appalled by the rightward shift of the party and wanted a return to what Disraeli called 'Tory democracy' as opposed to class-based politics. The 1910 election had also convinced many that the Unionists needed to develop a programme of social reform. Although the party had gained 105 seats it had failed to win back the working-class constituencies lost in 1906, particularly in the industrial north.

Balfour, who remained Unionist leader, sought to appease this progressive sentiment. The result was the long-forgotten Unionist Social Reform Committee (USRC), chaired by the charismatic F. E. Smith, later Lord Birkenhead, who had the respect of the 'young men'. Importantly, he had also supported Balfour's campaign call for tariff reform to be submitted to a referendum. Of the USRC's sixty-odd members more than thirty-five were MPs, many of whom had first been elected in 1910, including the future Prime Minister Stanley Baldwin. It published reports (or 'bills') on six areas of social policy, which together amounted to a comprehensive programme for an election expected in 1914. Furthermore, it developed a remarkably progressive ideology of social reform – an eclectic blend of traditional Toryism, Fabian socialism and contemporary ideas about rural regeneration.

Smith, in his tract *Unionist Policy*, argued that Tory social reform was a 'third alternative' to Lloyd George's 'Radical Socialism' and the 'Whig Individualism' popular with many Conservatives. While both incited class conflict from opposing perspectives, Toryism (argued Smith) by contrast was pragmatic and more concerned with 'the facts of life as they are'. Rather than encouraging conflict, Toryism urged the reconciliation of class interests under a higher national and imperial unity. Smith claimed the support of Disraeli, Randolph Churchill and Joseph Chamberlain in these views, while this progressive thinking also served a cruder political purpose. Tactically, the committee aimed to outbid the radicals by proposing social reforms that were even more collectivist than the Liberals could contemplate. It seems likely that the ethos of the USRC, together with its individual reports, captured Skelton's imagination. Despite his defeat in December 1910, he had not retreated back to Edinburgh to lick his wounds. Instead he embarked on an extensive speaking tour of Unionist platforms; indeed, it seems he became something of a star orator for the then beleaguered party in Scotland.

In 1911, under the auspices of the East Perthshire Women's Unionist Association, Skelton declared that Unionism was

> more than a set of solutions of problems . . . Unionism, rightly considered, was a faith. They did not want to raise the angry passions of the masses, which once roused were extremely difficult to quell, and whose existence was a danger to national life. This great country could not advance if there was not a proper, kindly, humane, and sensible relationship between man and man. Unionists were engaged in more than a political fight. They were fighting to show that in the interests of the people of this country it was not necessary to fire up class hatred.[18]

This became the basis of what Skelton later called 'Constructive Conservatism'.

In Blairgowrie, Skelton again defended tariff reform, despite the election defeat, and asserted that the Unionists' 'was the only policy of land reform which had been approved by experience in every other European country'.[19] And at another meeting on 9 July he pointed out 'the importance of a closer union between the mother country and the colonies'.[20]

By July 1911 Skelton had also revived his court work, defending, among others, a farm servant who had 'conveyed manure along Thistle Street [in Kirkcaldy] in a cart so loaded that part of the manure fell on to the street contrary to by-law made by the commissioners of the burgh'.[21] It must have come as a relief, therefore, when on 4 August the executive committee of East Perthshire Unionist Association recommended that Skelton be adopted to fight the next general election, giving him the prospect of escaping such a mundane professional life. It was passed unanimously and *The Scotsman* reported that at the last poll Skelton had 'created a most favourable impression, the result being a very large reduction in the Liberal majority', but that 'Mr Skelton was not present at the meeting, being absent on holiday in Norway'.[22]

Energised by his reselection, Skelton continued his speaking tour of Scotland. In October 1911 he told a Primrose League[23] demonstration at Dunblane that whereas Unionism had been on the defensive in Scotland, 'they would soon be on the aggressive'. He spoke of the 'harm that would be done to Ireland if the Unionist policy, which was rapidly making that country more prosperous and developing its resources, was destroyed by the granting of home rule'.[24] Skelton also accused the Liberals of 'neglecting the unification of the Empire by clinging to free trade' while assuring the crowd that the 'Unionist Party also stood for social reforms, which would develop a sense of unity amongst the people'.[25] But the recent Insurance Act – which introduced health and unemployment benefits for British workers – was the focus of Skelton's ire. At a meeting in Forteviot he said it must be regarded as 'in the nature of a huge experiment, the final result of which no man could foretell'. He went on to say that 'the Unionist Party did not promise that the millennium would come five minutes after they were in power, but the reforms they advocated—small ownership and tariff reform—would come slowly, and be all the more sure because of that'.[26]

The National Insurance Act, home rule and tariff reform became fixtures of Skelton's platform oratory throughout 1912. Speaking in Dunning he predicted that the 'years 1911 and 1912 would appear prominently as years in which industrial unrest was the most acute in recent history',[27] although he stopped short of directly blaming the Liberal government. In the course of a lecture to the Glasgow Democratic Unionist Association Skelton restated his growing belief that 'Unionism was quite as interested in questions of social reform as Radicalism or Socialism could possibly be'. Showing a remarkable sense of political foresight, he said 'he was convinced that the struggle of the future was between Unionist principles and Socialist principles'.[28]

Widespread industrial action continued in the middle of the year, and Skelton attacked reports of food stoppages in London at a speech in Perth's Conservative Club. He said he could 'say so with the utmost gravity, that there was no duty more stringent before the Unionist Party today than to uphold the interests of the community as a whole against those interests, which from time to time, from rather selfish motives, attempted to subordinate the interests of the community'.[29]

At around this time, the USRC's sub-committee on industrial unrest had been appointed and began a two-year inquiry. Its report, *Industrial Unrest: A Practical Solution*, was published in June 1914. It asserted that the state was duty bound to intervene in industrial disputes in order to protect the interests of the wider community. In this area, Skelton would later advocate a more radical approach, but the USRC believed the path to peace lay in merely allowing trade unions to nominate representatives to a conciliation board.

As the sub-committee got down to work, Skelton continued with his court work while the frequency of his speeches suggests that he believed another election to be imminent. At the annual general meeting of the East Perthshire Unionist Association in late November, he said that 'no one could be surprised that the Government should desire to put off the day of reckoning as long as possible, but in this constituency he did not believe that any delay would restore the confidence of their supporters or weaken the determination of the Unionists . . . Another year's experience of the constituency had only strengthened his conviction that the Unionists meant to win it.'[30]

More court work took Skelton into the New Year, and at a Primrose League demonstration in February Skelton expanded upon another of his growing interests, that of land policy. He said the Unionist aim

> was to give to Scotland and to England that race and class of peasant proprietors who were the backbone of France, one of the chief sources of well-being of Germany, the means of enormous wealth to Denmark, and, through Unionist Acts of Parliament, had brought to Ireland peace and growing prosperity. Subject, of course, to various natural differences, they proposed to carry out in Scotland and in England just what they had done in Ireland, and they hoped, by putting upon the soil a large number of small owners, owning the land they cultivated to achieve two great objects – to increase their rural population, now sadly on the decline, and to bring it about that the country districts should produce far more wealth for the people than they did to-day.[31]

At a meeting in Coupar Angus the following month, Skelton contrasted two opposing land policies: 'The Radical Party, both with regard to taxation and small holdings, were absolutely wrong. Land was simply an investment, like stocks and shares . . . With regard to the question of small holdings, he advocated the Unionist principle of ownership, and spoke in favour of the grouping of small holdings on the co-operative system.'[32] Later that year he said 'that the difference between the two policies was that the Unionists helped the individual who was willing to help himself, whilst the Radicals merely helped him to buy land not for himself, but for the

State. That was the essential difference between small ownership and small fixed tenancy.'[33]

Lloyd George's land inquiry and subsequent land campaign were by this point gaining wide publicity, but a few months prior to Skelton's last speech on land reform the USRC's agriculture sub-committee had published anonymously a pamphlet entitled *A Unionist Agricultural Policy*. Largely the views of its chairman Christopher Turnor, a Lincolnshire landowner and political eccentric, it espoused agricultural education, the reconstruction of village life and co-operative colonies of smallholdings and credit banks. *A Unionist Agricultural Policy* also defended the principle of state intervention to raise wages as entirely consistent with Toryism. Since the policy of laissez-faire had produced results inimical to the people, the state, it argued, was bound to step in, if only to ensure its own preservation. The report invoked the authority of Disraeli, who claimed that 'agriculture had a special claim on the consideration of the state'.

Another USRC report was also to shape Skelton's future thinking, although was not commented on by him at the time. *The History of Housing Reform* asserted that the aims of housing reform were essentially Conservative. 'The maintenance of the principle of property', it claimed, 'depends . . . on the existence within these Islands, of a vast majority of its inhabitants living under social conditions, which . . . permit them to believe in and practise the ordinary civic virtues. And this ideal clearly cannot be attained where the homes of people are in such a condition that nothing but squalor, vice or revolution is likely to issue from them.'[34] Skelton would have concurred, and later made this the central argument for his vision of 'a property-owning democracy'.

By March 1914 Skelton was confessing to crowds that 'he had fallen into the delusion that they would have had a general election by this time',[35] but remained convinced that the Liberals would not pass its Home Rule [for Ireland] Bill without another poll, which the Unionists were more than ready for. At a meeting in Kirkliston, Skelton said that if 'this country was a democracy, in fact, and not merely in name, it was a matter of vital necessity that before this Home Rule became law the people of this country as a whole must have an opportunity of saying whether they wanted it or not'.[36]

Skelton stepped up the rhetoric the following month, in particular attacking the provision that forty-two Irish members would continue to sit in the House of Commons, even under Home Rule, in order 'that they should push and squeeze, and drive and force, until their political independence was exchanged for complete national independence'. Ireland's demand for separation was foolish and wrong, he added, and he 'could not understand, and no honest man could understand, why the Nationalists should regard the English and Scots as an alien race, why they should hug such feelings in their breasts . . . He did not think that in the whole history of politics in the world there had ever been given an example of such a contemptible frame of mind as that in which they demanded entire separation from the British connection, and at the same time hugged the British gold.'[37]

Yet by contrast, Skelton was still doing his best to strike a progressive note. 'The best social reform policy', he said in early 1914, 'was that which enabled people to stand on their own feet, and that was the policy of the Unionist Party.'[38] Similarly, the 'so-called social reforms of the Radical Party were absolutely unsocial', he claimed, 'because the object was to set class against class, interest against interest'.[39]

Meanwhile, the USRC had completed its comprehensive programme for a general election expected in 1914 or 1915. A 1914 *Campaign Guide* was even prepared – a document that suggests the Conservative Party took social reform seriously – and Skelton was reaffirmed as the prospective Unionist candidate for the Eastern Division of Perthshire. In August the USRC broke up, most of its members leaving British soil to fight in the First World War, but it had filled the deficiency in pre-war Unionism by formulating a coherent social policy to be paid for by higher direct taxation on what F. E. Smith described as 'that luxurious class living entirely for pleasure which was treated with comparative indulgence by the Budget of 1910'.[40] Skelton would later call them the 'peach-fed classes', but whatever the term, that class was about to be given a nasty jolt by the calamity of the Great War.

As the storm clouds gathered in 1914 Skelton was commissioned, along with several colleagues from the Faculty of Advocates, to the Scottish Horse (Territorial Force), a regiment unique in that it was originally raised, not in Scotland, but in South Africa by the Caledonian Society of Johannesburg. Skelton became a second lieutenant on 25 August and initially served with the 4th Regiment on home turf. The Scottish Horse Brigade was formed in September 1914, and the following month Skelton was appointed a temporary lieutenant.

By January 1915 the Scottish Horse was attached to the 2nd Northumbrian Division to work on coastal defences, and two months later Skelton was made a temporary captain. In August 1915 the regiment dismounted and moved to Gallipoli, landing at Suvla Bay, Transylvania, on 2 September, where it became attached to the 2nd Mounted Division. In Gallipoli Skelton was assistant military landing officer and acting staff captain in the Anzacs.

Near the end of December the Scottish Horse was evacuated from Gallipoli and moved to Egypt; in February 1916 it was absorbed into the 1st Dismounted Brigade to work on Suez Canal defences; on 1 June Skelton was promoted to full lieutenant and on 18 June was made a temporary major; and in October the 1/1st and 1/2nd regiments formed the 13th (Scottish Horse Yeomanry) Battalion, the Black Watch, and moved to Salonika, where Skelton became second in command of the squadron when it joined 81st Brigade, 27th Division. Skelton remained at the rank of major until August 1917 when he reverted to lieutenant, having served in France from June that year.

Skelton's War Office file, now held at the National Archives in Kew, gives some indication of the conditions officers and their men endured during the Great War. A recommendation written by the

Lieutenant-Colonel Commandant Scottish Horse Yeomanry, dated 12 August 1917, reads:

> I would draw to your attention the rather hard case of some Officers at present holding the temporary rank of Major. Some of the best Officers in the Scottish Horse will be very hard hit for the following reasons:- On mobilization Officers were first appointed into the rank which they actually took up – i.e. a Captain joined as a Captain. After a short while, this was discontinued, and Officers were all made 2nd Lieutenants, irrespective of their age or qualifications. They then received accelerated promotion. For example:-

Lieutenant Archibald N. Skelton,	
Appointed 2nd Lieutenant	25-8-14,
Promoted temp Major	18-6-16,
Relinquished	15-8-17,
Promoted substantive Lieutenant	1-6-16,
Date of birth	1-7-80,
Medical Board	Nil.

Skelton was still in command of a company during the 4th Regiment's advance on Le Cateau, when he was wounded on 17 October 1918, just weeks before the Armistice. His Medical Board report records that Skelton 'was hit by shrapnel causing a severe flesh wound of back'. The wound was dirty so Skelton left his unit immediately, embarked for England on 20 October and arrived at Southampton a day later. There, he was examined by the Medical Board and boarded initially at Portsmouth before being transferred to a hospital in Chelsea, London. His condition was soon 'quite recovered, with no disability'[41] and he was recommended for three weeks' leave, after which he was deemed to be fit for general service. Skelton's misfortune even earned a mention in *The Scotsman*, which observed on 30 October that the Edinburgh advocate had 'seen a great deal of hard fighting'.[42]

Skelton was demobbed on 27 January 1919, the year in which his regiment was disbanded. He received the Victory, British and Star medals, and finally relinquished his commission on 30 September 1921, when he was granted the rank of captain. Skelton, one might say, had had a good war. As one obituary noted in 1935:

> To a man so constituted the War was an opportunity for experience and (even in these days be it said) enjoyment, and full use did he make of his opportunity. He served on three fronts, rose to be Major, was torpedoed in the Mediterranean and severely wounded in France. After the War he used to say that (although one might not guess it from some prominent examples) the ideal soldier was 'invariably courteous to his inferiors and rude to his superiors'. Whatever method Skelton adopted in his own soldiering I never heard his superiors or subordinates speak of his war activities with anything other than unstinted admiration.[43]

While Skelton was still recovering in London, the thoughts of Conservative associations across Scotland turned to the impending 'khaki' general election. William Young, who had defeated Skelton at the December 1910 poll, had not yet been recognised as the official candidate of the Liberal–Tory coalition (led since 1916 by David Lloyd George), so the Perth Conservatives unanimously resolved to invite Captain Skelton to contest the seat for the newly formed Perth Division.[44] Although he was still recovering from his wounds, it was 'hoped he will be able to take part in the forthcoming campaign'.[45]

But it was not to be. William Young did, after all, receive the Coalition ticket and Skelton withdrew, allowing Young to be returned unopposed. Instead, Skelton resolved to return to the courts and by July 1919 was well enough to do so. Yet, as in Skelton's later parliamentary career, despite diligence and obvious intellect, he failed to progress as quickly as his contemporaries. 'In his chosen profession he never attained the position to which his abilities entitled him,' observed one obituarist in 1935.

> But although he never had a great practice, he was an outstanding and loyal member of the Faculty, and was 'well heard' in the Courts before which he appeared. He even – such was his zest for life – imparted an element of exuberance and enjoyment to the discussion of legal points before the Divisions, and his exchanges of dialectics with the late Lord President and Lord Skerrington in revenue cases are still a happy memory. But the restraints of Parliament House irked him and when he left the floor in 1931 it was with the definite intention of never returning.[46]

Despite the frustrations of his legal career, Skelton was, in January 1920, nominated by the Lord Advocate, Scotland's most senior law officer, to be junior counsel to the Post Office, and to the board of Inland Revenue the following year, in which capacity he tackled a case involving the North British Railway Company – alongside his friend Stair Gillon – in early 1922. That year proved fortuitous for Skelton. In October, in a meeting at the Carlton Club, the Conservative Party finally voted, following much political unrest, by a majority to withdraw from the Liberal-led coalition government. A general election followed, and Skelton – who had last stood for election to the House of Commons nearly twelve years earlier – finally had a realistic chance of moving from Parliament House in Edinburgh to the Houses of Parliament in London.

TWO

'A GRACEFUL AND WITTY PEN' (1922–3)

The Carlton Club meeting of 1922 was integral to the development of the Conservative Party as a more democratic organisation, and to a country struggling to come to terms with the realities of the post-war era. A revolt by a group of junior ministers was the first hint that something was afoot, and in October backbench Conservatives decided to overthrow their leader, Austen Chamberlain, and withdraw from the coalition. Following speeches from Andrew Bonar Law, a Canadian Scot, and Stanley Baldwin, a half-Scots laird who affected a 'man of the people' image, MPs voted 185 to 85 in favour of discontinuing the six-year coalition and filed out of the Pall Mall club to face the consequences. It triggered an immediate general election and marked, in effect, the beginning of modern British politics.

Skelton was selected as the prospective candidate for the Perth Division at a meeting of the local Unionist Association on 14 October. The executive committee had failed in its negotiations with the National Liberals to form a joint committee with a view to finding a Unionist candidate acceptable to both parties, and so Skelton (who had already been adopted at a previous meeting) outlined his analysis of 'the present political situation and the future of the Conservative Party'.[1] He was unanimously endorsed.

The campaign opened on 25 October. Skelton said it

> was a time for sober government, sober action, care,
> prudence, and common-sense. The Unionist Party believed
> in moderate opinion, careful, moderate action, and wise
> and moderate policy towards the best thing so absolutely
> essential to the welfare of the country just now. They had
> done with [the] Coalition, and wanted some form more
> suited to the present state of affairs. He had not the slightest
> doubt about the country as a whole, regarding Mr Bonar
> Law as 'a . . . prudent, wise, experienced Scotsman, and
> he had no doubt that the country as a whole regarded Mr
> Bonar Law as much the man to deal with this phase. It was
> clear that most moderate men of every shade of opinion
> were rallying to the new Government.'[2]

At this election, however, Skelton could not look forward to
a straight fight with the Liberals. The Perth Liberals chose Sir
William Henderson, while William Westwood, a Glaswegian, was
selected as the Labour candidate. Meanwhile, the National Liberals
also chose to field their own candidate, a W. R. Gourlay, just to
complicate things further.

In policy terms, certain elements of Skelton's pitch were simply
a rerun of his 1910 campaign. Addressing a meeting at Methven, he
said he

> believed a great deal could be done for agriculture,
> not by directly handing over cash, but by some such
> organisation as land banks – no State capital, but State
> credit and State guarantee. It was necessary to have a
> proper credit system behind the Scottish farmer to-day,
> and he believed that only could be done by the land
> bank system known in other countries.[3]

Skelton added that he deplored the fact that only 25 per cent of the population lived in the country, and the continued tendency for young men to leave the country for cities. Not everyone, however, took Skelton seriously as the farmers' friend. Sir William Henderson, the Independent Liberal candidate, attacked Skelton's candidature on the basis that he was a lawyer, and not even resident in the constituency (Skelton still lived in Edinburgh). As *The Scotsman* reported, Skelton reminded Henderson 'that for 4½ years he had not been a lawyer but a soldier. The colour and texture of the Unionist cloth were as bright and as strong as ever, and he (Mr Skelton) had never been tempted to change it nor had he considered any invitation to turn it.'[4] Skelton might have added that his alma mater, Glenalmond, lay just outside Perth.

On 6 November Skelton addressed an audience of more than 2,000 electors in Perth City Hall. He was now clearly in his element, and

> ventured to say that there could be no contrast more glaring than that too often seen between the quiet efforts of private men and women who exercised thrift and the wanton extravagance that too often characterised Government Departments. But there was a worse extravagance than that, the wanton, crazy, wicked extravagance which the Socialist party would wish them to enter into. He was determined to the utmost of his ability to fight the . . . policy of the Socialistic-Labour ideas.[5]

The Perth Division declared on 16 November. The result was:

Skelton, A. N. (Unionist)	11,387
Henderson, W. (Liberal)	5,874
Westwood, W. (Labour)	4,651
Gourlay, W. R. (Nat Lib)	2,689

With a decisive majority of 5,513, Skelton became one of 344

Unionist MPs, an increase of twelve on the 1918 election. Bonar Law became Prime Minister, having gained a majority over Labour, led by John Robert Clynes, and a Liberal Party divided between National Liberals led by Lloyd George and simply 'Liberals' who followed Asquith. The number of seats won signalled that the sands of British electoral politics were shifting. Labour gained 142 seats (an increase of 85), making it the official opposition, while the National Liberals secured just 53, a loss of 74 (the 'Liberals' notionally gained 26, winning 62 seats). The Irish Nationalists were no longer an electoral factor, autonomy having recently been granted to the Free State that covered twenty-six of Ireland's thirty-two counties.

Nevertheless, it was the Unionists' first clear election victory in more than two decades. A party conference scheduled for the following month became a victory jamboree. It was, wrote the party chairman Sir George Younger, 'the story of a great recovery'.[6] In Scotland, however, Labour made significant advances in the west and south-west of the country. But, reasoned Skelton at a meeting in the Perth Conservative Club shortly after his victory, 'if it came to a question whether Perth and Edinburgh or the Gorbals more truly represented the views of Scotland, he believed it would be Edinburgh and Perth that would decide'. He added that

> they had to show the people of Scotland that Conservatism and Unionism was a faith, and that it truly was what Socialism pretended to be, a true line of advance, whereby the great masses of the people of the country would have an opportunity – and the only opportunity – of leading a wider, richer, fuller, more interesting, and more developed life, in years to come. Conservative principles put into practice offered the solution to national problems for which Socialism was groping vainly. Socialism performed a junction in showing up the troubles and difficulties of our national life, but it was wrong when it tried to suggest remedies, and it was hopelessly wrong, utterly foolish, and wanton in its folly. The future duty of Conservatives

was clear. They could not separate their politics from their work-a-day lives. In a democracy their politics must be all pervading. A democracy could only live if all were trying to do their best in their ordinary lives for the country, and a democracy must surely die if they said one thing as politicians and another thing as citizens. They must not only be Unionists on polling day but every day, and all the day. Unionism was based upon fair play between all classes and the desire of each to farther the common weal.[7]

The basis for Skelton's belief in what he would later call 'constructive Conservatism' was gradually becoming clearer. Soon he would commit his thinking to paper.

Perth in 1922 was a predominantly industrial city, albeit one surrounded by fertile farmland. It had, since the nineteenth century, been a focal point for Scotland's prosperous whisky industry, which continued to grow despite prohibition in the United States and the economic aftermath of the Great War. Famous brands such as Bell's and Dewar's were local firms, while the gateway to the Highlands was also home to the international headquarters of General Accident, a local insurance company which had been built up by Francis Norie-Miller, later Sir Francis, and a frequent Liberal opponent of Skelton's in elections to come. Perth generally mirrored Scotland's fluctuating economic and social fortunes, and its mixture of town and country concerns was ideal for a man of Skelton's political outlook.

If only Skelton had taken silk. The new government quickly found itself in trouble, at least when it came to manning the Scottish Office. The Secretary for Scotland, the unimpressive Viscount Novar, was in the House of Lords, and therefore it was important that the Lord Advocate, William Watson KC, should have a seat in the House of Commons, which he did not. A by-election was considered risky and *The Times* mentioned that, among others from the Scottish Bar, 'Skelton was a possibility' although he 'had not taken silk'.[8]

Despite this early disappointment, Skelton made his mark during a highly irregular maiden speech in the course of the Second Reading of the Rent Restrictions Bill, which amended the 1921 Rent Act. The House was already tense when Skelton rose to criticise the motives of the Labour Party, implying that it was not so much motivated by legality as by loot. The Labour benches, particularly its Red Clydeside contingent, erupted, but Skelton carried on amid heavy heckling.

> It is perfectly well known that in Glasgow for two years a Lord Provost's Fund has been collected for the purpose of either helping or entirely paying the rents of most necessitous tenants, and that that fund, which, in all, I believe, amounted to over £100,000, was earmarked to the extent of over £58,000 for the direct purpose of paying rents. It was so used. Why were we not told about it? Why was not a word said about it?[9]

This allegation simply made matters worse. 'I am a lawyer,' continued Skelton, 'perhaps a very indifferent lawyer, but I must say I am thankful that I do not run the danger that the most eminent lawyer runs when he tries to suggest constructive ideas to deal with this problem, and all he can do is to suggest constructive ideas which certainly do not commend themselves to any person in the House'.[10] When speaking, Skelton would emphasise his points by beating his clenched right hand upon the open palm of his left, creating an impression of aggression.

The following day's *Times* described what happened next.

> When he quoted Mr Ramsay MacDonald as saying that they should behave more like a kindergarten and less like a bear garden pandemonium broke out. Mr Ramsay MacDonald sprang to his feet in the hope of challenging the quotation, but, encouraged by his fellow-Unionists, the member for Perth refused to give way.[11]

Parliamentary convention dictated that, having mentioned him by name, Skelton ought to have accepted MacDonald's intervention. 'I can only say how much I regret having committed any breach of order, and I beg to apologise,' said Skelton contritely. 'I was rather surprised that the hon. Member opposite did not give way,' replied MacDonald. 'All I desire to say is that the hon. Member has very grossly misrepresented the remarks of mine to which he referred.'

'I repeat my apologies to the leader of the opposition,' responded Skelton amid angry cries and mocking cheers, before getting back into his stride, arguing that 'to mulet [sic] the property owners would be unjust and inequitable, and I think Parliament should shoulder such a sum of money as any tenants are entitled to and may demand.'[12]

MacDonald had by then resumed his seat, but his followers were determined not to allow Skelton to proceed. 'Mr [James] Maxton, with his dark locks surging tumultuously,' observed The Times, 'quivered with passion, flung out a threatening arm, and shouted, "Not one word." Mr [David] Kirkwood muttered unutterable things in untranslatable Doric. Mr [George] Buchanan wished to cross the floor and administer correction.'[13]

Skelton's maiden speech had certainly been a lively experience, and was also the first example of a pedantic manner that did little to endear him to opponents. His distrust of socialism was instinctive, but within months he was to urge the Conservative Party to compete with Labour not through invective, but by tackling the socialists on their own ground.

During the early 1920s, Skelton's pre-war fight against Liberal dominance had turned into a belief that only progressive Conservatism could defeat the new challenge from Labour. 'Here, for a backbench MP,' observed Phillip Williamson, 'he had an unusual and enduring influence.'[14] In four articles published by The Spectator during April and May 1923, Skelton sought to redefine Conservative thinking in what one historian called 'the age of illusion', but which he saw as the 'new era'. Skelton, through his journalism (and later an influential pamphlet), addressed the central question of what the Conservative Party should stand for in the post-war age. After the fall of Lloyd George and the rise of Labour, the Conservative Party – led by Bonar Law and then Baldwin – had been content to represent the status quo and defend itself against whatever assaults the Labour Party mounted. As the historian D. R. Thorpe observed: 'For Noel Skelton this was not enough; he believed that where there is no vision the people perish, and he sought to give focus to that vision.'[15]

In so doing, Skelton had an important and enthusiastic patron in the form of John St Loe Strachey, the then editor and proprietor of *The Spectator*. Twenty years Skelton's senior, Strachey nevertheless gelled with the newly elected MP. Like Skelton, he had been called to the Bar, but he never practised, having been distracted by journalism; he was also energetic, self-righteous and confident, and believed that journalists should be the nation's preachers. *The Spectator* was his pulpit, and editorial meetings were a flurry of ideas, instructions and amusing anecdotes.

Strachey and Skelton shared an uncompromising attachment to freedom and individualism, opposition to Irish home rule, state socialism and the previous Liberal government's social reforms (although unlike Skelton, Strachey opposed tariff reform). Generally speaking, they also agreed about the direction in which the Conservative Party should be heading, not least through the use of the referendum. Without Strachey, Skelton would have lacked an influential outlet for his political ideas.

Skelton's first article, 'Constructive Conservatism I – The Opportunity', appeared in *The Spectator* on 28 April 1923. 'The fate of Conservatism and Unionism hangs in the balance,' he proclaimed.

> It must lead or perish ... Free nations do not live by caretakers and policemen alone; and if the Conservative Party were to redefine itself to a caretaker's job and make *per viltate il gran rifiuto* [from cowardice the great refusal] when faced with the architect's, it would itself be the bar to its principles

– principles which are the point of attraction for all those better and braver elements of the nation that instinctively abhor the political mentality and morality of the Socialist. If so, it will have no second chance in our generation.

Skelton's prose was lively, colourful and more than a little florid. It also contained, for many Conservatives, some uncomfortable home truths. Skelton argued that an erosion of pure political principle was an inevitable side effect of legislation, but

the compromise of thought, the hybridization of underlying principles, is in quite another category. It produces sterility of action; it turns the organic into the mechanical.

It does not help at all to recall how often, in the past, the Conservative Party has failed, when in power, to realize and express its principles, has mumbled instead of speaking out, has drawn back instead of moving on, and how, despite it all, confidence in the essential truth of these principles remains one of the deepest-rooted political instincts of Britain. But let there be no such failure this time.

'To-day Conservatism,' Skelton continued, 'rightly understood and widely applied, can bring something like a real solution of our problems. It is, most certainly, more fitted to express the hopes and aims of the British people than any other set of political principles.' It was only with deeper analysis 'that we can realize how deep would be the ignominy and how poignant the irony of a Conservative failure'.

What then, asked Skelton, was the potential of such a situation? 'The opportunity is this: Conservatism is in control of the national destiny at the very beginning of a new political era. For a new era it is; one of these times when old values have lost their meaning, old prejudices their force, old axioms their sanctity; when opinion, ideas, the minds of men are plastic.' He likened the 1922 general election to 'that national miracle which turned the water of the Carlton Club meeting into wine'.

Skelton recalled that a 'political friend' had told him that the Coalitionists in 1918 believed themselves to be 'the accepted heirs of the new era'. No doubt they did, he wrote pithily:

> They hoped it was a prologue; it was really an epilogue. The Coalition was, in fact, a War product. It could never rid itself of the smell of blood and antiseptics. It had a hospital outlook, and, regarding the nation as its patient, characteristically spent its last breath in urging it to remain 'under treatment'.

The article then reached its questioning conclusion:

> It is a remarkable paradox, of course, that the party which is instinctively trusted and understood by the people should at times, it would seem, have feared the people and therefore misunderstood them . . . Has the Conservative Party the imagination, the will, the courage to seize the opportunity and do an architect's work?[16]

Skelton attempted to answer this loaded question in the second instalment of 'Constructive Conservatism', entitled 'The New Era', which appeared on 5 May. In it, he stated that Britain was 'now, electorally, a complete democracy' with all classes and both sexes enjoying full political rights. Conservatism, as a result, was now 'face to face with democracy'.

'Secondly,' Skelton continued, 'the new era is one not merely of democracy, but of an educated democracy. Education is so gradual a process that its growth is easily overlooked. Yet, as in all continuous processes of growth, there are decisive moments when change is apparent.' One such moment, he said, was the Great War.

> In a flash, the distance which Britain had gone along the road of education was revealed. The technical ability,

the rapidity in acquiring new kinds of knowledge and in mastering new duties, the self-reliance, the self-respect, the power to accept responsibility, the spontaneous facing of sacrifice, the large grasp of the issues at stake, the firmness and fineness of temper, the general spaciousness of character and outlook displayed by the men and women of Britain meant, and could only mean, that the influences of education had penetrated deeply and strongly into their minds and character.

Like many politicians of his generation, the 'war to end all wars' had left an indelible mark on Skelton:

The present writer, who on four fronts saw men under the most varying conditions of danger and of dullness, has never wavered in his conviction that it was largely to the extent to which the mass of the people has absorbed the benefits of some forty years of strenuous education that we owed our achievements in the War.

The Conservative Party, therefore, had to adapt to this new, educated, frame of mind. Yet, it was

to no purpose to reply that Socialism finds its strength in appeals to cupidity, envy and hatred. That may be true also: but . . . the real strength of Socialism lies in the fact that it is making an intellectual appeal at the very moment when the craving for mental nourishment is so universal.

It was, said Skelton, 'presenting a "view of life" to the nation in a method admirably suited to the mood and atmosphere of the new era'. And the Unionist response?

A view of life, a statement of fundamental principles, can only be met by the presentation of a truer view and

of principles more fundamental. If Conservatives are not
to fight with one hand tied behind their backs, the active
principles of Conservatism must be felt anew, thought
anew, promulgated anew. The whole intellectual content
of Conservatism, its moral and economic foundations,
its practical applications, must, whatever 'the mental
strife' involved, be made plain to educated democracy.
Conservatism must expound its 'view of life'.

Skelton even argued that the very word 'politics' ought to be
redefined. 'Conservatism believes in a restricted field for the
action of the State,' he asserted, 'and most emphatically the view
of life, the ideal of advance, it must present to the nation cannot
be exhaustively embodied in Acts of Parliament. In the new era
we must step outside the old limits and depart from the view that
politics mean only public affairs, and that public affairs mean only
public business.'

The article continued with another uncompromising home truth.

The prosperous, peach-fed classes do not readily understand
the angle from which the mass of the people approach
political life. To the former, politics is not a medium of
education, of general culture. That side of life they have
an infinite number of other means of enjoying – fastidious
living, beautiful homes, the enjoyment of literature, art,
travel, the closeness and variety of their points of contact
with human culture and civilisation. Because their general
interests are wider, the intellectual area they allot to politics
is correspondingly narrower. And for those who are the
heirs of 'the governing classes' of the past, politics naturally
means, above all, administration.

But to the 'mass of the people the opposite is the case. Politics
is their main point of contact with general ideas; the paramount
expression of the life of the community; the chief, if not the only

means of satisfying their *goût des grandes choses*.' He added: 'If the British people do not now take their pleasures sadly, they certainly take their politics seriously.'

Such, then, concluded Skelton, was the situation:

> A people at the dawn of a new era, equipped with full political power, educated, and still more, highly sensitive to educative influences, presented by a powerful and devoted Socialist Party with a view of politics which is really a comprehensive 'view of life', and yet instinctively trusting to their natural Conservative instincts: a Conservative Party, inclined perhaps, in common with other parties in the past, to regard politics with only a caretaker's eye, and yet, obviously, from the wider point of view, charged with the duty of expounding the Conservative 'view of life', since in it lies embedded the true solution of the fundamental problem the new era presents.[17]

John Strachey was clearly delighted by the first two parts of 'Constructive Conservatism'. 'The first was very good, but the second was really one of the best things we have ever had in *The Spectator*,' he told Skelton on 8 May. 'It was dignified and distinguished in style and had a true sympathy with democracy, which is one of the things I care for most in the world. Every word of it is true, and I feel sure that we ought to win a victory for the constitution on these lines if we handle it properly.'

When the articles were finished, Strachey proposed to write a critique with which to introduce another series of articles on future Conservative policy. 'Then I should like to consult you about those articles,' he added, 'so that later on we might issue them in book form. I think such a plan would give you a good show, and I am sure nobody deserves it more than you do.'[18] Strachey also invited Skelton to discuss his 'Referendum book, about which I still remain very keen'.

'I am very glad you liked my two articles,' replied Skelton the same day. 'I fear 3 & 4 are less interesting & not too well written [but I have] been able to say some things [about] which I feel very strongly.'[19]

It was in his third article for the 12 May edition of *The Spectator*, 'Problem and Principle', that Skelton coined his most enduring phrase, 'a property-owning democracy'.

But what of the 'fundamental problem of this new era'? 'Beneath the tangle of immediate anxieties', Skelton replied rhetorically, 'unemployment, the housing of the people, the agricultural emergency, the financial burdens of the State – it is possible to detect a master-problem which, while it remains unsolved, exercises a profound and malign influence upon the mental outlook and the material condition of the people?'

Skelton argued that one did not have to look far: for 'the mass of the people – those who mainly live by the wages of industry – political status and educational status have outstripped economic status. The structure has become lop-sided. It is therefore unstable. Until our educated and politically minded democracy has become predominantly a property-owning democracy, neither the national equilibrium nor the balance of the life of the individual will be restored.'

To restore that balance, continued Skelton, was 'the master-problem of the new era'. The wage-earner, he added, had long been attempting to solve the problem for himself, through the Co-operative movement, friendly societies, savings banks and even some trade unions, 'he has made a most determined effort to build up for himself . . . "something of his own" behind him, and the large amounts of wealth thus accumulated show how strong and persistent the impulse has been.'

Yet this effort, argued Skelton, had not solved the problem. The Liberal, he said, had been distracted from tackling it by his obsession with political rights; the Conservative, although helpful, had not considered it within a social context; while the socialist had used it to pervert the impulse behind it into an element in the view of life which he presents; he declares, that is, that ownership by the State is ownership by the people, implying that that means a property-owing democracy.

In fact, of course, it does not. What everybody owns, nobody owns; and far from expressing the wage-earner's ideal, Socialism makes it unattainable, while communal ownership, when obtained, neither interests nor influences a single human being. We have yet to hear of a man who, in the Great War, rushed to arms to preserve his share in the London County Council Tramways or in Battersea Park.

[But] whatever his savings may be in the Co-operative Society, or in War Savings Certificates, the wage-earner, as industrialist, has only the economic status of a machine; for his wages, as such, are, and can only be, part of the costs of production, occupying the same position as the expenses of running the machine of the factory or workshop in which he is employed.'

Skelton went on to identify what he considered the defining characteristics of the Conservative 'view of life'. The first was stability of the social structure, although he was careful to note that 'stability is not stagnation'. The second was

that the character of the individual citizen being the greatest asset of the State, the primary object and best test of all legislation which deals with the individual is its influence upon his character.

Everything that weakens individual character and lessens individual effort and initiative is anathema to the Conservative. Everything that strengthens and increases these is very near to his heart. The consequences flowing from this principle are so manifold that they cannot be elaborated here. The main and most essential one is the insistence by Conservatism on the necessity of limiting the

action of the State as far as possible to 'helping the individual
help himself'. Further, it follows that the best kind of social
legislation is that which gives to the citizens a better chance
of helping themselves during their working lives, and that
only second best (though admittedly essential in many
cases) is direct State intervention to sustain, shelter, and
support those who have failed in health or occupation. For
these failures only touch the fringe of the life of the nation.
It is improvement in conditions during the working life
which marks the real advance.

And these fundamental principles of Conservatism, continued
Skelton, 'which form the basis of its whole view of life, lead
inevitably to the development of the political, the educated
democracy into a property-owning democracy.' He then elaborated
on the special allure of property, although it is interesting to note
that not once did he specifically refer to home ownership.

The beneficent effect upon human character both of the
effort to acquire private property and of the opportunity,
after it has been acquired, for its wise or foolish use, can
hardly be over-estimated. For what is the effect of property,
its proverbial 'magic'? In the getting, the exercise of thrift, or
control, of all the qualities which 'the rolling-stone' knows
nothing of; in its use, an increased sense of responsibility,
a wider economic outlook, a practical medium for the
expression of moral and intellectual qualities.

It was therefore for Conservatism, said Skelton, 'to see to it that
this pathway to the development of character is opened wide
to the people; and to expound to the nation – what no one else
apparently dares or cares to – the vital inter-relation between
character and private possessions.' He also noted a certain irony:
'Mocked and jeered at in the past as "the Party of Property", it is
precisely as such, now that the wheel has turned full circle, that

Conservatism in the new era holds in its keeping the key to the problem.'

Between the traditions of the Tory democracy espoused by Disraeli and Skelton's new formulation, there existed some fundamental differences. While previously it had been collectivist, paternalist, and radical only on matters of social reform, in Skelton's hands it was individualist, egalitarian and radical in its political and economic implications. The old Tory democracy was the ideology of a landed class threatened by industrial society, while Skelton, in contrast, unflinchingly accepted the capitalist ethic and sought its wider diffusion.

Skelton was essentially arguing that the Conservatives could only counter Labour's 'phoney' appeal by responding to the real aspirations of the people. They could no longer afford to pander to the narrow perspectives of business or the upper classes because of the wider democratic mandate; democratic rights were no longer one among many political issues, but the very medium within which all politicians functioned. So Skelton wanted to empower the people, although in a different way to Labour. In the nineteenth century Conservatives had argued that only those who owned property should have the vote; so it followed that when all had the vote, then all should own property.

The third quarter of 'Constructive Conservatism' concluded thus:

> To make democracy stable and four-square; to give the wage-earner property and status; to bridge the economic gulf set between Labour and Capital; to present a view of life in which private property, instead of being reckoned, as the Socialist reckons it, a shameful thing, will be recognised to be an essential vehicle for the moral and economic progress of the individual; these are the tasks which the opportunity, the problem, and its own principles alike call Conservatism to perform in the new era.[20]

Skelton saved substantive policy proposals for his fourth, and final, article, which appeared in *The Spectator* on 19 May 1923. 'Democracy Stabilised' laid out exactly how he believed a property-owning democracy could be realised.

> (1) for the wage-earner, whether in factory or in field, industrial co-partnery, or its halfway house, profit-sharing; (2) for the agriculturist, who seeks to become completely his own master, small ownership; (3) for the rural world as a whole, agricultural co-operation; (4) for the community, to secure it against sudden assault, the Referendum.

Skelton argued that one common principle underpinned each proposal, 'for each, in its own way and in its own sphere, at once develops the character of the individual, and the stability of the social structure'. He conceded that of those, co-partnery and profit-sharing could not successfully be implemented by acts of Parliament, although he lamented that the extent to which they could had 'never been zealously or exhaustively explored'.

First, Skelton tackled what he called 'industrial co-partnery'. In short, he believed that 'Capital and Labour by it are to the full recognised as partners in the work of the production of wealth'. His reasoning was admirable, although perhaps a little naïve.

> Thus status and property-owning grow together; the wage-earner, as industrialist, from a machine becomes a man. Nor is this all. To the wage-earner, co-partnery brings a new incentive and a new kind of interest in his work, arising out of his new relation to it; a union of his thrift effort and his work effort; a wider industrial outlook, since, as his savings in the business increase, so does his interest in its general prosperity, for that prosperity affects him directly as a shareholder.

Co-partnery, argued Skelton, would also have a knock-on benefit to the community, for example in reducing the number of strikes, while it was 'clearly on the broad highway of economic evolution, for it is the next available incentive to increased productivity'. Increasing wages and reducing the hours of labour, said Skelton, had both contributed to this, but were 'from a purely economic point of view' not now 'squeezed oranges'.

Skelton went on to acknowledge the criticism that tariff reform 'had acquired almost the character of a substitute for, instead of a part of, a general policy of improving the status of the wage-earner'. Certainly, he added, 'many opponents have made haste to point out to the working classes that, in the existing industrial system, the lion's share of any advantage would, in their opinion, fall to Capital rather than Labour'. Such a criticism, Skelton asserted, 'would be of no avail under a system in which employer and employee clearly shared alike in the increased prosperity'.

> Yet there are objections. It is said, 'Some industries are not suited to the system.' Possibly not. But has there yet been any determined effort to work out in practice the modifications necessary to make it suit the special circumstances of particular trades? The overcoming of practical difficulties is a matter for resource and will-power, once the value of the underlying principle is realised. Conservatism in the new era must refute Anatole France's mocking remark that moderate men are those who have only a moderate belief in moderate opinions.

There was also an overtly political consideration, for

> co-partnery is the ideal ground on which to fight socialism, for it emphasizes the distinction, fundamental but neglected, between a property-owning democracy and the socialist ideal, and if the Trade Union leaders hide from their followers the more excellent way, so much the worse, when the truth is discovered, for them and for their leadership.

Next on Skelton's policy wish list was the ownership of land. He began with a critique of recent UK land policy, which in his opinion failed both landowner and farmer. 'The resettlement of the land of England and Scotland,' he said, 'the development of intensive cultivation, the reconstitution of the rural community, are matters so vital that every effort to devise sounder methods of instituting small holdings than those presently in operation must be made by Conservatism.' The Wyndham Land Act,[21] he added, returning to a theme from his election campaign, 'was the last and greatest constructive work which Unionism did for Ireland'.

Third was agricultural co-operation, which Skelton claimed was 'inextricably bound up with the Conservative view of life, because it is essentially the means whereby in the cultivation of the soil the individual can be helped to help himself'. On this, he said, 'there can safely be neither silence nor indifference' from the Conservatives, for

> without active and ardent Conservative support and exposition, confidence in co-operative principles in agriculture would advance only at a snail's pace, since distrust of Liberalism is complete in rural England, and is rapidly increasing in rural Scotland, while the country populations of both nations agree in their contempt for the town-bred fallacies of Socialism.

And finally, Skelton enthused about the referendum – 'crown and apex of a constructive Conservatism in the new era' – which he considered essential for resolving constitutional disputes. Here, above every other proposal, journalist and editor (Strachey) were singing from the same political hymn sheet. Skelton harked back to the constitutional crisis of 1910–11, in the midst of which he first stood for election. 'It was called for then to save the House of Lords,' he said; 'it is needed now to protect democracy.'

> For if democracy, faced in the new era by Socialism as its

scarcely disguised enemy, is, from a constitutional point of view, to be made stable and safe, if its property and liberty are to be preserved, the people, in the last resort, must directly and for themselves develop their own fate. And for this duty they are ripe. Meantime, it needs only a blunder or two on the part of a Cabinet, a General Election dominated by passion or prejudice, and the flank of the Constitution is turned. The task of Conservatism in the new era would be only half done if the British democracy were to be denied a means of protection the value of which has been amply proved elsewhere.

Quoting another of his Conservative heroes, Arthur Balfour (now the Earl of Balfour), Skelton concluded his definition of modern Conservative philosophy by asserting that 'the Conservative Party cannot leave it a matter of guesswork what its outlook is. "Democracy", Lord Balfour once said, "is government by explanation."' The mass of the people, he said, 'are profoundly perplexed by the paradox that Conservatism, in which they have so deep an instinctive belief, is apparently content to leave its view of life unexplained, its principles unstated, while Socialism, which they distrust exceedingly, is fearless and untiring in setting out its aims and ideals.'

Liberalism, added Skelton,

> is dying because its principles are dead. It will fare ill with Conservatism unless it breaks its silence and makes clear to the nation that it, too, has a vision of the future – of a property-owning democracy, master of its own life, made foursquare and secure, and able therefore to withstand the shrill and angry gales which, in the new era's uneasy dawn, sweep across the world of men.[22]

A lot of the ideas in Skelton's four Spectator essays were not new. Many had been explored first by the Unionist Social Reform

Committee (USRC) before the war, while broader themes had already been articulated by figures such as F. E. Smith and Edward Wood. But although Skelton's 'Constructive Conservatism' could be described as merely the latest feature of a longstanding debate about Unionist ideology, such an assessment would sell it short. Whereas the USRC had been largely ignored because of the First World War, Skelton's *Spectator* articles were not. And in terms of energy, style and coherence, the policy platform espoused by Skelton was altogether more attractive and, as we shall see, influential.

The political backdrop to 'Constructive Conservatism' was interesting. While Skelton polished his prose the Unionists were enduring a less than happy period, in stark contrast to the euphoria that followed the Carlton Club meeting and the 1922 general election. Although Andrew Bonar Law was popular personally, his Cabinet were not an impressive bunch, constituted, as it were, from the so-called 'second eleven'.

There had also been little legislation, the prevailing view in early 1923 being that industrial confidence required time to settle down. In terms of domestic policy, however, there was modest progress. Neville Chamberlain was in charge at the Ministry of Health, where his Housing Act resulted in the construction of more than 300,000 homes. Of this, Skelton must surely have approved.

Then a major internal crisis blew up. Stanley Baldwin, as Chancellor, unilaterally secured a deal on American war debt over which Bonar Law made it known he was prepared to resign. The Prime Minister, however, gave way on 31 January 1923, significantly eroding his authority. Meanwhile, there was backbench unrest at the lack of a positive programme, and the government's majority sank to twenty-two on a motion calling for universal old age pensions. On 10 April the government was defeated by five votes in a snap division on unemployment among ex-servicemen.

Even more unsettling was Bonar Law's increasingly fragile health. Already seriously ill with cancer, the 'unknown Prime

Minister' finally resigned in May 1923. The only real contenders for the premiership were Lord Curzon and Baldwin, the latter of whom was in the Commons and therefore in a stronger position. Baldwin therefore became Prime Minister on 22 May 1923, just days after Skelton's series of articles concluded in *The Spectator*. Skelton's relationship with his new leader would be by no means harmonious, but it was important nevertheless.

With the *Spectator* articles, Skelton had made his mark. 'He had a massive commanding presence,' remembered Lady Tweedsmuir years later, 'deep-set blue eyes, an aquiline nose, and a very pleasant voice, salted by a Scottish flavour. When I first met him he seemed almost too good to be true—the hero of a Disraeli novel come to life. He was young and impressive-looking, a convinced and earnest Conservative, successfully mounting the first steps of the political ladder.'[23]

As we shall see in the following chapter, Skelton's articles had even more of an impact when published as a pamphlet the following year, although a response of sorts did appear in the *Spectator* letters page on 26 May. More than a little patronising in tone, although not necessarily unfriendly, it commented on 'four articles of very charming word-spinning – which convey an impression of the writer's temperament rather than a picture of the situation – Mr Noel Skelton unfolds his plans for stabilizing Democracy.'

'But let us', continued the critic, who simply signed the letter 'C.P.R.', 'assume that Mr Skelton's programme is practical politics and fills the bill. He has remained content with floating his ideas in *The Spectator* and has stopped short of the active steps upon which there are in the Tory ranks many thoughtful younger men like Mr Skelton and that they mean business; that they are, in fact, prepared to take their coats off and have a real go in to drive their convictions home to the people.'

> The first thing for Mr Skelton and his friends to do is to collect themselves together and settle definitely how they propose to set about stabilizing Democracy. At the same

time, they must elect a leader who can lead and whom they are prepared to follow. The next step is a competent staff and adequate financial resources. These things are much easier said than done, but Mr Skelton and his friends must face the fact that they will necessarily be exposed to the criticism of insincerity or futility unless they manage to do them.[24]

Feedback from other quarters was more positive. In July 1923 Robert Boothby (who would the following year join Skelton in Parliament) wrote that he 'felt almost a personal pride in Noel Skelton's admirable articles in *The Spectator*, as I was responsible for his original introduction to John [Strachey]'.[25] And when the articles were published, Strachey wrote to Baldwin saying that an opportunity existed 'to remake the Unionist Party as a democratic and constitutional party . . . opposed to all forms of oligarchic and Jacobin rule, but with a full constructive policy instead of mere negation'.[26] Strachey also told the Prime Minister that it was his intention to make *The Spectator* adopt 'a kind of independent and non-partisan position from which it could preach the new gospel of democratic Conservatism'.[27] This brought only the odd response from Baldwin that 'the worm is turning . . . things are moving, it is the spirit of spring rather than autumn'.[28]

In September Strachey sent Skelton a copy of his new book on the referendum. Skelton replied on 2 October, saying:

I feel that your economic outlook is based upon what I consider an unjustifiably optimistic Free Trade view. I should not, for example, regard unlimited output as . . . suitable for all economic ills . . . If only we could take a leaf out of Denmark's book, develop co-operation, more intensive & scientific cultivation we should be getting onto the right lines . . . I should like, when Parliament is in session, to write an article or two on this.[29]

Strachey agreed, but in the meantime asked his star writer to furnish him with a few book reviews, including J. A. Spender's recent biography on the former Liberal Prime Minister Sir Henry Campbell-Bannerman, whom Strachey thought 'that queer, old, but really rather fascinating, creature'. Skelton, he said, was 'just the man to do the article fairly and squarely, and yet to do nothing which will hurt all sorts of feelings which ought now to be respected'.[30]

Away from this good-natured whimsy, the UK economy remained sluggish, trade stayed low, production had only revived very slowly, and unemployment flat-lined at around 1½ million. British agriculture was also depressed, a situation that continued throughout the inter-war years with 100,000 acres going out of cultivation per annum. The Labour Party, still led by the articulate Scot Ramsay MacDonald, was performing well, having harnessed the spirits of the Red Clydesiders to form a formidable opposition.

Baldwin, by contrast, was in difficulty. By the summer of 1923 tariff reform was back on the political agenda. The Prime Minister was minded to U-turn on the issue, having decided tariffs were necessary, but felt bound by a pledge made by his predecessor, Bonar Law, not to introduce any without first having another election.

On 23 October 1923 Baldwin informed the Cabinet that he would reveal as much at the party conference. Instead, he announced it two days later during a seminal speech in Plymouth.

> I have for myself come to the conclusion that owing to the conditions which exist in the world today, if we go pottering along as we are we shall have grave unemployment with us to the end of time, and I have come to conclusion that the only way of fighting this subject is by protecting the home market.[31]

An election atmosphere almost immediately ensued, and it became clear that Baldwin had miscalculated. By November it seemed that an early election was unavoidable and Baldwin announced on 13 November that Parliament would be dissolved, with polling day set for 6 December. There was much grumbling about the move, but only one resignation, that of a junior minister.

Few MPs favoured the election, and the future Home Secretary William Joynson-Hicks told Baldwin that 'it would be most unpopular with our party in the House. They have all paid one thousand pounds to get there and their wives do not want to pay another thousand with the risk of being thrown out.'[32] Skelton, of course, was not married, but a similar feeling probably weighed upon his mind during an ominous election campaign.

Skelton combined increasingly frequent journalism for *The Spectator* with his third battle for Perth. Reviewing a fellow MP's book on the functions of a second chamber, he dismissed it as 'a lamentably shallow contribution to the discussion of a vital question'. House of Lords reform was not the issue it had been in 1910 or would be again by the mid-1920s, but for Skelton it was another convenient opportunity to dwell upon one of his favourite political issues:

> For legislation affecting the fundamentals of the Constitution, introducing new principles or raising issues whereon the opinion of the country may appear to be almost equally divided, the only adequate expression of the country's opinion is its vote. Anything short of that involves the risk that such legislation may be passed against the wish of the people. Reference to the people is then the only absolute safeguard of democratic institutions. And clearly this, if it be the function of either House, must fall to the Upper to perform; for, ex hypothesi, the legislation has the approval of the Lower . . . But whatever the difficulties, the attempt to construct a Second Chamber fit for this task must be made; for where the safety of democratic government is at stake, no easy assumption that the task is impossible can be permitted.[33]

Back in the fray, *The Scotsman* assessed that the Perth MP's chances of re-election were pretty strong. One correspondent wrote:

> Mr Skelton has close local associations with and an intimate knowledge of the constituency. The bond of sympathy he formed with the younger men of Perthshire during his and their war service is still maintained. He has special gifts as a platform speaker, as he proved, during the last election, when his persuasive power over audiences was largely responsible for the emphatic victory he gained.

The newspaper also noted that

> Mr Skelton has been making personal investigation of the conditions of local industries, and the causes of the special difficulties of each . . . In this way he is bringing himself into close accord with the workers, who are showing by their general attitude that doctrinaire theory has much less attraction for them than the problem of their means of livelihood.'[34]

Skelton, concluded the report, would probably be returned, although perhaps with a reduced majority.

Skelton extended his battle against the Labour Party to the pages of *The Spectator*. Attacking the 'intellectual exhaustion of Socialism' in a review of *Towards a Christian Sociology* by Arthur J. Penty, Skelton wrote:

> All varieties of Socialism suffer from the same basic delusion. They all attack the modern method of producing wealth. 'Industrialism' and 'Capitalism' are their arch-enemies.
>
> But the real problem is distribution of wealth after it has been produced. The development of the present wage-system into one in which Labour shares with Capital the

profits they jointly produce is the clear, logical and obvious
evolution of our present social and economic system . . .
[and] here lies the road along which the industrial army
will presently march. But the Socialist will not have the
satisfaction of having helped to blaze the trail: for the
coming relations between Capital and Labour flow naturally
from the work of Shaftesbury and the thought of Disraeli.
They are based upon the profoundest of social truths –
that private property is the foundation of civilisation and
the extent of its distribution the measure of a civilisation's
stability and success.[35]

When Skelton captured Perth in 1922 there had been four
candidates; this time it was a straight fight with the Liberal
candidate, and Skelton's fellow advocate, Macgregor Mitchell. An
issue in the election was inevitably protection, which had directly
affected the town and in particular two of its main industries –
linen and glass-making. Both had suffered seriously because of
foreign competition and the head of a local linen factory had
indicated that closure was imminent unless help was forthcoming.
Mitchell did his best to capitalise on this. What is more, he had
once played cricket for the county, although he lacked Skelton's
military record.

Skelton touched upon the trade issue in another article for *The
Spectator*. Reviewing J. A. R. Marriott's *Economics and Ethics: A
Treatise of Wealth and Life*, he responded to the question of how
far moral law should govern the organisation of industry and
control the mechanism of trade. Skelton was unequivocal: 'The
more the moral law governs and controls, the more successful
from an economic point of view the industry and trade will be.' He
continued with a now-familiar critique of the moral foundations of
the present economic structure:

Of that system, private property is the basis, and the real
question which is 'perplexing many minds' is whether

private property itself has a moral basis. Is it right or is it wrong?

The orthodox economist rests his whole economic structure upon it and obviously regards the economic soundness of private property as axiomatic. What does the moralist say? If he were to decide it is wrong, and the proposition here suggested is correct, that what is ethically unsound cannot be economically sound, then private property should be replaced by something ethically sounder. This is clear, at any rate, that 'the social conscience' of to-day will not allow the retention of private property on economic grounds unless it is satisfied that it has an ethical basis also.

Skelton also took exception to John Marriott's assertion that 'State Socialism is no more immoral than individualism or syndicalism'. 'Is there any foundation for that statement?' he asked. 'Is it not . . . that between the possession of private property and the development of human character there is the closest possible link, and that if you destroy private property the chances of the individual for ethical development are reduced?' Skelton maintained that

it is only when they [the economists] have satisfied themselves that private property has a moral basis, and serves an ethical end, that they will fully understand that the next step in economic development is to promote the extension of private property, so that as many men and women as possible may share in the moral and economic stimulus it provides.

Noble sentiments, but even they could not salvage a shambolic (national) election campaign, in which all the advantages of the 1922 contest were absent. When the results were declared in early December, the Unionists had suffered a net loss of eighty-eight seats, including Skelton's in Perth; the Liberals, meanwhile, gained ninety-six seats, and Labour forty-nine. Skelton was doubly unlucky in that Scotland had returned almost the same number of Unionist MPs as in 1922. The result was:

Mitchell, R. M. (Liberal)	12,655
Skelton, A. N. (Unionist)	11,134

Mitchell had a small yet respectable majority of 1,521. 'Though on balance the Unionists have gained a seat in Scotland,' commented *The Scotsman*, 'and are not without hopes of further successes, their personal losses have been grievous. Deplorable . . . is the defeat of Mr Noel Skelton, who with his keen interest in social questions, his independent outlook, and his gifts of speech, promised to be one of the most valuable of Scottish members.'[37]

Although the Unionists had won the most seats (258, 86 fewer than the last election), the combined strength of Labour (191, an increase of 49) and the Liberals (158, an increase of 96) put the government in an uncertain position. Baldwin's administration limped along until 17 January 1924, when a Labour amendment to the Address resulted in a defeat by seventy-two votes. Baldwin resigned the following day and Ramsay MacDonald became the first Labour Prime Minister, albeit in command of a minority government that had the tacit support of the Liberals.

Ironically, the Unionists were by then in a good position, having united under the protection banner and successfully depicted the Liberal leader, Asquith, as having been complicit in the formation of a Labour government. As Austen Chamberlain remarked to the Secretary of State for Air, Sir Samuel Hoare, 'We have got (unexpectedly and by our blunders and Asquith's greater folly) a second chance. Have we got the wit to take it?'[38] Skelton, even out of Parliament, was determined to ensure that they did.

3

'A POLICY TO INSPIRE CONVICTION' (1923-4)

The Conservatives' loss of the 1923 general election was viewed as a calamity for which Stanley Baldwin received most of the blame. For Skelton personally, it was a blow to lose his seat after barely a year in the House of Commons, although he continued to contribute regularly to *The Spectator*, no doubt hoping another election was not far away.[1]

Baldwin then faced a fight to maintain his leadership of the Conservative Party. Tariff reform was effectively abandoned, while he turned his mind, as had Skelton in the months before, to the future direction of the Unionists. 'Our great enemies of the future are not going to be the Liberals, who are moribund,' said Baldwin in a landmark speech at the Hotel Cecil on 11 February 1924, 'but Labour, which is very much alive. You are not going to beat Labour on a policy of tranquillity, negation or sitting still. There is vitality in Labour at present in the country, and unless we can share a vitality of that kind we shall be unable to conquer.' He continued:

> The great source of strength of Labour in the country at present is that they have in their ranks a large number of men who believe in their policy. They have the type of man, and many of us who have mixed in the industrial world know him well, who will give the whole of his strength and

the whole of his time to bring about, as he believes he can, a better condition for his fellow-men – with more equality of opportunity, and giving to them a better chance of enjoying more education and more of the good things of life – a perfectly genuine and altruistic feeling. It is that feeling which sends so many of the workers of the party to canvass, to do propaganda, and to conduct the business of elections without payment or reward. It is a spirit which can only be beaten by a similar spirit in our party.[2]

Loud cheers greeted Baldwin's refreshing analysis of the 'new era' and he survived to fight another day and, before too long, another election. His message must also have been music to Skelton's ears, not to mention many others. 'A strong Conservative Party', wrote Winston Churchill to his wife the following month, 'with an overwhelming majority and a moderate and even progressive leadership is a combination which has never been tested before. It might well be the fulfilment of all that Dizzy and my father aimed at in their political work.'[3]

Baldwin's conversion to progressive Conservatism was simply the product of a straightforward analysis of the political zeitgeist. Although the Labour Party was still an unknown quantity, it had managed to form its first administration, and without any talk of revolution. The new socialist ministers even wore morning dress as they received their seals of office at Buckingham Palace.

Skelton, meanwhile, kept himself occupied. In January he was appointed an external examiner in constitutional and administrative law at his alma mater, Edinburgh University,[4] while the following month he lectured at the Unionist School of Study. He also continued to supply *The Spectator* with reviews, including J. A. Spender's *Life of Sir Henry Campbell-Bannerman*, in which his admiration for the great Liberal statesman is obvious.

A singularly individual and spicy personality was hidden behind an exterior rather smug, somewhat clumsy and pre-eminently respectable. No distinguished Scot indeed had more belied his looks since James I had gobbled and sparkled at Whitehall. Highland in blood, lowland in environment, with a touch of Cambridge, a dash of Paris, in mood something of the Whig aristocrat, in morals of the Radical Nonconformist, Campbell-Bannerman was pawky but cultured, an idealist but cautious, a Scottish 'buddy' and a cosmopolitan man of the world, shrewd but innocent, provincial yet urbane, awkward but formidable, with, under it all, a sterling character, an implacable sense of duty and in what was the real centre of his existence – his relations with his invalid wife – wells of devotion, sympathy and self-sacrifice which never ran dry.

Skelton also compared 'C.-B.' with another of his political heroes.

He was utterly imperturbable; he never lost his temper; he always kept his head. In coolness, indeed, he rivalled Disraeli, and if there was something amazingly impressive in Disraeli's iron control of his highly-strung, sensitive genius, very engaging and effective in its own way must have been the lumbering, blundering, pachyderm imperviousness of 'C.-B.'s' good sense and good humour.

He concluded by praising the late Prime Minister's handling of the Second Boer War. 'Having once thus seen the problem, no unpopularity or contempt or ridicule could make him abandon the solution he approved.'[5] Those words could also be applied to Skelton's own political approach.

Skelton also turned his mind to publishing his four *Spectator* articles as a pamphlet. He wrote to John Strachey from the New Club in Edinburgh on 20 January, asking for permission to do so. Strachey replied the following day, saying:

I am only too delighted to do anything I can to help you, and you are fully at liberty to say to any publisher that I was very much impressed by your articles and should be very glad to see them republished, holding as I do that they express the essential need of the Unionist Party.

Strachey also referred to the recent election, confessing that he could

never again feel confidence in Baldwin's judgement. He was a trustee for Unionists who, like myself, believe that the unity and welfare of the Unionist Party is essential and who wanted to draw to it men of intent throughout the country. He smashed this hope and has given an excuse to hundreds of thousands of voters to say they can never vote Unionist.

'His was an act of treason against the Unionist Party,' continued Strachey somewhat melodramatically, 'and, like all treason, it would, no doubt, have been justified by success; but when it has failed, then it seems to me we are obliged to regard it as treason.'[6]

'It was his duty and he did',[7] replied Skelton mysteriously the following month, also enclosing an article he had on Unionist prospects. He could be forgiven for feeling aggrieved at Baldwin's actions given that he had lost his seat, but Skelton appears to have taken a philosophical stance, perhaps reassured by Baldwin's speech at the Hotel Cecil. Strachey, however, was evidently less forgiving. 'Did I tell you what a splendid letter I had from [Sir George] Younger?' he wrote to Skelton in February.

My latest day-dream, – of course, quite impossible, – is that he should be the next Unionist Prime Minister with [Sir Robert] Horne as Leader of the House of Commons.

Meantime, I really am afraid for the first time in my life that the ship is drifting on to the rocks. I have always held that there was only one revolutionary danger in this country, and that is the inability of men of moderation and intelligence to understand issues and carry on the government . . . The Socialists, the Communists, and the Reds do not frighten me in the least; but the Unionists and the Liberals fill me with fear.[8]

Skelton shared Strachey's concern, albeit in reverse, replying that he was 'afraid this Labour Govt is going to prove incapable of carrying on [the] administration of this country in this perilous time . . . Their failure will certainly aggravate the situation, if only because it will change the hopes of their supporters . . . [to] despair.'[9]

But essentially, and as Skelton said in his article on Unionist prospects which finally appeared in *The Spectator* in May 1924, he did not think Strachey's fears about the Conservatives were typical of the party's rank and file. Instead, he said, 'Among these, indeed, there is a striking increase of interest and energy in the constituencies. It would be difficult to recall a defeat which has produced less depression. And it is not irrelevant to mention this, for the spirit of a party is an essential factor in its prospects.'

Nevertheless, Skelton believed the next election would find the country in a very different mood than the last. He argued that the actual formation of a Labour government would prompt the average 'left-centre' voter back to the Unionist fold.

> For these voters, far from being 'left-centre', are perhaps the most inclined to be stationary, if not reactionary, in their political outlook, and their new mood will enable Unionism to advance with more boldness than seemed possible to many when a stagnant, rigid Liberalism stood ready as a harbour of refuge to the backsliders.
>
> No one would deny that amongst Conservatives there tends to be a section which dislikes change for its own sake – as well as a large non-party body of similar opinion. But that body of opinion is alive now to the impracticability and folly of standing still, and when it moves – as move it is now prepared to do – it will prefer to move with progressive Conservatism towards a property-owning democracy

rather than towards the *Sturm und Drang* of Socialism or
the manoeuvres of a suspect Liberalism.

Although Skelton was a protectionist, he had no sympathy for
the presentation of a policy which seemed to penalise the worker
in favour of big business. A tariff, he said 'will fall automatically
into its place as one of the means – perhaps an essential condition
precedent – to the end' of a property-owning democracy. Even
so, 'the real danger to Unionist prospects comes not from fear of
Protection, but from the doubt lest the party should not be in
earnest about social reform . . . Britain, unlike France, passed from
political aristocracy to political democracy without the disaster
of a revolution. Can we make a similar advance in the economic
sphere? It depends entirely upon Conservatism.'[10]

Soon after his Hotel Cecil speech – which had secured him a
resounding vote of confidence – Baldwin embarked upon an
extensive speaking tour of the country, which included a visit to
Skelton's old seat of Perth in March 1924. Speaking at the city hall,
he said 'the love of an almost divine individualism was possessed by
the Scot', which was 'a spirit as alien from the Socialism preached
to-day as light was from darkness'. Socialism and the destruction
of individual liberty inherently embodied in this creed, so Baldwin
argued, transgressed 'the blood of Scotland'.
    But on industry he did not fully back up Skelton's recent
proposals. Baldwin wanted

> to give men more opportunities of learning something
> about the industries in which they work with their hands
> . . . so that in all the great trades of the country the men
> might know the things which are absolutely essential to be
> known – how the goods they make are sold, where they are
> sold, and, above all, what competitive goods they have to
> meet, where those goods are produced, and how the labour
> is remunerated and treated that produces those goods.

'The whole policy of the Unionist Party', Baldwin continued, 'was to unite and not disintegrate. The modern Socialism sought to separate classes, whilst Unionists sought to unite them.'[11]

Convenient stories had begun to circulate about the harmonious labour relations within Baldwin's own family firm. The Conservative Party, meanwhile, began to professionalise itself, creating a secretariat for the Shadow Cabinet and introducing a more rigorous approach to policy-making. Lancelot Storr, who had been Baldwin's secretary at Downing Street, headed up the secretariat, whose staff included a young man called Robert Boothby, who would later become, as an MP, a Skelton acolyte.

For the first time since 1915 the party was reconsidering a wide range of policies, with ex-ministers in charge of various committees (comprising MPs and advisers) that reported weekly to the party leader. When their work was completed, the findings were summarised by Neville Chamberlain in a pamphlet called *Looking Ahead: Unionist Principles and Aims*, which was published on 20 June 1924. The writer John Buchan, another friend of Skelton's, was recruited to oversee Conservative Party literature, and with his help Baldwin began to emerge as a national leader with a clear policy agenda.

Baldwin often invoked the spirit of Disraeli to convince Conservative members and voters that his progressive shifts in political tone had in fact been party policy all along, while presenting the First World War as a great watershed which simply did not allow for a return to the bad old days of reactionary Conservatism. 'It is more than fifty years ago that Disraeli was calling the attention of the country to housing and health problems and they mocked him with a policy of sewage,' said Baldwin in one typical speech. 'The sanitation, or let me say the spiritual sanitation, of our people should have the first call on the historic Tory Party.'[12]

This view of Tory history had just received a powerful reinforcement from Maurice Woods's *History of the Tory Party*, which Skelton reviewed, somewhat caustically, for *The Spectator*. On the whole, he liked it, but it was 'when Mr Woods deals specifically with Tory principles and the Tory Philosophy' that his analysis became 'inadequate and, it must be added, somewhat superficial'.

Woods argued that the party's 'innermost belief' was that stability and order were of fundamental importance to the community. This conviction, he elaborated, led inevitably to a profound sense of the importance of the Crown. But, Skelton argued:

> Toryism to-day would be a laughing-stock if 'its innermost belief were such as to make it, above all else, the defender of institutions on which there is no attack. For that is really to present to the twentieth century Toryism in fancy dress, complete with black-jack and churchwarden pipe. Far from Toryism being Opportunism, its thought, action and statesmanship are based on the most fundamental conception governing the organization of human society.
>
> This once realized, Tory philosophy becomes intelligible and Tory policy consistent and logical. Take, for instance, the light thus thrown upon the underlying unity of the views of Bolingbroke[13] and Disraeli – the two dominating minds of Toryism. It was the search for stability which made Bolingbroke call for the Patriot King and made Disraeli, imbued and thrice imbued as he was with the views of Bolingbroke, reach forward towards Tory Democracy.

He concluded:

> Only monarchical rule or democracy can produce stable conditions – democracy being, as Lord Salisbury once said, 'the safest form of government'. For democracy means actual representation of the nation as a whole. Failing it, no one can represent a nation except its king. Oligarchy, whether Whiggery or Socialism, can represent nothing but itself.[14]

So-called 'Young Conservatives', or at least *younger* Conservatives, were beginning to agree, and what is more, actually echo Skelton's thinking. In a letter published in *The Spectator* – 'The Young Conservatives and the State of the Party' – the future MP John Loder articulated his apologia for youth:

> The Conservative Party has the great chance of becoming the constructive party in the State, of being more liberal than the Liberals and more socialist than the Socialists, because if it appeals, as it can if its principles are what they seem to be, to the British spirit of individual freedom and unfettered co-operation, it will rally to its banner all who are not blinded by theory and dogma. Is the Conservative Party going to make the best of this chance? Is it going to be a positive or a negative force?[15]

Work, meanwhile, continued on Skelton's pamphlet, *Constructive Conservatism*, during the summer of 1924. He scored a notable coup by persuading Sir Robert Horne, a fellow Scot and former Chancellor of the Exchequer, to write a short introduction.

Skelton probably knew Robert Stevenson Horne, a son of the manse, from the Faculty of Advocates, which Horne had joined ten years before him. Like Skelton, Horne had unsuccessfully contested the general election of 1910, and was elected eight years later to represent the Hillhead Division of Glasgow. As Minister of Labour from 1919 to 1920 Horne dealt with a wave of industrial unrest, and was also responsible for the Unemployment Insurance Act 1920, which extended the limited pre-war scheme to cover the majority of workers. As president of the Board of Trade in March 1920, Horne also addressed the delicate issue of trade policy, negotiating, against die-hard Conservative criticism, a trade agreement with Soviet Russia, while as Chancellor from 1921 he had to grapple with a threatened national coal strike, an economic downturn and spending cuts.

Horne was, therefore, on the same political wavelength as

Skelton. Like the former MP for Perth, he was urbane, an excellent raconteur, and inevitably a fixture on the London party circuit. But unlike Baldwin, Horne had resisted the break-up of the coalition in 1922 and refused to serve under both Bonar Law and his successor. By mid-1924 he was back on the Unionist front bench, but Baldwin disapproved of Horne's lifestyle and frequent exchange of directorships in search of higher fees. He concluded that Horne was 'that rare thing – a Scots cad',[16] but Skelton had no such objections.

Constructive Conservatism was finally published by William Blackwood and Sons in September and was available by early October 1924, and is easily the most enduring of Skelton's written work. It opened with his own preface, which noted that 'The Opportunity' he had described in his first *Spectator* piece had now passed. 'Yet defeat has been no unmixed evil,' he wrote. '1922 preserved Conservatism: 1923 consolidated it. It may well be that 1925 will see it engaged on its task of laying the foundations of a national future consonant with the traditions and the character of the race.'

Horne's introduction opened in a similar vein:

> In a time of political unsettlement like the present it is well to review our principles and test our creeds. We have been the witnesses of a political revolution in Britain without fully realising it. The results, however, are now here for men to see. No longer do Conservatives and Liberals face each other in serried ranks, monopolising almost the whole field of party conflict. The once powerful Liberal Party has shrunk to exiguous dimensions, and a formidable Socialist group has snatched from it pride of place amongst the political sects which appeal for the suffrages of the people. Nor are the issues which divide political camps the same. The old party war-cries have for the most part died away, as a new set of problems have clamoured insistently for solution. In these circumstances we may well ask ourselves – as does the author of this admirable essay – whether the Conservative

faith provides the elector with adequate guidance in our present difficulties; whether its gospel contains such a message of inspiration as will make men fight for it with conviction?

Horne continued by asking if the faith and conviction of 'those who have hitherto called themselves Conservative and Unionists . . . [will] be adequate to the needs of these tremendous times, so fateful to our future? Mr Skelton has provided in this brief essay both a philosophy to sustain faith and a policy to inspire conviction.' But, he added, Skelton had

> also dwelt with some insistence upon a besetting sin of which Conservatives have need to beware. Stagnation must not be allowed to masquerade as stability. An exaggeration of a virtue may very easily become a vice, and we shall be signally lacking in our duty if we fail to put into action practical remedies for our present distresses which will commend themselves to the common-sense of the people.

He followed this with an unequivocal endorsement:

> The reader will find in these pages a sketch of some of the practical proposals which the author commends to his Conservative comrades. Of these not the least important is that which he mentions last – namely, the institution of the Referendum. I would venture to add my own plea to Mr Skelton's argument in favour of this reform. It is in line with our democratic development – for what in a moment of doubt could be more democratic than a clear and unambiguous reference to the people? At the same time it is a safeguard which none who have reflected upon the usurpation of power in recent times by tyrannical minorities would readily forgo.[17]

Although referendums were later employed in the UK – over Europe in 1975 or devolution in 1979 and 1997 – in 1924 they were still a novel concept. Their use was not only favoured by Horne and Skelton, but found an enthusiastic proponent in John St Loe Strachey, the editor of *The Spectator*. That journal had been advocating the referendum for almost a year; an editorial in December 1923 had even reprinted Lord Balfour of Burleigh's Referendum Bill of 1911, which had been drafted and paid for by the newspaper. 'We are prepared to say that the Referendum Bill would pass at a Poll of the People by an enormous majority,' boasted a leader column penned by Strachey himself. 'Then, both in the case of the Tariff and the Capital Levy, an appeal to the electors could and would take place.'[18]

Its use in the UK had first been mooted during the second general election of 1910 when Arthur Balfour pledged to refer the question of tariff reform back to the electorate should he secure a mandate. Large newspaper adverts ostentatiously promoted this pledge, although the Unionists lost to the Liberals and therefore the promise went unfulfilled. And even earlier than that, Salisbury had considered its use to settle the Irish question in 1892, encouraged by the judgement of the constitutionalist Professor A. V. Dicey that the referendum was 'at once distinctly and undeniably democratic and in practice Conservative.'[19]

Nowadays the use of referendums (the more Latinate plural of 'referenda' is frowned upon by the *Oxford English Dictionary*) is recognised as a form of 'direct democracy', as practised in countries such as Switzerland. The main argument in favour, and one which Skelton more or less used, is that certain decisions are best taken out of the hands of political elites and determined directly by the people, while others argue that only certain questions, such as the adoption or amendment of a country's constitution, the secession of a state or the altering of national boundaries, should be determined by the directly expressed consent of the people. The counter-argument runs that representative democracy is a system in which elected officials exercise independent judgement rather than robotically carry out the wishes of voters. The referendum, therefore, is a political cop-out.

While Strachey, Skelton, Horne et al. were advocating its use, contemporary precedents were thin on the ground. Australia had conducted referendums occasionally since federation in 1901, most recently over conscription in 1918; Sweden had held its first in 1922 on prohibition, while Norway held one, also on prohibition, in 1919. More significantly, Chile had held a plebiscite on a new constitution in 1925. The 25 October edition of *The Spectator* backed up Horne's endorsement of the referendum with a lengthy editorial, while also identifying the whole of *Constructive Conservatism* as being representative of the paper's political stance.

Following Horne's complimentary introduction was the only substantially new portion of the pamphlet. Part I, 'Architect or Caretaker', replaced 'The Opportunity', which had opened the series back in April 1923. Skelton asked:

> Is Conservatism prepared to supply, in the new era we are entering, the main creative and moulding influence in the national life?
>
> Liberalism cannot. Its thought is barren: its fires are cold: it sees no objective: even if it did, its energies are too exhausted to let it reach it.
>
> Socialism, on the other hand, has force, fire, energy indeed; but its objective, if attained, spells economic disaster and moral despair; it can neither increase wealth nor develop character. The omnipotent State, the kept citizen, responsibility checked, initiative crippled, character in cold-storage, wealth squandered – towards such a goal, Britain, it may be said, will never consent to be led very far; but every step taken is a step wasted, and if a safer road with a better ending be not found for the people – if the alternatives are to be between Socialism and stagnation – the national choice will not fall on stagnation.

'It is Conservatism which must do the architect's work,' Skelton
continued. 'Nothing else is worth its while.' Not only were the
principles of Conservatism unexhausted, he argued, they were
'exactly fitted to lead the country along the next stage of its journey.
To adopt the caretaker's attitude now and refuse the architect's task
would be to deprive the country of the benefits of a constructive
Conservatism at the very time when most it needs it.' Skelton was
beating the political establishment with a heavy polemical stick.

> Yet faith in Conservatism – subconscious, intuitive –
> remains to-day, as ever, the deepest-rooted political instinct
> of Britain. It has been a tragedy too often repeated, indeed,
> that the broad, sound, living national Conservatism has
> found itself reflected, in the purely political sphere, by a
> bloodless, rigid, paralysed habit of mind, which has traded
> on that subconscious, intuitive faith, and has often imposed
> what would have proved an intolerable strain on any loyalty
> less patient and less profound than is that of the people of
> Britain to the underlying truths of Conservatism.

Heavy, then, claimed Skelton, 'is its responsibility, if the
Conservative Party refuse to apply its active principles to the deeper
troubles of the new era; for in these principles alone can a cure be
found'. He then repeated his view that private property was 'the
basis of civilisation', for on it rested the character and economic
freedom of the individual.

> To Conservatism, therefore, the way lies open to expound
> the greatest of all social truths – that the success and the
> stability of a civilisation depend upon the widest possible
> extension amongst its citizens of the private ownership of
> property.
>   And round private property the political combats of the
> future will rage, their issue will decide whether wholesale
> pauperisation is in store for the people, or an advance to

new levels of character and responsibility: the issue itself depends upon the vision, the courage, the resource of Conservatism.

And whatever the analysis, he concluded, 'the statement, the application, in these pages attempted, be correct or not, this much is certain – that the battles ahead cannot be won, or the moulding, creative influence exercised, by the use of a caretaker's mop'.[20]

Encouraging possession of private property among the working population was perhaps an obvious response to socialist collectivism, but Skelton's presentation of the concept was a fresh restatement of Conservative 'philosophy', concisely summed up in the pregnant phrase 'a property-owning democracy'. In this spirit, he supported the Housing Act of 1924 (steered through Parliament by the Red Clydesider John Wheatley), which aimed to build 190,000 new council houses at rents working-class people could afford. Paradoxically, Wheatley regarded local authority housing as a transitional step towards more home ownership, which, despite his firebrand left-wing background, he favoured.

Skelton had already expanded upon his view of property – which still excluded housing – in a *Spectator* essay entitled 'Private Property: A Unionist Ideal'. 'It is not for nothing that the Conservative Party used to be called the "Party of Property",' he argued. 'Private property is, so far as history gives us a clue, the foundation and *sine qua non* of all progressive civilizations.'

It follows that the extent of the distribution of private property is the measure, on its economic side, of a civilization's stability and success. Similarly, character and a sense of responsibility are rooted in a man's possession of 'something of his own'. A democracy without scope for the development of economic character and responsibility, cut off from private ownership, cannot be expected to understand the material foundations of civilization.

'It will perhaps be a slow process,' concluded Skelton, 'but great parties must take a long view, and if an objective is sufficiently important must not fear the toils of the march.' What was more, the Unionist Party had at once to 'make it clear that the elevation of the status of the wage-earner to that of a property-owner lies at the root of its social policy.'[21]

The publication of *Constructive Conservatism* came at a pertinent moment. On 8 October 1924 the minority Labour government fell after a successful Liberal amendment over a treaty to formally recognise the Soviet Union, and polling day was set for 29 October. Five days later Skelton was, once again, unanimously adopted as the Unionist candidate for the Perth Division.

Skelton sent Strachey a copy of his pamphlet on the day the government fell, noting smugly that 'Horne in his little introduction definitely states his approval of this Referendum as a democratic [system]'.[22] Strachey replied on 21 October offering his congratulations. 'I am fearfully over-driven,' he wrote, 'but I must write and tell you how splendid your pamphlet is, and how admirable is Horne. I am afraid I have been sometimes a little unfairly critical of him, but I withdraw it all after that introduction. However, I am much too busy to say anything, except to make you a salute.'

Strachey not only wanted Skelton 'to do some [more] writing for *The Spectator*', but he told him that he had 'sent for a lot of copies of the pamphlet, and mean to scatter them broadcast'.[23] Skelton wrote again two days later, this time from the Station Hotel in Perth (his berth during election campaigns). 'I am so glad you like this pamphlet in its new form,' he said gratefully. 'At any rate, it is as near as I can get, in the space, to what I regard as the "fundamentals". I thought you wd approve of Horne's preface.' The election campaign, said Skelton, was going well.

> I have legitimate hopes . . . of getting back to the House of Commons. I should . . . do some writing for 'the Spectator'

> & I am quite certain that 'the Spectator' will have a most
> important part to play . . . Unless we treat it [the election]
> as an opportunity and not as a justification . . . we shall fail
> at the end of the Parliament.[24]

Strachey responded on 25 October.

> I do hope you are quite safe. It will indeed be a 'damp
> haystack' General Election for me if you are out. Of course,
> we may have a great victory and all be able to sleep in the
> way that the majority of Conservatives prefer. Deflation,
> paying off debt, and unemployment treated as a necessary
> evil to which it is best to close one's eyes, does not seem to
> me, however, a very hopeful programme.

Strachey suggested that he, Skelton and Horne should 'get together
and try to make the Constitution, at any rate, less dangerous than
it is'. Why not, he added, 'a Referendum League with Horne as
President and you as Secretary?'[25] Nothing, however, seems to have
come of this particular idea.

Baldwin's organisational and policy reforms appeared to have
paid off. The difficulties of the 1923 election campaign were gone
and in many seats a Labour intervention helped split the radical
vote, allowing Unionists to win back seats previously lost to the
Liberals. The 1924 Conservative campaign deftly emphasised the
safeguarding of industry and assistance of agriculture, both to
counter unemployment, while stressing imperial unity, defence
and the fostering of an Empire-wide foreign policy.

On the eve of poll, Skelton delivered a rallying cry for his
'property-owning democracy' in Perth. 'Let it be all for each, and
each for all,' he said. 'Let the great principle of united effort be the
principle of their legislation.' He declared that

> the British community was an immense power and why not

aid it in building up a property-owning democracy, master of its own fate, secure from outside attack, and able to look after its own affairs, secure and safe from all the winds of revolution; Bolshevism, and despair which in this post-war period swept across the world of men? Surely it was an ideal worth fighting for? It was the Unionist ideal, and it was because he believed there lay in the ideal of a property-owning democracy being the due for the future of their people – he was not . . . speaking now on the threshold of defeat, as last year, but, as every man and woman in that hall knew, on the threshold of victory . . . Their time was coming, and on these principles he was prepared to stand or fall.[26]

When the polls closed on 29 October a total of 412 Unionists were returned, an increase of 154 in all, including Skelton in Perth. The result was:

Skelton, A. N. (Unionist)	13,022
Mitchell, R. M. (Liberal)	7,998
Roberts, C. (Labour)	5,316

A healthy majority of more than 5,000 was a substantial achievement for Skelton, although the Labour intervention had played a part and the *Perthshire Advertiser* commented that he had polled more votes than expected. *The Scotsman* recorded its satisfaction at Skelton's return to Parliament, as a former member 'of experience and high promise',[27] while Strachey wrote with 'hearty congratulation' for 'so splendid a victory'.

I think that Horne, Boothby, and you, and the other young Unionists, not only in Scotland, but in England, should play a very great part in keeping the Unionist Party off – I will not say the rocks, – but the mud banks of fatuous optimism. We have got the chance to clear up all the gunpowder that is lying about loose and which it is the cheerful aspiration of Labour to explode under our feet.[28]

Baldwin's 'New Conservatism' now had a huge mandate, and a host of younger, zealous Tory MPs who wanted to make it a reality.

4

'A GREAT POLITICAL
TEACHER' (1924-9)

The 1924 general election was a watershed in British politics. With the Liberals reduced to a rump of just forty seats, the House of Commons was now polarised between the Conservatives (with an additional 154 MPs) and the Labour Party, which despite losing forty seats remained the official opposition with 151 MPs.

The parliamentary demographic also underwent a marked shift. While in 1918 the number of MPs aged under forty constituted only one sixth of the Conservative Party, after the 1924 election they made up just under a quarter of the 412 Tory MPs, with many Members – like Skelton – returning to Parliament having lost their seats in 1923.

The size of the government's majority, however, took the party by surprise, and ironically, Skelton was no longer a young man. He was forty-four in 1924, although his relative seniority did nothing to prevent him becoming the recognised leader of a parliamentary group called the YMCA (Young Men's Christian Association). Initially, the sobriquet 'Eager Young Men' also attached itself to the group.

For many, the 1920s was an exciting decade: the age of illusion, of nightclubs, jazz, champagne cocktails and racing cars. The wireless boomed as the medium of mass entertainment and information, while the movies became talkies. The spirit of the age chimed with the youth of the YMCA, forged from a handful of radical Scottish Unionist MPs and more moderate English members. Most had served in the Great War, a conflict which resembled a social melting pot, where the professional and landed classes recognised for the first time the mindset and culture of working men.

The YMCA, therefore, captured the zeitgeist of what Skelton had already called the 'new era' in *Constructive Conservatism*. Skelton's ideas, already articulated in a pamphlet many new MPs had read earlier that year, appealed strongly to the group because it was so forward-looking in terms of Tory democracy. They set out to support the progressive elements in Baldwin's Conservative government against what they regarded as the party's reactionary business members – often referred to as the 'Forty Thieves', or more simply, 'Diehards' – industrialists such as Sir George Balfour, Henry Page-Croft and Patrick Hannan.[1]

Skelton became the intellectual leader of the group (though not in a formal sense) and took a leading part in the lobbying and journalistic activities of the YMCA, aided in the latter task by Bob Boothby and Duff Cooper.[2] Others began to notice the dynamic spirit of the group. The Beaverbrook Press took up the young Conservatives' cause, while Oliver Harvey told John Loder[3] that the only hope lay 'in the younger Conservatives insisting on something being done and not allowing the old rascals to stamp out the enthusiasts'.[4] At around the same time, Harold Macmillan wrote to Loder saying that 'we shall be able to do our small part in stirring up the old fogeys and making this Government get on with the job'. It was, he noted, 'the best chance we shall have and we are uncommonly lucky to have it'.[5]

The 1924 Conservative manifesto had included commitments on housing, comprehensive pensions, education and amending the existing factory law. The YMCA were especially keen on such social issues, knowing that ignoring them would risk alienating the working-class voters many of them depended upon for their majorities (not least Skelton in Perth). The YMCA was drawn mostly from bourgeois, or 'haut bourgeois', families, and in this sense Skelton was typical. Like Harold Macmillan he had entered Oxford on a scholarship, and belonged more to the professional wing of the YMCA than the aristocratic. Oliver Stanley,[6] son of Lord Derby, perhaps best typified the latter. Even before the 1924 election brought most of them together, many in the group already knew, or at least knew of, each other through the London social circuit.

It is important to note that the YMCA lacked any formal organisation, and was a loose grouping at best. It also lacked a clear statement of intent, although to be fair this was well enough known. 'Perhaps those who worked most consistently together', recalled Macmillan in his memoirs, 'were Noel Skelton, Oliver Stanley, John Loder, Rob[ert] Hudson,[7] Boothby,[8] and later Terence O'Connor.[9] These were the core; but others came and went, or were vaguely attached.' Macmillan continued:

> Undoubtedly, the most striking mind and real intellectual leader of our little company was Noel Skelton. It was he who developed and occasionally published in short but intensely interesting pamphlets the philosophy of the new Toryism. A little older than most of us, he commanded not only our affection but our respect.

Macmillan also remembered that *Constructive Conservatism* had 'a great effect on all the younger Members of the party'.[10] Other accounts of the YMCA, however, vary. Duff Cooper, for example, was not really a member of the group and Robert Boothby later claimed it was nowhere near as cohesive as Macmillan claimed. In one of his many books, Boothby recalled that

> it devolved upon the Scottish Tories, hitherto a small band without many personalities or traditions, or indeed much hope, to provide the main opposition to the Socialists; and to imbibe a sufficient quantity of the spirit of Liberalism to make themselves acceptable in that rôle. On the whole they succeeded remarkably well; and this was largely due to the

enthusiasm and unquestioned brilliance of a great political teacher, the late Noël Skelton. Neither Sir Robert Horne, the effective spokesman of big business, nor Walter Elliot with his diversified interests, ministerial pre-occupations and doubtful political antecedents – had he not been a Socialist at Glasgow University? – could have been a comparable mentor for the new Unionist Party, or done as much.

Like Elliot, added Boothby, 'Skelton was a superlative talker, with a tremendous gaiety and zest for life; but in the more concentrated Edinburgh tradition. He stimulated every gathering he joined; and in a flash generated the sparks of animated and provocative talk by means of audacious sallies and improvisations, flung out with reckless prodigality.'[11]

In his unpublished memoirs, Loder noted the debt owed by the younger, more inexperienced, members during the early days of the 1924 Parliament.

> Initially, when we were raw Parliamentarians, we owed much to Noel Skelton, the member for Perth, who had been first elected in 1922, was beaten in 1923, and who had regained the seat in 1924. He was our senior both in years and political experience. Just before the 1924 Election he had published a pamphlet called *Constructive Conservatism*, which called attention to the great differences between the party politics of the pre-1914 and the post-war era. He understood the aspirations of the new democracy.[12]

Skelton's acolytes, meanwhile, understood the appeal of 'a property-owning democracy', if only as a phrase. Stanley, Boothby and Hudson all used it in their Commons speeches, after Skelton introduced it to the House (during a debate on unemployment) on 26 March 1925:

> I believe, for reasons which I shall attempt to put before

the House, that the future of trade and employment in this country depends, first and foremost, upon a constant upholding of the principle of private enterprise and private property, and the great extension of the latter through the larger number of the people in this country. So far from believing that through any form of state control, far less of state ownership, you will get improved production, improved work and improved conditions, in my judgement the real hope of this country and in particular the real hope of the working classes, lies in the development of what I venture to call a property-owning democracy.[13]

Stanley Baldwin, once again Prime Minister and vindicated in light of his actions a year earlier, had also noticed the relative youth of a large section of his backbenchers and, more importantly, taken note of their views. Baldwin even told King George V of the 'band of keen and ardent young Conservatives with a genuine desire to serve the public interest rather than any particular class or faction, or their own particular selfish interest'.[14]

And at the Prime Minister's victory rally at the Royal Albert Hall on 4 December, Baldwin spoke of the 'disgrace of the slums' and the need to tackle housing conditions. Again, the Prime Minister drew particular attention to the commitment of his younger MPs to social reform. There was also evidence that Baldwin had read Skelton's pamphlet, when he said that 'even the philosophers justify property because it is something in the external world which is a material representation of human personality'.[15] The following year he went even further.

We want people to own their own homes. And we shall devise every fair means we can to extend the class of occupying owner. We want to see more and not less of private property. We want it more spread. It is impossible to exaggerate the value to the citizen, therefore to the State, of a good home.[16]

Baldwin was not only a great political survivor but also a deft operator. He was acutely aware that his party had to present itself as the natural party of both England and Scotland if it was to survive. The same logic applied to the party's handling of social issues. In this sense, Baldwin had bought into Skelton's view that the party had to articulate a 'view of life' in order to attract the Labour-inclined voter.

Following the election triumph, Boothby noted that Baldwin had kept his party united 'because he has throughout managed to retain the confidence of the extreme right, and at the same time given a clear lead to the Tory democrats of the left'.[17] Meanwhile, the *Spectator* editor John St Loe Strachey – who often despaired of the Conservative Party, even in victory – had pinned his hopes not just on Skelton, but also on Boothby and Sir Robert Horne. 'You will have some capital young supporters in men like Skelton', Strachey told Horne on 31 October, 'and also, I am glad to see, Boothby, and you may depend upon me and *The Spectator* doing everything we can to help on dynamic as against static Conservatism.' He added:

> To my mind, we want to make the giving of ownership to a far larger proportion of the population our main policy, – 'Ownership of land, Ownership of houses, Ownership in stocks and shares for the small man'. The worker, however good his wages, has not a good foundation for Democracy unless he has got some of the magic of ownership. Do put it on your banner.[18]

Boothby received a similarly effusive letter from Strachey the same day. 'I think that Horne, Skelton, and you,' he wrote, 'reinforced by one or two other good men and backed up by the Spectator might do a very great service in keeping the Unionist Party off – I will not say the rocks, – but the mud banks of fatuous optimism.' Strachey continued: 'We have got a chance to clear up all the gunpowder that is lying about loose and which it is the cheerful aspiration of Labour to explode under our feet.'[19]

And responding to Skelton's hopes that Baldwin would place himself firmly at the head of an 'orderly programme set down and worked through steadily', Strachey noted that he was afraid

> Baldwin is a touch-and-go man and would never do anything in that way. I admire him, but I have no confidence in his powers of leadership. He has not enough ambition, – that useful antiseptic in politics. I am afraid, therefore, that he is not one of the people likely to do the best with a vast majority.[20]

But Baldwin, too, recognised that the 1924 election was a key event in British politics, although Austen Chamberlain warned him that having such a large majority also brought reactionary dangers. The Prime Minister seemed conscious of this, summing up his political outlook in a speech at Stourport on 12 January 1925 thus:

> There is only one thing which I feel is worth giving one's whole strength to, and that is the binding together of all classes of our people in an effort to make life in this country better in every sense of the word. That is the end and object of my life in politics.[21]

'Appeasement from strength' was, therefore, Baldwin's approach, both abroad and at home. On the policy of intervention in industry the Prime Minister occupied a middle position, agreeing with the YMCA that the Tory tradition allowed intervention, but siding with the 'industrials' who believed that this intervention must be minimal and consistent with economic policy. Baldwin believed the role of his government was to stabilise the situation while industry sorted out its internal problems.

Skelton anticipated some of these issues in his first political essay of the year, entitled 'Labour in the New Era', which appeared not in *The Spectator* but in the *Quarterly Review*, a journal launched in 1809 by the Anglo-Scottish publisher John Murray.

'The General Election of 1924 has brought the country definitely into a new era,' proclaimed Skelton, before going on to assert that 'the Labour leaders have learned now that, in the new era, the oldest and most persistent of British instincts – detestation of foreign interference and horror of revolutionary methods – is as strong as ever. They stirred it, and it has destroyed them.'[22]

> The electors may give a Socialist party a parliamentary majority: they will never allow it to socialise Britain . . . It is of immense importance to the future of Britain that, within the next five years, Socialism should have been swept out of the field of practical politics. For if it survives, this danger survives with it . . . Of the present three parties, Liberalism seems fated to be ground out of existence between the upper and the nether millstones, leaving Labour to form the alternative Government of the future. And as Governments and parties suffer defeat more from their own faults and failures than on account of the principles or promises of their opponents, some day, soon or late, the Labour Party will be swept into office on a wave of popular support.

Skelton had already grasped that the future of politics would be an eternal battle between left and right, Labour and Conservative. 'It is by continuous and outspoken criticism of the defects of the existing industrial system that Socialism thrives,' he continued. 'Why, in sober truth, should the wage-earner be attracted by the idea of making the State his employer and the community the universal master of the individual?' Skelton argued that the defect of the present system was 'that under it he [the wage-earner] is industrially only a machine; that his wages are a mere part of the costs of production; that with the profits of the business in which he is employed he has no concern . . . The core of the problem is the status, not merely the remuneration, of the worker.'

Co-partnership, said Skelton, was 'the clue to the future'. It would leave the system of private enterprise intact, while giving to the wage-earner a share of the profits, an increasing interest in capital, and 'it contains, too, a great constructive ideal in fullest harmony with the character and genius of this industrial age, because in grappling with the industrial problem it also points the way to a new and sounder social system through the development of a property-owning democracy'. He added:

> All roads to-day lead to a property-owning democracy, for in such a democracy lies the remedy of industrial unrest, the application of the political principles of the modern world to the actual material life of the people.
>
> It would be inexcusable if the Unionist Party were to keep silence on a subject of such immense industrial, social, and national importance; it has no constructive task in the years ahead more important than to explain and expound to the country the principles and the practice of Co-partnership, and to use its influence, actively, consistently and continuously, to mould in its favour public opinion amongst both employers and employed. And it is a constructive task none the less because it is a matter far more for exposition than for legislation.

These were all familiar themes from Skelton, but he was consciously fleshing out his thinking and re-emphasising his central beliefs now that the Unionists were back in power. 'It is only a property-owning democracy which will permanently refuse to admit a Socialistic Government to its confidence,' he asserted.

> To the property-less man the distinction between nationalisation and individualism is too remote from his experience and his circumstances to stand out at all times with perfect clearness through the scud and spindrift of political storms; for if he have no property of his own, how can he be greatly interested in the fate of the possessions of others? But a property-owning democracy knows that

nationalisation is its bitterest foe: into the hands of a nationalising party it will never deliver itself.

However, conceded Skelton,

> to maintain the wage-standard would remain the function of the Trades Union, as necessary under Co-partnership as it is now . . . Just as Co-partnership alone can break the spell of Socialism, so its real effect upon the Trades Unions would be to exorcise some of the evil spirits that haunt them.
>
> Yet even the well-wishers of Trades Unionism must tremble for its future . . . [it] enters the new era employing methods which are grotesquely and intolerably tyrannous and corrupt . . . The practice of open voting on the most vital questions of course allows, and cannot but be meant to allow, the minority to feel the pressure and coercive power of the majority . . . Lastly, the use of the political levy to extract funds for the support of Socialist propaganda from members who are not Socialists is utterly base and unscrupulous. The Trades Unionist leaders will be mad to continue such practices . . . Unless the leaders are warned in time, they will find growing up against them in the Unions a powerful and determined public opinion.

But, and crucially in the context of imminent events, Skelton argued that 'reform of Trade Union methods must come from within, not from without. To attempt reform from without, and above all or an anti-Socialist Party to attempt it by legislation, would be an error and blunder gross indeed.' To alter, he continued, 'the present right of the Trade Unionist to contract-out of the political levy, by forbidding the Union to charge him with the levy unless he had contracted-in, would be obviously to legislate in advance of public opinion within the Union.'

> Once a party uses its power, under whatever guise, to weaken

its rivals, public life degenerates into a mere vendetta, and Acts of Parliament become instruments not of reform but of reprisals. Such legislation never achieves its object. In this case it would be regarded by the wage-earners as an attack upon the Trades Unions, and many who are at this moment beginning to regard their methods with suspicion would respond anew to the appeal to class loyalty, would rally to the cry of 'The Unions in danger.'[23]

Most Conservative opinion, including Skelton, had long been opposed to the 'political levy', under which the Labour Party gleaned revenue from trade union membership fees. In February 1925 Fred Macquisten,[24] the Unionist MP for Argyll, introduced a private member's bill which proposed reforming this system so that Labour-supporting union members had to explicitly 'contract in' to the political levy, rather than have their subscription purloined automatically.

At the outset, it appeared as if majority Cabinet and backbench opinion favoured the bill, or at least a similar measure from the government. Baldwin took the matter seriously and consulted extensively, including a delegation led by Skelton. 'After Questions', recorded Duff Cooper in his diary on 25 February, 'about twenty of us went on a deputation to the Prime Minister about the Political Levy. Skelton stated our case briefly and well.'[25] Harold Macmillan also recalled the delegation in his memoirs. 'When this [Macquisten's bill] was in the offing, our little group, under Noel Skelton's leadership, went in a deputation to [Baldwin], asking him to oppose the bill. He received us kindly, and the fact that he appeared to follow our advice was naturally a source of gratification to us.'[26]

Baldwin, to be fair, had probably already decided what to do, although his reasoning was remarkably similar to that outlined by Skelton in his *Quarterly Review* article the previous month. He explained eloquently his reasoning to the Cabinet, and later addressed a packed and hushed Commons. Speaking with quiet sincerity, he began with a nostalgic view of industrial life from his childhood, before making a dramatic peace offering, not only across the floor of the House, but across the gulf of industry.

> We have our majority. We believe in the justice of the bill . . . But we are going to withdraw our hand. We are not going to push our political advantage home at a time like this . . . We, at any rate, are not going to fire the first shot. We stand for peace. We stand for the removal of suspicion in this country. We want to create a new atmosphere, a new atmosphere in a new parliament for a new age, in which the people can come together . . . We abandon what we have laid our hands to. We know we may be called cowards for doing it . . . But we believe we know what at this moment the country wants, and we believe it is for us in our strength to do what no other party can do at this moment and to say that we at any rate stand for peace . . . I have confidence in my fellow-countrymen throughout the whole of Great Britain. Although I know there are those who work for different ends from most of us in this House, yet there are many in all ranks and all parties who will re-echo my prayer: 'Give peace in our time, O Lord.'[27]

Baldwin had triumphed, and his Commons speech – together with others in Birmingham and Leeds – sold half a million copies when issued as the pamphlet *Peace in Industry*. It had elevated the issue to a higher moral plane, while marking the first victory for the YMCA against the Conservative Party's reactionary element. Baldwin's speech killed Macquisten's bill and strengthened the Prime Minister's hand when it came to reducing wages in the coal industry. But, added Macmillan in his account of the episode, 'it was only as the Parliament proceeded that some of us began to feel some doubts, not as to his [Baldwin's] desire, but as to his power and determination to influence events'.[28]

For the moment, at least, the YMCA had reason to be content with the direction of government policy. In November 1924 Neville

Chamberlain had presented to Cabinet a list of reforms he wished to implement in housing, health and local government. Baldwin was supportive and most – including extensions of national insurance and widows' pensions – had been implemented by 1929. The former, however, suffered a cut soon after the triumph over the political levy, and when the Economy Bill was debated in March 1926, Skelton moved an amendment arguing that the reduction in the state contribution to national health insurance 'be regarded as a temporary expedient and not a permanent policy'.[29]

The first full year of the parliament also saw the formation of a 'Social Reform Group' of MPs, including Lady Astor, of which Skelton must surely have been a member. This group faced its first test in the guise of the Factory Bill, which was at risk of being dropped. Among those urged to lobby for its survival were Skelton and Macmillan. The Cabinet eventually dropped the bill on the basis of time limitations, but promised another – which would limit working hours for women and young children – during the next session.

Another crisis arose in May 1925 when the steel industry applied for safeguarding. Steel was a major industry, but was so vital to the economy that a decision to grant it protection would have led to demands for similar intervention in other industries. Thus the tariff issue reared its complicated head once more. Despite threats of resignation from Winston Churchill, Baldwin announced in December that the request would be refused.

There was, however, unanimous support among the YMCA for a proposed coal subsidy which John Loder thought was 'the best in the circumstances' and would allow time for the government's wider programme of industrial conciliation to work. Skelton elaborated on the Young Conservatives' views in a letter to *The Times* on 3 August 1925. Instead of polarising opinion, he argued, the subsidy would isolate extremists and rally moderate opinion to the government. Critics, however, saw it as capitulating to organised labour. Skelton retorted that the popular view among the press and politicians was that it constituted weakness, but only if the view of the situation was normal. 'There is, however, another [view],' he wrote.

It is that the national situation is for the moment, and promises for some months to be, of such exceptional gravity that industrial peace is an absolutely overriding necessity, to which all ordinary considerations must be subordinated.

The nation feels vaguely but strongly that this is so. Is it wrong? A coal strike, extending, as it would inevitably have done, into a railway and a transport workers' strike, would have been economically ruinous, and might have had national consequences no man can adequately assess . . . Moscow would have rejoiced and might have triumphed.

Skelton argued that the 'coming months have special anxieties of their own' and that British trade would continue to feel pressure from the Continent. 'In truth, a cyclone is raging. Its peak was passed on Friday. The house stands. It will weather the rest of the storm.' Skelton continued with a spirited defence of Baldwin's plain-speaking approach:

He has identified and concentrated upon this as the dominant issue. Whoever cares to may doubt whether he is right. No one can at present say he is wrong. To urge that his appreciation of the situation is at fault is to run the risk of under-estimating the seriousness of the crisis. That way, above all others, to nations come catastrophes.[30]

Away from the industrial situation, Skelton devoted much of his first full year in Parliament to agricultural matters. He was nominated as secretary of the Scottish Unionist sub-committee on agriculture in February, while the following month he made a lengthy agricultural speech during a debate on unemployment. He told MPs:

I have no doubt that . . . by small ownership and by the interest in the work which small ownership creates, results are being obtained which could not be obtained in any other way. You have there an example of what I believe to be the fundamental necessity. You have there a property-owning democracy.

I believe we must go along the line of giving a real stimulus to production by allowing the producer to know that he will become the owner of property, that he will have something of his own, and that he will not be a mere wage slave – to use the familiar term – of some socialist state, but will be an independent man with all the advantages of independence and his own position in life. I believe that there we have a clear line of advance. It is a line of advance which can only be developed by a Conservative government, because a Conservative government is the only government and the Conservative Party is the only party which fully realises the close relation between ownership and the character of the individual.

Therefore . . . we on this side, confident of the material, moral, and economic value of a system which is based upon private property, feel that we cannot stand still on that point, but believe that, in the development of that very instrument of welfare, namely private property, in which we so profoundly believe, lies the only hope of the working classes of the future in this country, lies the only hope of larger production, and lies the only hope of the development of an independent, sound, strong, and, may I add, absolutely non-socialist nation.[31]

Skelton also spoke regularly of the need to improve agricultural housing. In this regard his Perth constituency, surrounded as it was by rich and fertile land, was a pertinent illustration of his radical vision for land reform and he incorporated it into his second *Quarterly Review* essay of the year, 'The Nation and the Land', which appeared in July. Skelton began:

The Conservative party pledged itself at the polls to carry out a national and not a class or sectional policy, thus accepting anew Disraeli's massive saying: 'If the Tory party is not a national party, it is nothing,' and since the Election Mr Baldwin has convinced the country that this pledge will be honoured in spirit and in letter, in the sense, at any rate, that class or sectional interests will not prevail.

The first test, said Skelton, of a national policy

is that it can be stated, explained, justified, not only to a section, but to the whole of the nation. For it is not the country districts which can decide whether and how Britain is going to develop her country estate. Only the cities and the towns can make that decision. They, politically, are Britain. Nothing that they disapprove can be done. Nothing that they approve long remains undone.

Even on the subject of agriculture Skelton could be scathing about previous government policy. He said that Britain had behaved towards her country estate as 'a mere absentee landlord'. 'Its people are strangers: its problems a mystery: its life a dull farce played in front of a rural drop-scene.' What was more, 'Rural Britain does not interest the Stock Exchange, for it is not expressed in terms of shares.' And 'to Treasury eyes, rural Britain embodies the most unattractive features of a country cousin and a poor relation . . . If England has been an absentee landlord to her country estate, the Treasury, it would seem, has been a short-sighted and a heedless land-agent.'

Skelton contrasted one school of thought, which argued for larger, highly industrialised farms covering thousands of acres, with his own alternative.

Instead of fewer and larger farms, more and smaller holdings; instead of the formation of a new kind of large estate, the private ownership of land 'in widest commonality spread'; instead of industrialised production, intensive cultivation;

instead of profits for a few urban shareholders, a livelihood for a numerous property-owning democracy; instead of land exploitation, land settlement. It is land settlement, not land exploitation, which will commend itself to the nation as a whole, and will best reinforce and harmonise with our general social structure, predominantly urban as it is and as it must remain.

In Perthshire, said Skelton, a grazing farm of 550 acres 'on which three to five men were employed, now supports, and supports well, eleven small owners and their families'. The smallholder, therefore, 'has, as an economic unit, a specially high quality. It is the special virtue of the small cultivator that, as a consumer, he is, pound for pound of his income, of exceptional merit.' And 'family for family, a group of small-holders will absorb a much greater amount of industrial produce than the same number of persons, farmer and labourer in normal proportions, in the large-farm system'.

Certainly his heads of expenditure compare very favourably with the cinema ticket, the Saturday bet, the canary, the whippet, even the pedigree rabbit or the fancy pigeon on which the urban wage-earner of approximately equivalent income, lavishes the surplus of his earnings . . . [but] if anything can stop the drift to the cities and even entice the country-bred back to the land, small holdings, and particularly small ownerships, will do it.

Again, Skelton drew upon personal experience.

And . . . this is no mere surmise the present writer believes, because he knows how many of the small-holders of his acquaintance have some town-dwelling brother or cousin anxious to return to the land.

To the agricultural labourer in England, the farm-servant in Scotland, the opportunity of becoming in his middle life the master of a piece of land, brings what without exaggeration may be called a new horizon and a new hope . . . The policy of land settlement, in short, not only harmonises with our general economic structure; it raises a rural policy from a sectional to a national level. And if a small-holding system of intensive cultivation harmonises with the general interests of Britain, not less does Britain offer unequalled promise for such a system's success.

Skelton lamented that 'it is from overseas that the bulk of our bacon, butter, cheese, and eggs come to us, while our urban population is condemned, since round it lie half-empty the fields of England, to nourish itself and its children on condensed and tinned milk'. He added: 'The small-owner, indeed, is as valuable from a social and a civic point of view as he is from an economic. Nothing can compensate a nation for his absence. And in particular for a democratic state he is the surest of all foundations.'

Again, as with the industrial question,

the Unionist Party has at the present moment a remarkable opportunity for turning at last the attention of the nation to the development of its country estate. For Unionism to-day speaks with authority. In its leader, Britain recognises a man after her own heart, whose growing power over his fellow-countrymen is, in fact, the dominant feature of public life. Understood in town and country alike, Mr Baldwin will be listened to in both.

It may take more than one generation before its full fruits are gathered . . . with its social structure underpinned by the wide extension of the private ownership of land, [Britain] will reap the harvest of a constructive statesmanship and, in its daily life, will realise, with a completeness to which it has long been a stranger, that the nation is one and that factory and field are only parts of a single whole.[32]

The article certainly impressed John Strachey, to whom Skelton had sent it on 14 July. 'I have looked at your Quarterly article and think it excellent,' he replied. 'You need not mind there being nothing new in it, because if there was on such a theme as the Land it would probably be wrong. As you say, however, there is a distinctly new angle of vision.'[33]

Skelton also continued to occupy himself with constitutional considerations, largely egged on by Strachey. Although Sir Robert Horne had been excluded from Baldwin's government (albeit by his own refusal to serve), therefore depriving Skelton of a high-level ally (leading, perhaps, to ministerial preferment), he remained enthusiastic about the referendum. 'In the present Parliament, Skelton, a clever young Scottish Member, is very keen about the Referendum,' Strachey told Lord Selborne on 27 February.

> He rang me up on the first day of the meeting of the Commons for a copy of Balfour of Burleigh's bill[34] because if he had won a place in the ballot he intended to introduce it. He tells me that he finds a great number of the younger Conservatives in favour of the Referendum, and he is going to do his best to further the cause.

Strachey suggested that when Selborne got back to London he 'should come and meet Skelton here, and, if possible, Horne, and we might see whether it might not be possible now to form some kind of committee for keeping the Referendum issue before men's minds'.[35] Strachey reported to Skelton on 8 May that he had met with Selborne and Horne, and that both were 'very keen for action'. He continued:

> Horne spoke very nicely of you and of how well fitted you would be to run the thing if you would. As far as I am concerned, I most strongly hope you will, because I know your ideas are sound.
>
> We all three agreed yesterday that the necessity for the

Government to do something in regard to the Parliament Act gave a tremendous opportunity for the Referendum. I get more and more proof every day of how much the Labour people dread the Referendum. It really does put a curb on them . . . It seems to me that you two members would be ideal people to get recruits. Selborne, between ourselves, was rather appalled by the ignorance on the whole problem shown by many of the new members.[36]

The *Spectator* editor saw Skelton soon after on the subject, but it seems the author of *Constructive Conservatism* – which devoted a considerable portion to the referendum – was beginning to have some doubts. Skelton wrote to Strachey from the Conservative Club that same month, asking if he would 'consider this point which has been giving me some trouble in my own mind?' 'You & I', he continued, 'start off from the general policy on the Referendum as the next stage in democratic development and also as a . . . constitutional safeguard.' But what if, he added, a future Labour government was to include a 'wide Capital Levy' in that year's Finance Bill, 'and I suppose that you & I am in agreement that in principle Finance legislation must be referable, like any other'.

But, suppose a Finance Bill introducing such a provision were referred and rejected by referendum, what about the Govt? Could it be argued that a government, when financial arrangements for the year had been destroyed, could remain in office? I really doubt it, for what could they do. Cd the Socialist Ch. of the Exchequer be expected to frame a new Budget Day in H of C . . . or indeed, at all? This point is the neg[ative] one, which to my own mind, is difficult – always assuming that I include Finance Bills [in] the operation of the Referendum. [This would] clearly impair its usefulness. If you admit that defeated on its year's Finance Bill, a Government would have no practical alternative to resignation, then the Referendum could be attacked . . . [as] destroying a government.[37]

Strachey, always more interested in grand schemes than troubling details, does not appear to have shared Skelton's anxiety. 'On the whole I am satisfied,' he replied on 14 May. 'I mean by this that here is the first step in getting the problem of veto over snap-votes in the House of Commons considered. If it is considered, I feel that in the end reason and experience will drive people to the Referendum solution.'[38]

That same day, Selborne chaired a talk with Unionist members about the referendum – at which he distributed copies of Strachey's book[39] – and Skelton wrote to Strachey to tell him that the outcome had been to form a committee to consider the position of the House of Lords in relation to the 1911 Parliament Act. *The Scotsman* thought this 'significant' and hoped that it would 'ensure that the subject is not relegated to the domain of pious hopes'.

> It is suspected with good reason that in the Cabinet there are varying degrees of enthusiasm. Some members are keen for reform, others are in the Lord Melbourne mood of 'Why can't you leave it alone?' Such an attitude will not satisfy the rank and file of Unionist members. They accept for the moment the plea that the Government cannot deal with it this session . . . But they are determined that the Government shall not reserve it for a deathbed declaration of intention, and once again face the country with nothing done. The Committee which has been formed is influential and representative of both the younger and the older members of the party. It includes Sir Robert Horne, Mr Noel Skelton, and Major Strang.[40]

Strachey also encouraged Skelton to raise House of Lords reform in the Commons, but he instead summarised his thoughts in a concise memo drafted in July 1925. This proposed that the House of Lords should consist of 250 hereditary members elected by the whole body of peers, 'plus a number, not exceeding (say) 100 "Peers of Parliament", to be appointed by the Crown, on the advice of the Prime Minister, after a General Election, for the duration of a Parliament'.

Skelton also proposed that 'a new authority, in place of the Speaker, should be established for certifying money bills, in terms of the Parliament Act'. This authority, he added, might be a joint standing committee of the two Houses, or a specially constituted judicial tribunal. The proposals were deliberately narrow in scope, the memo stated, so as to formulate a scheme that at least stood a chance of attracting general Unionist support.

The proposals, reasoned Skelton cautiously, had 'the advantage of introducing no absolutely new constitutional method or principle'. In 1707 and 1800 Scottish and Irish peers, respectively, had elected representatives from among themselves to sit in the House of Lords,[41] while bishops and the Law Lords represented a non-hereditary element in the Second Chamber.

> The creation of Peers of Parliament to sit for the duration of a Parliament would meet what is perhaps the greatest practical difficulty in the present position when a non-Conservative Government is in office – namely, the almost complete absence of any but Conservative members in the Second Chamber. Yet it avoids the obvious danger of and opportunity for a new 'democratic' agitation which would arise if the principle of popular election (whether direct or indirect) were partially introduced into the House of Lords.

Skelton's memo summarised opinion on the future of the House of Lords as falling (roughly) into four groups: those who believed the Parliament Act should be repealed and the pre-1911 position restored; those who thought that increased powers of delaying or the right finally to reject bills should be granted to a reformed Second Chamber with a partially elected (direct or indirect) element; those who believed that the Second Chamber should be entirely elected, directly or indirectly, with increased powers; and finally, those who felt that 'the Referendum should be introduced, for the purpose of securing a final decision when the two Houses are in conflict'.

With so many divergent views, however, the choice was between doing nothing, or doing something everyone could agree on. The memo continued:

> The Parliament Act has not proved itself, in actual operation, to be a failure. Public opinion in this country is notoriously averse to large constitutional changes unless and until the existing position has been found, in practice, to be impossible . . . The conclusion is almost irresistible that, as a result both of the general and the party situation in which the question has to be approached to-day, any proposals introduced must be limited in scope and be of the nature only of amendments of the present position. It is because the proposals here made seem, both as regards the change in composition of the House of Lords and the alternations of the Parliament Act, to fulfil these conditions that they are put forward with the approval or acquiescence of representatives of all the four groups of Unionist opinion set out above.[42]

So together with doubts about the referendum, Skelton also appeared to be blowing hot and cold on Lords reform. 'Our young Conservatives are as troublesome as ever,' lamented Robert Sanders in his diary on 14 July. 'Skelton, who is on our committee, has now come to the conclusion that nothing ought to be done at all for fear of the Government being thought reactionary.'[43] The YMCA believed that any reform would be perceived as anti-Labour and would not attract wide enough support even in the Conservative Party. Further evidence of Skelton's unease came when his name appeared among those on a censure motion against Lord Cave's proposals for Lords reform.

Writing in the *Quarterly Review* in October 1926, Skelton quoted Baldwin speaking in Perth four days before the 1924 poll: 'It is our duty to consider, within the framework of the Parliament Act, whether it is practicable to make provision for the machinery of the Second Chamber for preserving the ultimate authority in legislation to the considered judgment of the people.' But, said Skelton, 'there was no suggestion, in these words, that a drastic reform of the House of Lords was to be the central measure of the central session of the ensuing Parliament'.

Skelton reasoned that 'a drastic alteration in the powers and composition of the Second Chamber cannot be accomplished in this Parliament without destroying either the reputation or the solidarity of the Conservative Party.' To construct, introduce, and carry a complete scheme of vital constitutional change 'without giving the electorate an opportunity of expressing their views upon it, would be an abuse of a parliamentary majority such as has never yet been attempted in modern politics'. He said the experience of 1910 showed there were only two practicable methods. 'The first is to introduce during this Parliament a complete scheme of reform of the House of Lords, for the purpose of full discussion and criticism in both Houses, and . . . if it commands the approval of at least the Conservative Party, a leading issue at the next general election'. This, said Skelton, would avoid splitting the party, while the 'other course is to proceed by stages, abandoning the attempt to reach constitutional finality even in the next Parliament'.

That Labour had no 'authentic representation' in the Lords was a problem, and Skelton revived his memo's suggestion of allowing the Crown, through the Prime Minister, to summon a certain number of Labour representatives to sit in the Second Chamber for the duration of the Parliament. 'The present writer approaches the question from the position that the final objective is a reduced but reinforced House of Lords, entrusted with powers of reference to the people.'

The hereditary Peers, it may safely be premised, would

never consent to the complete withdrawal of their right to sit in the Second Chamber. Thus an insurmountable difficulty would confront a Conservative Government which proposed a purely elective body. Yet the partial introduction of the elective principle is the most unsatisfactory of all expedients. It brings the hereditary and the democratic principles into direct conflict and opens the door to a new phase of political agitation, undertaken with a view to making the Second Chamber elective only.

The referendum, Skelton acknowledged, though necessary, 'is viewed with doubt and suspicion by some Conservatives and nearly all Liberals'; therefore 'it is clear that the policy of endeavouring to pass in this Parliament a final and drastic scheme of reform of the Second Chamber is unsound, dangerous, a gamble, and a folly.'[44]

If 1925 narrowly avoided serious industrial strife, then 1926 faced it full on. What is more, some of Skelton's political predictions came startlingly true. Although the first half of the year was relatively serene, the row over the Factory Bill rumbled on. The King's Speech of February 1926 failed to mention it, and instead a private member's bill was introduced in the name of Ellen Wilkinson. Harold Macmillan gave notice on 10 March of an amendment, which Skelton signed, lamenting so important an issue being left to a backbencher. Wilkinson et al. were essentially trying to bounce Baldwin into producing the desired bill, and it worked. Just two days before Macmillan was due to speak to his amendment, the government announced plans to bring forward a bill and give it prominence in the next session.

Skelton, meanwhile, became more closely involved with UK and Scottish Tory party organisation. Already active in the Unionist Workers' League, which promoted young Tory speakers, in March 1925 Skelton was elected to the governing body of the Association of Conservative and Unionist Clubs, an umbrella group for around 1,520 clubs across the UK. The patron was Skelton's political hero, the Earl of Balfour, and Skelton helped make arrangements to hold a series of regional conferences over the following three months in 'various industrial centres . . . to develop the political work undertaken by members of party clubs in their respective constituencies and with this end in view to inaugurate educational classes, study circles, lectures, and debates'.[45] In Scotland, meanwhile, Skelton was elected to the executive committee of the Scottish 1924 Club, which had been founded for a similar educational purpose. He attended its first annual meeting in the Conservative Club rooms on Princes Street[46] in Edinburgh in June 1926. Skelton believed, after all, in an educated as well as a property-owning democracy.

Departing from the *Quarterly Review* for a solitary article, Skelton contributed an essay somewhat ominously entitled 'The Safeguarding of British Democracy' to the *English Review* in July 1926. It was, for Skelton, a rare foray into foreign affairs and was essentially a reaction to the rise of Benito Mussolini in Italy. 'A new chapter in the history of political ideas has opened,' he wrote. 'An immense new fact has appeared in Europe. Democratic government, for which the great war was going "to make the world safe", is being discarded by a whole group of Continental nations.'

The rise of dictatorships in the Latin or Catholic nations of Europe was, argued Skelton, 'nothing very significant or unexpected, for it would only be extending to the old world what has for years been the rule in Latin America'. But, he added,

> [the] world is witnessing, in truth, a movement without parallel in Europe since the Counter-Reformation, in which authoritarianism in religion, reforming and remodelling itself under the stern and far-sighted principles of the Jesuit organization, first checked and then confined to the Teutonic countries the whole body of spiritual ideas which had found expression in the Reformation.
>
> Here, then, is no black frost of reaction nipping in the bud a young and delicate shoot. The new authoritarianism claims to be, and bears all the marks of being, an

evolutionary movement discarding and supplanting an outworn form. The whole status of the democratic theory has already, in the eyes of the world, been changed by its advent, for democracy is no longer the young Siegfried: it is held up to scorn as the old, effete, disillusioned and dispossessed Wotan. The clash of the new-forged sword upon the ancient spear can be clearly heard in the utterances of Signor Mussolini, with their energy, their driving force, their robust and searching intellectual power. What then is the new Gospel of authoritarianism to which Fascism has given both philosophical and material form? It is that the individual citizens exist for the State, not the State for individual citizens.

Skelton did not live to see the Second World War, but he would witness the rise of Hitler in the last few years of his life. This, then, even down to the Wagnerian imagery, was prescient stuff. 'But is it all?' he asked. 'Is there not spreading in England also an opinion that democracy is outworn?'

For it happens, firstly, that in England to-day, democratic principles, if their open and avowed enemies are few, rather lack effective and unreserved supporters . . . And the Conservative Party, though its instinct is to rally to the defence of any threatened institution, has always contained a school of thought, not even yet extirpated, which tolerates rather than approves democratic government.

Skelton quoted Balfour in describing 'democracy as "Government by explanation"'. But, he added, 'The process of explanation is intolerably tedious to many politicians: it consumes an amazing amount of time and energy: it seems to have no necessary connection with the work of government – indeed to be rather opposed to the idea of governing.' And the burden, argued Skelton, had been much increased by the extension of the franchise in 1918.

'At such a moment, Italy discards democracy. The repercussion in England cannot but be immense.'

Therefore, continued Skelton, the question must be considered: 'Is democracy worth preserving in England, and if so, how is it to be strengthened and safeguarded? What, in fact, is the essential virtue, the core, the inner value of democracy? Why retain a system which superimposes on the work of governing the separate distracting and conflicting duty of explaining?' He quoted Lord Salisbury, that democracy was the 'safest form of Government', since it was the only system of government 'fitted with a safety valve'.

> Dictatorships, for instance, end, as they begin, with revolution. But might not democracy become, in practice, so cumbrous, so ineffective that these hypothetical risks would be worth running?
>
> In Britain democracy will not fail through the inability of the citizen to exercise them well. Immense and repeated extensions of the franchise, shifting the centre of gravity in the State, demanding, all of a sudden, millions of men and recently of women to take up the citizen's task, leave the character of the British electorate unaltered in its common sense, steadiness, and balance. The danger lies elsewhere . . . The functions of a democracy must advance step by step with its education and its capabilities.

'To strengthen, invigorate, stabilize democracy something more is needed,' said Skelton. 'The means lie ready to our hand – it is the introduction into the British Constitution of the Referendum, for the direct, effective, definite and final decision of large and fundamental questions.' So his earlier doubts, as articulated in a rambling letter to Strachey, appeared to have subsided. 'The present position of the House of Lords is admittedly make-shift only,' Skelton continued. 'Its future composition and its future powers raise, without the Referendum, a perhaps insoluble problem. With the introduction of the Referendum, however, that problem disappears; for conflicts between the two Houses are solved not by the victory of either, but by the direct decision of the country.'

Although it stretched the imagination somewhat to accept that constitutional safeguards could protect nations from fascism, Skelton was at least consistent. 'The issue between democracy and the new despotism is already clear,' he concluded. 'It is for Conservatism to take up the challenge and re-establish as the fundamental axiom of our politics that, however it be elsewhere, in Britain at least, the free citizen is still fit to be master of his own and the community's life.'[47]

Skelton was by mid-1926 in an enviable position: influential within the Conservative Party, well known in Parliament, and able to reach a wider audience through his political journalism. 'I dined one night with a group of young Tories,' wrote Neville Chamberlain, the Minister for Health, to his sister Ida, 'one of whom Noel Skelton, MP for Perthshire impressed me as being remarkably level headed as well as clever.[48]

The major event of 1926, however, was the General Strike. It lasted just nine days, from 3 May to 12 May, although the impact lingered for much longer. It was instigated by the general council of the Trades Union Congress (TUC) in an unsuccessful attempt to force the government to prevent wage reduction and worsening conditions for coal miners. The British coal-mining industry had recently suffered an economic crisis through heavy domestic use during the Great War, low productivity, increased European competition, a strong pound (through the recent reintroduction of the Gold Standard) which hampered the export market, and the actions of mine owners who wanted to normalise profits even during periods of economic instability, often leading to wage reductions and longer working hours.

It was the last issue that brought matters to a head. The TUC pledged to support its members in their dispute with mine owners, while Baldwin decided to intervene, declaring that the government would provide a nine-month subsidy to maintain the miners' wages while appointing a royal commission (chaired by the Liberal Sir Herbert Samuel) to examine the problems of the mining industry.

Samuel published his report in March 1926. This rejected outright nationalisation but advocated reorganisation, a withdrawal of the government's subsidy and a wage reduction to ensure the industry remained profitable. Mine owners responded by publishing new terms of employment for all miners, including an extension of the seven-hour working day, district wage agreements and, crucially, a 10–25 per cent reduction in wages. If miners did not accept these new terms then from 1 May they would be locked out of the pits. Unsurprisingly, the Miners' Federation of Great Britain (MFGB) rejected both wage reduction and regional negotiation with the slogan: 'Not a penny off the pay, not a second on the day.'

The TUC met on 1 May and subsequently announced that a general strike 'in defence of miners' wages and hours' was to begin two days later. In the interim, frantic efforts were made to reach a compromise between the mine owners and the government, but to no avail. The TUC feared that an all-out strike would bring revolutionary elements to the fore, so it decided to bring out workers only in the key industries: railwaymen, transport workers, printers, dockers and iron and steel workers. As with the miners' dispute nearly sixty years later, the government was well prepared. The recently created Organisation for the Maintenance of Supplies, together with the armed forces and volunteer workers, kept basic services running.

On the day the strike began, the House of Commons held an emergency adjournment debate on the 'Industrial Crisis', in which Baldwin presented the dispute as a threat to the constitution. His tone throughout was one of sorrow rather than anger, and he depicted the strikers as misled rather than dangerous. Above all, the Prime Minister appealed for trust in his handling of the situation. Skelton backed him all the way:

> Any government, from whatever quarter of the House it is drawn, representing whatever policy, or brought into office

under whatever circumstances, would be forced to take
exactly the same decision as His Majesty's present Ministers
had to take . . . If this be an attack on the constitution and
established government of the country, there can be neither
humiliation nor ignominy in the withdrawal of such an
order . . . A mistake has been made. Let that mistake be
fully acknowledged and remedied, and let negotiations on
the true subject of discussion, the future of the coal trade,
be resumed. When this threat, which the government of
the country must resist to the utmost, when this foolish,
ill-advised, but I hope not irremediable, threat has been
withdrawn and the situation once again made clear, then
there can be an entire resumption of negotiations.[49]

Meanwhile, between 1½ and 1¾ million strikers refused to work
and the British transport network ground to a halt.[50] By 5 May
the government propaganda machine was in full flow, with the
Chancellor, Winston Churchill, editing the pro-Baldwin *British
Gazette*. The following day, Baldwin said the General Strike was 'a
challenge to the parliament and is the road to anarchy'. And on 7
May the TUC met with Samuel to work out a set of proposals to end
the dispute. They were rejected by the MFGB, but on 12 May the
TUC's general council announced its intention to call off the strike.
Baldwin shrewdly avoided triumphalism, and offered further
negotiations and government help.

Skelton wrote to *The Times* later that month, arguing that the
nine-month subsidy was all the government could have done until
reorganisation brought larger returns to the mining industry. 'But
such a subsidy, indefinite in duration, disastrous in amount, neither
the nation nor Parliament will ever grant,' he wrote. 'Nor could it,
in reason or justice, be granted; if only because men, no less skilled
than miners, are working to-day for longer hours at lower wages.
That way, once and for all, no road lies.'

Therefore, Skelton argued, the question was rather what the
nation could do to ensure the miners' standard of living was reduced

by as little as possible. He said the seven-hour limit on time spent down the pit or at work on the coalface should be withdrawn.

> Parliament then, it would seem, has a plain, though unpalatable, duty here. It must itself correct its own mistake. It would be a gross, a dangerous, and a pitiable dereliction of duty to postpone undertaking it until the task is made easy by others 'eating the leek'.
>
> It is said that to withdraw this crazy restriction would injure the credit of the Conservative Party. I write, as every private member of Parliament must, for myself only, but as one who is devoted and pledged to a national, democratic, and constructive Conservatism, having for its own objective the development of a property-owning democracy in Britain, as the soundest and surest means of bringing new energy and interests into the life of the individual citizen and new stability into the structure of the State. But a national party, however much it believes in its usefulness and its power for good, must, at times, be surgeon as well as architect, taking the surgeon's risks and responsibilities. And, in fact, the risk of discredit is trifling. No man, by the withdrawal of the restriction, will be forced to work for eight hours, if that figure be substituted for seven. A permission is given, not an order. A burden is removed, not imposed.

'Future mining legislation,' concluded Skelton, 'if new legislation be required, is, it must be added, in a different category. Parliament may well wait before undertaking it, to hear the agreed views of the interested parties. But the correction of its own error "brooks no delay". And why should there be delay, he asked, 'when to correct this error is to save, to the utmost extent to which it can be saved, the miners' "standard of living," and also, perhaps, to bring at length a solvent to a situation daily more disastrous?'[51]

But although Skelton espoused the government line, Baldwin's handling of the coal industry dispute had pushed progressive

Tories onto the defensive. This was illustrated in the debate on the Coal Mines Bill, in which Skelton, Robert Boothby and Cuthbert Headlam all defended the repeal of the Seven Hours Act. 'Let us never forget,' said Skelton in the debate, 'and this has not once, so far as I have heard it, been mentioned in this debate – that alone among the industries of this country the profits of the coal-mining industry are so arranged that the men receive 87 per cent of the profits and the owners 13 per cent. That is so.' And he suggested that 'hard as are the alternatives, the government are pursuing the course which enables the miner to select the least hard alternative'.

Skelton 'humbly' agreed with Labour members that the miners' standard of living should not be reduced.

> It is because, so far as I can see, and I make no claim to be an expert, this is the only means whereby you can bring to an absolute minimum such reduction of the standard of living as is necessary that I support this bill. That is the hard alternative, but, surely, there is no man, no statesman, no party who would not attempt to solve it in the way we are trying to do.
>
> . . . I venture to say to the government, to the Prime Minister, and to Hon. members opposite that, in carrying out what we believe to be right in these hard and difficult times, we are providing the sound solution, because it is the solution which most maintains the miners' standard of living, and we are taking a decision which once again is showing that democratic government in this country, with a Conservative government in power, is not too afraid [or] too weak to face the situation, however hard and difficult it may be. I shall venture to record my vote when the time comes against this amendment and in support of the bill, with the full conviction that it is the right way, and not the cowardly and weak courses which are commended to us from the other side.[52]

Skelton, however, together with Macmillan, Boothby and Robert Hudson, abstained on the second reading.

For several months the miners maintained their resistance, but by October 1926 hardship had forced many men back to work and by the end of November few remained on strike. Thus the issue of trade union reform once again raised its head. The views of the YMCA were summed up in a letter Skelton wrote to Baldwin following that year's annual Conservative conference in Scarborough. Writing 'as one who thinks legislation can do little and dreads these sham remedies introduced chiefly to propitiate the rank and file of the party', he urged the Prime Minister to refer the whole question to a royal commission. 'It would do everybody good', he wrote, 'to have the trade union question put in cold storage.' Moreover, such an inquiry would provide 'clear proof that this Conservative majority is determined not to use its present parliamentary strength unfairly in a class or party way'. To act unilaterally, he argued, '*de haut au bas*', would preclude Labour from any constructive contribution at a time when divisions within their ranks were widening. Legislation, Skelton concluded, would fragment opposition and divide the Tories with 'Die-hards pressing strong Amendments, [and] progressives trying to get the clauses toned down'.[53]

That Skelton had to remind Baldwin of his own 'peace in our time' philosophy of the previous year said a lot about how much the situation had changed. Baldwin's public standing was high in the wake of the General Strike, but the stress had left him physically and mentally drained. Skelton ruminated at length on the state of both the Prime Minister and his party in his next *Quarterly Review* essay, which appeared in October 1926.

> At the beginning of a year so momentous for the Conservative Party, it is surely wise to survey the situation and attempt an appreciation of it . . . What Britain needs and what public opinion demands is the continuance in power of a steady but progressive Government . . . not merely until the end

of the present Parliament, but for another term of years thereafter.

The trauma of the General Strike appeared not to have altered Skelton's thinking. 'What is the main task before such a Government?' he asked.

> It is the achievement of 'Peace in Industry'. The reconciliation of Labour and Capital is the sine qua non of national prosperity. Peace in industry is no sentimental catchword. It is the first and greatest practical need in a country so highly industrialised as Britain.
>
> At present the workman's life is hopelessly lopsided. He has full political status: he has full educational status. Economically, he is on the level of a machine; for, in the language of political economy, his wages, the sole reward of his industry, are only part of the cost of production. The status of ownership must be introduced into the economic life of the wage-earner . . . Peace in industry as well as the general stability of the community rests eventually upon the steady development of a property-owning democracy . . . by exercising its influence to guide public opinion towards this objective and by developing such cognate policies as the extension of small ownership in land (which is by no means without influence on the psychology of urban labour) and of individual house ownership, the Conservative Party can, if it will, act as a powerful directing force towards industrial peace.

Skelton praised Baldwin's handling of the policy, 'but it must be admitted that there has been, since the General Election, a distinct and definite movement to the right, an obvious hardening of opinion in the party as an organisation . . . and to some extent among the rank and file of its members in the House of Commons'. The tragedy of the situation, said Skelton, 'if tragedy be not too strong a word, is that the right is perhaps not greatly interested in peace in industry'. He continued:

> The General Strike and the measures of necessity taken to meet it are another matter. The combination of moderation and strength shown by the Cabinet was perfect. But an emergency which arms the Executive with dictatorial powers and exhibits it in untrammelled authority and activity naturally stimulates, as it seems to justify, the point of view of the right.

With regard to the trade unions, Skelton lamented that it seemed 'to have been too readily accepted that the General Strike and the coal stoppage are new circumstances which make amendment of the law imperatively necessary'. On the contrary, he argued, the main result of the strike had been 'an absolute and disastrous failure for its users'. And anyway, he added, 'the secret ballot would not have prevented the coal stoppage. Men do not go idle and wageless for nineteen weeks, unless, at the outset at least, their hearts are in the policy of resistance.'

Skelton then repeated the contents of his recent letter to Baldwin:

> The best way by which the Conservative Party can help to divorce the Trades Unions from politics is to refrain from legislation against them . . . an attack upon the Unions is an attack upon the wage-earning class, and the wage-earning class as a whole will rally in their defence . . . The State, the Government, the Conservative Party, and the Nation have shown their strength, which proved, naturally enough, to be irresistible. Let them now show their patience, and from the vantage-ground on which they stand, concentrate upon a healing policy. The position is really the same as that with which Abraham Lincoln was faced at the conclusion of the Civil War. Measures of vengeance and oppression were pressed upon him, and by the very people who when the

struggle appeared doubtful were faint-hearted. But Lincoln, who was adamant during the war, refused to treat the beaten side with harshness. Such, indeed, is the lesson of high statesmanship always; let it be applied now, and in its application it may lay the foundations of industrial peace. If, on the other hand, the contrary policy is pursued, not merely will the chances of industrial peace be imperilled, but also the Labour Party, like the Trades Unions, will find a rallying ground on which to restore the forces at present demoralised.

Skelton concluded:

The national regard and respect for the Conservative leader is deep. Across this prospect there falls the shadow of a grave danger, originating within the Party itself – the desire to use its power to obtain a mechanical security, instead of an organic – in industry by 'curbing the power of the Unions,' in the Constitution by erecting a bulwark against the next Socialist Government.

He said it was 'driven by the desire to achieve incompatibles. To pursue incompatible aims is to court failure: to achieve them is impossible.' So,

faced with the alternatives of 'a smack at the Trades Unions' or the reconciliation of Capital and Labour; of the alteration of the constitution by a Parliamentary coup d'état or the continuance of the national confidence in the moderation, fair-mindedness, and disinterested outlook of the Conservatism of to-day, the Conservative Party enters a fateful year. How will it stand in October 1927?[54]

The answer turned out to be much the same, both politically and in the narrower parameters of Skelton's career, although his prospects appeared good when a vacancy had arisen at the Admiralty in December 1926. 'Men like Colonel Headlam, Captain Harold Macmillan, Mr Oliver Stanley, Mr Skelton, to name no others,' commented *The Times*, 'are all of them more than equal to the standard which has been expected of Under-Secretaries in the past.'[55] Instead, the post went to Headlam, while Boothby was appointed Churchill's PPS. Skelton's congratulatory note to the former clearly masks his own disappointment. He jokingly expressed delight that 'the P.M. should select you instead of some filthy Die Hard. I feared so much that one of the latter would be chosen. Your appointment and Bob Boothby's in conjunction show that progressive Toryism isn't dead yet.'[56]

The year 1927 also marked the point at which the YMCA began to lose its earlier coherence. In his thesis on the group, Paul Gatland, observed:

> Though the young radicals may have found a focus for their early activity in the person and ideas of Noel Skelton, he gave no indication of any interest in the new ideas the more radical of the group developed from the middle of the Parliament. His only constructive proposals throughout the Parliament remained those of co-partnership and the creation of a class of small landed proprietors, which included the re-settlement of displaced industrial workers.[57]

There was a lot of truth in this analysis. In September 1926 Macmillan had suggested to Boothby, Stanley and Loder that they collaborate in the composition of a manifesto that summed up their views. The context was the authors' disappointment that the government, and especially Baldwin, had failed to get to grips with the settlement of the coal dispute. The result was *Industry and the State: a Conservative View*, which included a detailed programme for the constructive reform of trade unionism. Most likely written by Macmillan, who believed above all in legislative action, this marked a split with Skelton, who was cynical about a legislative response, believing the major role of government was the education of public opinion. In his view

> the measure of the possibility of developing the individual rights of the individual trade unionist in his industrial capacity is entirely, solely and purely the degree of the enlightenment of the employer . . . as soon as you get the great mass of organised labour in this country and the community satisfied that the great mass of the employers in the country mean, under all circumstances, to play fair with the labour which they employ, then it will be possible for the trade unions to relax their precautions, to consider more the rights of the individual, and to regard themselves less as a fighting force and more as men of peace.[58]

Skelton, therefore, was conspicuous by his absence in the book's list of authors, although his thinking was acknowledged in the text.

The book argued for a 'middle land' on the basis that unrestricted individualism was just as unrealistic as socialism. The problem, its authors argued, was less a matter of theory than of practice, and they suggested that the Conservative approach should be guided by 'two outstanding characteristics of British history', which they classified as 'empirical evolution' and 'unbroken continuity', leading eventually to the Skeltonian ideal of a 'property-owning democracy'.[59] The book attracted a range of opinion, indicating, in Loder's words, 'the progressive reaction of reviewers from the chuckles of the left to the "Boys will be boys" attitude of the centre and the apoplectic fury of the right'. The *Sunday Pictorial*, under the headline 'What's In a Name?', went so far as to say that 'this amazing production . . . preaches nothing more or less than thinly disguised Socialism . . . Apparently these bright "Conservative" MPs belong to what is known contemptuously as the "YMCA" group. They neither appreciate nor understand the principles they are supposed to uphold.'[60]

Industry and the State was, despite these barbs, an influential text, later expanded upon in Macmillan's *The Middle Way* (1938), which set in stone the acceptance of state intervention. The inclusion of co-partnership was, however, important for Skelton. The idea had been included in 1924's *Looking Ahead*, but was dropped from the subsequent manifesto.

In 1925 the MP Reginald Shaw introduced a private member's bill to give tax breaks and other perks to companies implementing co-partnership schemes, but the government did not react favourably. In August 1926 Baldwin's support was sought to set up a committee on the subject (the Conservative 1922 Committee having already examined it with the help of Macmillan and Skelton), but the Prime Minister simply stressed the impracticality of developing a constructive policy. The Conservative Research Department was also cynical, believing co-partnership to have limited electoral appeal. That, combined with the limited scope for government action in promoting it, meant co-partnership never became a major element of Tory policy.

The Parliamentary session of February–July 1927 turned out to be one of almost continual attrition by the YMCA against the reactionary drift of the party, and as early as June 1927 the speeches of the Young Conservatives were seen as providing the basis for the formation of a 'Fourth Party', although that never came to pass.

On trade union reform, the group focused its attention on the Trade Disputes and Trade Union Bill, a generally moderate government response to the General Strike, although it included 'contracting in' for the political levy and aroused bitter opposition from the Labour Party, further souring the mood and denting Baldwin's conciliatory image. Only Stanley and Skelton, however, spoke against the bill in the Commons. By November 1927, meanwhile, they had more cause for concern when the government introduced its Unemployment Insurance Bill.

Baldwin viewed this unease as pre-election jitters so appointed Skelton, Macmillan and Loder to a standing committee charged with examining the bill. Any possible revolt, however, was averted when, in the King's Speech of February 1928, a new industrial policy directly related to the concerns of the YMCA was announced. The only sizeable revolt turned out to be over House of Lords reform.

John Buchan, the novelist and administrator, entered Parliament in 1927 at a by-election and became a useful ally for Skelton, who had by then drifted apart from Macmillan and Boothby. Born in Skelton's spiritual home of Perth, Buchan already knew the author of *Constructive Conservatism*.[61] Skelton was a regular guest when the Buchans stayed each winter at the Edinburgh home of Alec and Rosalind Maitland. There, Maitland's colleagues at the Faculty of Advocates, including Skelton, Johnnie Jameson and Stair Gillon (with whom Skelton had fought in the Great War), would engage in vigorous conversation. '[Buchan] enjoyed those evenings immensely when the talk was fast and furious,' recalled Lady Tweedsmuir; 'it had a way of going back to the shared experiences of their light-hearted Oxford days.'[62]

Buchan's maiden speech took place during a key debate on the future of the House of Lords, which Baldwin had promised to strengthen in response to Diehard pressure. Macmillan and Skelton led backbench Tory opposition, while Buchan's speech pointed out the scheme's contradictions, questioned its usefulness and urged his party to trust the people, for 'there will be no constitutional revolution in Britain until the great bulk of the British people resolutely desire it, and if that desire is ever present, what statute can bar the way?'[63] In the event, more than 100 Conservative MPs opposed the measure, which was then dropped.

Baldwin congratulated Buchan personally, no doubt relieved that he had been saved from an impossible political situation. 'Another ministerial organ has referred to this revolt as a "YMCA",' observed Oswald Mosley during the debate, 'which, I understand, is a reverent tribute to the evangelical character of that group of young Conservatives.'[64]

Evangelical was one adjective for Skelton, although others considered him pedantic and blunt to the point of rudeness. 'He showed more performance than promise'[65] was his remark upon the maiden speech of one slick young orator in the House of Commons. And Lady Tweedsmuir recalled that

> John Buchan liked to sit in the House of Commons and listen to speeches. Skelton once asked him why he did so. John replied, because he was interested. 'You can't possibly be,' retorted Noel.
>
> 'Well, then, because it's a cheap way of acquiring popularity,' said John.
>
> 'Cheap,' scoffed Noel, 'it's the most expensive waste of time possible.' (It may be noted that Noel was not nearly such a busy man as John, but he much preferred talking to listening.)[66]

'Of course, my dear,' Skelton would tell friends in another common refrain, 'everything is going to the dogs,' particularly if pressed for his opinion on the Conservative or governing party. 'But to those who regard conversation rather as a wild adventure than a pedestrian plodding among facts,' commented Tweedsmuir, 'Noel's talk was a perennial delight.' She also made another amusing observation:

> Skelton would delight in breaking up what he foresaw would be a very dull dinner-party followed by a long spell of boredom. As he sat down to dinner he noticed that his neighbour had a slight cold. He remarked to her how dangerous it was to go out in the evening if one was not in the best of health. He turned to the lady on his other side, remarking, 'I am afraid you have caught a bad cold too!' and he painted an even darker picture to her of the dangers of catching 'flu. He worked upon their feelings so skilfully that both ladies left for home immediately after dinner, and the whole party broke up in alarm and confusion.

But Skelton was not all consumed by politics, and particularly disliked anyone who could talk of nothing beyond public affairs. 'She may do good, and I don't say she doesn't,' he once said of a 'well-known lady philanthropist' to Tweedsmuir, 'but she has completely destroyed her own atmosphere'.[67]

Skelton was also frustrated that other personal hobbyhorses were not making any progress, despite having been included in the 1924 manifesto. During a debate on Scottish agriculture, he said:

> Without going into ancient history, into pre-war history, let me recall to the secretary of state the fact that the Prime Minister at the last general election definitely stated in his election manifesto that the policy of smallholdings would be developed if the Unionist Party were returned to power.
>
> . . . I do not care whether you study Fascism in Italy under Mussolini, the work of the Belgian government, the work of the German government or the work of the Denmark government, you will find one of the main pre-occupations of modern governments is the utilisation of the power of the state to develop land settlement amongst their people . . . I appeal to my right hon. Friend not to give up a piece of social work which is essentially Unionist in character.[68]

Skelton also mused upon 'social work' in relation to the Labour and Conservative parties in his only political essay of 1927, 'The Labour Party',[69] which appeared in April's *Quarterly Review*. Despite recent events, Skelton's political faith was undiminished:

> It is because democracy has the capacity of exhibiting the features of a living organism, the tissue and substance of which are the characters and personalities, the aims, the outlook, the ideals, the hopes, and the wishes of the individual men and women who compose it – that it can claim to be the highest form of human government.

'To-day,' Skelton observed, 'the world is full of machine-made democracies crumbling before our eyes.' But 'it seems at least probable that for the years immediately ahead, the Labour Party must share with the Conservative the conduct of the political life of England. Is it fit for that task? Is it founded upon an organic conception of politics?'

> They have yet to learn the bitter lesson that a caucus, a machine, expounds these principles, views and aspirations for the purpose of exploiting them, not for the purpose of promoting them. It uses emotions and beliefs; it does not share them . . . If a party is to be great, its principles must express something that is good in men; something that is common to them, without distinction of class or position in life; if a party is to be permanent, it must draw its nourishment from tap-roots that reach far down into the instincts, the hopes, the beliefs of a people.

Skelton went on to lament the performance of Ramsay MacDonald, a Labour MP who then enjoyed cross-party respect. 'Even his speech has suffered from the work he has had to do,' wrote Skelton. 'Only now and then, when he can speak freely, does he give Parliament a taste of his true quality. Otherwise he is sombre, lowering, clouded, hiding his real thoughts under a loud, empty, and bombastic oratory.' As a result, he added, 'the House of Commons receives from his personality an impact rasping and exhausting. Once and again comes a moment when he is formidable; it passes and ennui succeeds.' Had MacDonald been a member of a 'real party', continued Skelton,

> he might have been a great leader and a great statesman. But the construction and maintenance of a political machine is, in truth, no school for statesmanship.
>
> The organic conception of politics will beat the mechanical, if only it does not imitate the tricks of its rival: if it will but be true to itself. Its sole defender to-day is the

Conservative Party. Conservatism, indeed, has more to defend than any policy. At a time when Liberalism hawks its moneybags and Labour, after more than a generation's stealthy approach, is about to make the last rush and spring upon the Co-operative flock, only Conservatism is left to justify the instinctive belief of the English people that the political life of a nation is the expression of the best and not the worst characteristics of the individuals of whom the body-politic is composed.[70]

By 1928 Baldwin's New Conservatism seemed to be in tatters, while his party appeared to have reverted to type. The Conservatives were also losing seats to Labour and Skelton had reason to fear for his own ability to hold on in Perth. But there were also successes. Trade union talks finally got under way in 1927, ushering in an unprecedented period of calm that almost removed the industrial relations issue from mainstream politics.

Nevertheless, Baldwin maintained a moderate course during the last full year of his government, and in 1928 the franchise was equalised for both sexes at the age of twenty-one, a reform the YMCA must surely have embraced. During a debate on 13 February the Prime Minister said:

> I thank him [MacDonald] for the few words he said in praise of the younger members of our party. I think he meant half of what he said – and I may assure him that I have every confidence in them, and, when the time comes for him and for me to move on, I have no doubt they will be able to settle many problems in their time which baffle this generation.[71]

But far from preoccupying himself with lofty matters of state, Skelton spent 1928 concentrating on Scottish administration and, as we shall see later, his private life. Although Skelton was proud of being a Scottish Unionist (as opposed to an English Conservative), he took little part in affairs of a strictly Scottish nature. The

Secretary of State for Scotland since 1924, Sir John Gilmour, did little to change Skelton's habits. Tweedy, occasionally reactionary and, according to some accounts, dull, Gilmour had also voted to retain the Coalition back in 1922, so he and Skelton were not exactly on the same wavelength.

Gilmour was particularly keen to consolidate Scottish administration, both local and national, during his five years at the Scottish Office, and introduced the Reorganisation of Offices (Scotland) Bill in March 1928 to that end. Scotland had been governed for decades through semi-autonomous government 'boards', two of which – the Scottish Board of Health and the Board of Agriculture for Scotland – were to be abolished under Gilmour's plan and replaced with English-style departments run by civil servants.

'I rise with anxiety to discuss this bill,' said Skelton during the bill's second reading, 'because after the most careful thought which I can give I find myself in complete opposition to the Secretary of State for Scotland with regard to it.' In short, he could see nothing wrong with the status quo in terms of Scottish administration, and believed that the loss of two distinctively Scottish institutions would merely play into the hands of the Scottish nationalists, who were at that time gaining a higher public profile. Alluding to his father's administrative work, Skelton asserted that 'nobody, so far as I know, in this House or in Scotland has ever suggested that the administration of health and of other things for which the Board of Health is responsible is less efficient in Scotland than it is in England'. On the contrary,

> there appears to me to be real administrative value in having these departments not under individual civil servants, who perhaps know little about Scotland, but under a body of representative Scotsmen who can convey to the Secretary of State, who is much occupied in London, a kind of general Scottish view upon topics.

He even argued that the 'present system unquestionably gives to Scotland a certain degree of administrative home rule', although he did not believe in a 'separate Scottish Parliament'. 'I am certain that it is a mistake to diminish those aspects of administrative individuality which Scotland still possesses.' He concluded:

> If it can be shown that the Boards in Scotland are inefficient then we should willingly consent to a change, but on this question the Secretary of State for Scotland seems to me to be like a dentist playing about with his infernal machine upon a piece of perfectly sound smooth tooth when he is only a hair's breadth away from the nerve.[72]

At the end of the debate, Skelton went into the lobby against the bill.

Four months later, Skelton still held the same view. 'I see no substance in the argument that boards are inefficient,' he said. 'I remain of the opinion that there has been for Scotland a very great advantage in a system which brought into direct contact with its administration a considerable number of people drawn from various sections and districts in the country.' And, he said, 'I hope that my fears about the bill are ill-founded, because it would be an ill day if any step taken by a Unionist government brought nearer by a single inch the possibility of home rule for Scotland.'[73] Ironically, and politics is full of ironies, three years later Skelton would find himself in charge of the very departments – health and agriculture – whose creation he was so vociferously opposing.

In May, Skelton again clashed with the Scottish Office during a debate on the Western Highlands and Islands of Scotland.

> It will not be the first time that I have voted against my right hon. Friend in matters of Scottish affairs, much as I respect the character and the quality of his administration, and the day to day work of Scottish government. It has never been better done by a Secretary of State for Scotland. But

I suggest that, in the wider questions which undoubtedly arise, we want a little more constructive thought, and a wider range of vision.

According to the honourable member for Perth, there were three main questions facing contemporary Scotland: 'The first is the constant decrease of the rural population; the second is the constant increase of Irish blood in Scotland; and the third is the whole position of life of a third of the Scottish soil, namely, the Western Islands.'[74]

Sir John Gilmour's second reform came as part of a UK-wide shake-up of local government, which had been virtually untouched since its formation in 1889. The Local Government (Scotland) Bill sought to streamline Scottish local authorities by, among other measures, scrapping parish councils. Skelton asked:

> What does it matter if the parish council or some local institution in the rural or village districts should be abolished? It matters for this reason, that they act as a focus, as a central point of the rural life, as a means whereby people of different classes, different outlook, different points of view, meet on a common basis.

This time, however, Skelton was part of a much larger lobby opposed to these reforms. He went on:

> It is true that the life of the ordinary rural parish is not very exciting and that therefore the subjects for discussion at the ordinary rural parish council are not very exciting. But the fact is that in Scotland they are the sole connecting link, the sole focus of the life of the small rural district. It was along that line of argument that I was greatly alarmed at the idea that they should be abolished. I think the whole situation has been radically altered by the statement which my right hon. Friend made to-day, that he had now come to

the conclusion that there should be some elected body of a smaller area than the county council.[75]

But as the bill completed its progress through Parliament in February 1929, Skelton indulged in a political volte-face, principally over the issue of agricultural rates, which were to be scrapped.

> We all know that the future of democracy and the nature of this country lie in building up a strong property-owning democracy, four-square and independent, and, as far as Scotland is concerned, the sweeping away of owners' rates on agricultural land is an essential step towards bringing that about in the agricultural districts.[76]

During an adjournment debate on the coal industry in May, Skelton had another suggestion for helping to build a property-owning democracy. Once more, he used an example gleaned from his Perth constituency:

> A working engineer returns from the war and cannot find employment. His mother has a certain amount of savings. The opportunity opens for the purchase of 10 acres of land, 6 miles out of the town of Forfar. He purchases them. He builds his own house. He is enabled subsequently to purchase 10 acres more. On those 20 acres, he has been for the last five years engaged in a very special form of agricultural work, the cultivation of raspberries. He is making thoroughly good; he is thoroughly happy.
>
> I had this only last Saturday from his brother-in-law who is a gardener in my constituency. If one searches for examples, one will find countless examples of men of urban training who can make good on small parcels of land, and I venture to say . . . it is a mistake for the government not to try to work out a scheme whereby a few hundreds or thousands of our mining families could be put upon the land.[77]

Skelton, however, was more than content with other aspects of the government's programme, and eagerly supported Winston Churchill's first Budget and Neville Chamberlain's reforms of housing and pensions policy.[78] The YMCA was also committed to the League of Nations, and in 1927 one of their number, Walter Elliot, joined the UK delegation to Geneva, a trip Skelton would make himself seven years later.

Skelton's diminished political and parliamentary activity during 1928 can perhaps be explained by his burgeoning, yet complicated, personal life. James Johnston had noted back in 1925 that the elegance of the YMCA's ideas was matched by their sartorial sense.[79] Indeed, they mostly mixed in fashionable London society, where Skelton often found himself at the Lord North Street home of Katharine Tennant.

Katharine Tennant, or 'K' as she was invariably known, was born in 1903, the third of four daughters of Sir Charles Tennant, the Gladstonian politician and industrialist. Sir Charles was seventy-nine when K was born, and had earlier fathered the politician Harold John Tennant, briefly Secretary for Scotland in 1916, and more famously Margot Tennant, who married the Liberal politician Herbert Henry Asquith, later Prime Minister, in 1894.

As a child Katharine had played in the nursery at 10 Downing Street, and aged eight she threw a toy from the second-floor nursery window onto the heads of protesting suffragettes. She grew up, however, with strong Liberal ideals. Educated by governesses at home, at Abbot's Hill School in Hemel Hempstead, and finally in Paris, she was presented at the court of George V as a debutante. But, as she later said, 'I was more interested in politics than parties'.[80] K studied at the London School of Economics under Harold Laski and William Beveridge, became an accomplished violinist, acquired fluent French, and was a keen rider and golfer of genuine skill, including Balfour and Asquith among her sporting opponents.

Tennant and Skelton, therefore, were separated not only by

age but also by social background. They probably met during frequent and eclectic gatherings at Katharine's Westminster home, described as 'a salon for the stimulating fringes of all parties'.[81] A sexual affair seems to have begun in the summer of 1928, and Skelton began writing to Katharine – sometimes daily – at the end of July. 'K, my dear,' begins his first surviving letter. 'A single word between trains – in which nothing can be said, except that I spent a wakeful night thinking of you, & wondering whether you were thinking of me.'[82]

Skelton proposed to Katharine at around this time, but there were obvious difficulties, not least an age difference of twenty-three years. Katharine, however, was surprised and indecisive. 'I think it is far far better that you should search your own mind, undisturbed by me,' he wrote on 3 August.

> I see most clearly all the disadvantages for you in marrying me . . . But I feel in my bones that I should have a real chance of making you happy & I know that . . . it is something to which I wd devote everything that is in me: trying to make life pleasant and real for you. What I feel for you I really can't write, except that you have always seemed to me to have a largeness of soul & spirit all your own & that I can imagine nothing better than to try to clean & burnish my musty spirit to make it fit for your society.[83]

Still Katharine had sleepless nights.

> You mustn't worry yourself. You will soon realise whether you want to marry me or not. I hate to think of you having disturbing thoughts & disturbed nights . . . besides I have known for a long time that I was going to ask you to marry me & whereas apparently, this idea has come as a surprise to you. But I *know* you like me. I know I have never felt anything but happy in your society.[84]

Skelton wrote again, more frankly, the next day. 'What must be written about are the disadvantages to you,' he said. 'Let us look at them fair and square.' The result is worth quoting at some length.

> 1st I am much older than you. I was 48 on 1st July. That is bad. You are what 23 or 24. That means that when I am 58 you will only be 33 and when I am 68 (!) you will only be 43. But I am bound to add that there is this compensation – that when I am old . . . then you will begin to lead your political life, if you still want to & when I am out of the way altogether you will have still a . . . side of life with all its immense interest & variety to live & move in.
>
> 2nd I am perfectly poor. At present I make about £1000–1100 a year and have about £300–350 of my own, which will increase in a few years to about £400. I suppose I could make more, if I only wanted to – as I should want to, if I were married to you: for I could write more . . . but it is quite clear that I shall never have much.
>
> 3rd You wouldn't be marrying a man with a great 'future' to make up for not much of a 'present'. I suppose I am not quite useless in politics . . . but politics for me has always been above all interesting as an experiment which I have been from the first determined to conduct along lines I approve of . . . . On the other hand, I am not . . . without political significance. (No, I don't mean that its vital interest is of course something else – what I mean is that 'success' has never, I think, been my object, except in so far as it can be got by [means] & outlook I approve of) . . . Oliver Stanley said to me the other day that I write on politics better than any one on the Unionist side & I do feel most deeply that [if] I were married to you, there would be . . . a real accretion of power & value: because I know that life would have . . . new meaning & character to me. At present, I know that I am only scratching the surface of life.
>
> 4th There is 'myself'. That can't really be written about.

> I do feel, however, that I am still capable of improvement & development . . . All I can say is that I don't feel that the possibilities are exhausted. And I feel that with you I could be what I have always hoped to be & never have been – but what that is, I cannot describe & don't even exactly know.

The fourth point clearly hinted at a depressive tendency. He concluded:

> Now, my dear, there is a lot of words chiefly about myself but still more about the disadvantages to Katharine Tennant of her marrying Noel Skelton. Are there any advantages? None, unless she loves him & even then that wd be his advantage not hers. And yet I say, despite the disadvantages, – so selfish a creature is man – yet I say, – love me. Your Noel.[85]

The anguish is obvious; deep love combined with an acute sense of selfless practicality. 'The kind of man you should marry is a man like [Herbert] Henry Asquith,' Skelton wrote while staying in Gullane, East Lothian, 'a man worth everything you [are] & wd like . . . your brains, energies, affections – but your Noel is something very small in comparison with such a character or personality as his was.'[86] They saw each other in East Lothian later that month, on what Skelton said was the 'most wonderful & delightful day of my life', although he later lamented that 'such sureness of heart is a pain & a blessing'.[87]

Yet still Katharine could not reach a decision. 'Anyway, if you marry me, I shall dedicate everything that is in me to making you happy & if I can't do it, then I wd willingly take myself out of your path forever,' he wrote on 20 August, 'but, oh my darling, don't hurry. Don't be rushed into "declarations". You are so wonderful . . . But darling I am 48 & you are 25. So be careful!!'[88] And a few days later: 'You ask me if your feelings mean "yes". I think they mean something of the sort: but I still say caution & patience.'[89]

Tennant and Skelton spent several days at the end of August and beginning of September together at Ivy Lodge in Gullane, a regular haunt where they could indulge in a shared passion for golf. He continued writing to her despite the regular contact. '*I* know that I want *your* companionship always: but it may well take a little time before you decide that you want mine.'[90] On 4 September he wrote in anticipation of another meeting.

> Since I wrote so far, your letter has come. My dearest, what can I say . . . that I am totally undeserving, but that I love you & love you more & more each day . . . I have this feeling that I shall never myself be interested in anything but you again . . . my dear, I must 'shut up'. I shall write things so foolish – & get so tired that I can't go on.[91]

By October, there was still no decision from Katharine, and Skelton tried vainly to nudge her in the right direction. He wrote from the New Club in Edinburgh.

> In any case, you mustn't let any thoughts of me enter into your final view. I can get on without you. I have got on without you. The only proper basis for our marriage would be that you should feel that you can't get on without me. Then I should know that all is well & that the sacrifices, if any, involved in marrying me would be less than the sacrifices of not marrying me & that wd give a . . . basis for our joint lives.
>
> If you feel you can get on without me, then dismiss altogether the idea of marrying me . . . the real question – can you or can't you get on without me? . . . When I say that I can get on without you, it only means that by my time of life, one simply has to learn to get on with what one has got.
>
> If you read this letter carefully, it will, I think, give you the best clue as to what your decision should be.[92]

But Skelton soon became exasperated, as is evident from another letter written from 21 Northumberland Street, the Edinburgh New Town residence he shared with his spinster sister Evelyn.[93] 'K, my dearest, you are going to marry me, aren't you? . . . I believe we are in fare danger of [producing an] unnecessary shipwreck. If you are not careful, I think there is a good chance that you will kill the happiness of . . . yourself & me & that very greatly alarms.'[94]

By 10 October Skelton wrote to tell Katharine of his fear 'that you are deciding that you are not going to marry me. However, I shall soon dare you to make any such decision.'[95] And a week later, his tone became rather more blunt: 'I don't wonder you don't like the business of deciding but you *are* going to marry me.'

> Meantime, I am struggling to make speeches & am having quite good meetings & am, in consequence, quite enjoying myself: but I wish that you had not succeeded in convincing me quite so thoroughly that you will not marry me – indeed cannot! – Yet I daresay you are right & that I wd never make you very happy or pleased that you had done it . . . I feel that I ought to advise you not to marry me: but somehow I don't find it possible to do that, strangely enough.[96]

And two days later, Skelton wrote again to sympathise with Katharine's depression but, he said, 'the time for decision is clearly approaching . . . I have no desire to beg at love-making with you or to bandy compliments and comments about each other's qualities. We know each other . . . Are you going to marry me or not?'[97] He arranged to have dinner with her in Edinburgh the following day. 'I suppose then or thereabouts the decision must be taken.'[98]

But it was not good news for Skelton – Katharine said no. He wrote to her on 21 October from Edinburgh:

> I know that of all the women I have known, I have never felt to be so absolutely mutual, at ease & at one with any of them . . . I believe that to some extent the same is true of you with me. . . You may very well be right. You may find

someone whom you like better & who . . . understands you
better than I do . . . & makes you a more complete & full &
dominant part of his life.[99]

Skelton wrote to Katharine for the last time (at least for around
nine months) two days later, underlining wistfully the words 'you
are right not to marry me'.[100] As 1928 drew to a close, Skelton must
have regretted that more than anything in his political career.

The year 1929 was dominated by the general election. Although
the YMCA (and particularly Macmillan) had welcomed the
government's last major measure, the Local Government (Derating)
Act, as a necessary reform, it came too late to affect employment
and was too complex an issue to provide an effective election
platform.[101] After its passage through the House of Commons
Baldwin decided to hold the election in the spring and polling
day was fixed for 30 May. Some Conservatives suggested trying to
arrange some kind of coalition with Lloyd George's Liberals but, as
Cuthbert Headlam recorded in his diary on 7 April, most of those
in the YMCA, including Skelton, were 'quite prepared to see the
Party break rather than that such a thing should come to pass'.[102]

It was therefore an unhappy party – and an unhappy Skelton –
that approached the 1929 poll, and when Parliament was dissolved
on 11 May there was no option but to fight a campaign under the
slogan of 'Safety First'. As the Conservative Party historian John
Ramsden observed, that slogan was a failure 'precisely because it
showed up the party's real stance in the election; safety first and
nothing second'.[103] Indeed, the Conservative Party entered the
campaign with few positive cards other than the appeal of Baldwin
himself; the slogan 'Trust in Baldwin' was intended to highlight the
poor reputation of Lloyd George, whose revitalised Liberal Party
posed the greatest danger to the seats the Conservatives had won
in 1924.

Baldwin was considered to have performed well during the
election campaign, but a party that had been so closely attuned

to the national mood in 1924 was by 1929 almost completely
out of touch. The YMCA, however, rallied to Baldwin's, and the
government's, defence. Although the previous five years had
included its share of disappointments Baldwin remained, in their
eyes, the only realistic leadership option.

Skelton was again adopted as the Unionist candidate for Perth at
a constituency meeting on 11 May, although he had reason to think
he would not be returned to Parliament. Alongside a reinvigorated
Labour Party, the recent local government reforms in Scotland
had been highly unpopular. Nevertheless, as campaigning began,
Skelton tried to remain positive. He told one meeting:

> Whatever side of national life you look at, you will see
> as a result of the good government of the last four years
> there is happening what always happens – that the fruit of
> good government is order and peace and improved trade
> and prosperity, that by good government you can give
> the benefits of peace so that they flow into the smallest
> households in the land.[104]

Heckling from Labour supporters was particularly bad during this
campaign, but Skelton relished the cut and thrust of town hall
debates. He regularly attacked Lloyd George's pledge to spend
huge sums on roads and other public works schemes over the next
two years. Skelton said it showed a 'contempt for democracy to call
such a hotch-potch scheme a conquest. It was not a conquest, but a
fraud', as after two years everyone would once again be out of work
and the nation worse off financially. He said he was proud to follow
Baldwin's lead, as 'he was a wise, practical man, who understood
the needs of the hearts and the lives of our people. A man who
had raised the tone of public life by restoring to the utterances of
statesmen a degree of credibility, honesty, and truthfulness that
was not always expected of others.'[105] Skelton also commended
Neville Chamberlain's housing reforms, saying that the 'building
of some 930,000 houses in the last four and a half years is a world

record and has greatly relieved the housing shortage in our cities'.[106]

The Labour leader, Ramsay MacDonald, spoke at Perth City Hall during May, and Skelton responded by saying that

> he understood a man or woman being attracted by the Socialist policy, but he asked them to consider if this was the moment to put it into operation . . . It was an experiment that had never been successful wherever tried . . . In their own interests and in the interests of the wage-earners the real motto for this election should be 'Safety First'.

He said to Socialists: 'Take heed.'[107]

Once again, the Liberal candidate was Francis Norie-Miller, a major local figure in his capacity as the founder, vice-chairman and managing director of General Accident, while the Labour candidate was a Glaswegian schoolteacher called Helen Gault. Conscious of his left-wing opponents, Skelton was careful to emphasise the late government's progress in social reform and industrial relief during the campaign, mentioning in particular the improved Widows and Old Age Pensions Act. Nevertheless, it proved an ill-natured few weeks.

At a big Unionist rally in Perth City Hall on the eve of poll, Skelton said of Lloyd George's road scheme that 'this great picture palace has already begun to vanish and the picture on the screen has become trembling and vague and will very soon become indistinguishable'. Concluding his address, Skelton asked:

> Was it for nothing that mutual interests had been built up between the two partners [in] industry? Was it for nothing that they saw growing between their eyes the ideal of the Unionist Party? The future of Britain and its people was not under the heel of a Socialist Government, but under a system which produced an ever-growing, ever-strengthening property-owning democracy.[108]

The polls closed on 30 May[109] and the Perth Division declared at 12.40 a.m. the following day. The result was:

Skelton, A. N. (Unionist)	14,229
Norie-Miller, F. (Liberal)	12,699
Gault, Mrs. H. E. (Labour)	8,291

Skelton's stock had risen during the last few days of the campaign but the Liberal candidate had still taken about 3,500 Unionist votes. His majority was just 1,530, but he had been lucky – almost all the Conservative gains of 1924 had been swept away and only 260 government MPs remained. Labour was for the first time the largest party in the Commons (with 287 seats, an increase of 136), although still lacking an overall majority. Lloyd George's Liberals enjoyed a modest recovery, but secured only fifty-nine members. Nevertheless, Skelton was probably conscious that had a Labour candidate not entered the fray, Norie-Miller would probably have defeated him, while the growth of the socialist vote made the seat increasingly untenable if Skelton was to remain in Parliament.

Skelton and his supporters went to the Perth Conservative Club following the count, and from the balcony the victorious candidate addressed a large crowd. He said that 'when the centre was right everything was right, and Perth remained the great centre of Scotland'.

> He might say – and he was not using the language of exaggeration – that that part of Perthshire he had known so long had become something like a spiritual home to him. In the first place he had an intimate acquaintance with Perthshire when he went to school at Glenalmond, where he had days and years of unalloyed happiness and he believed of undesirable benefit to himself. That was the foundation. Then at the age of thirty he was honoured with the request to stand as Unionist candidate for East Perthshire and was met with a spirit of cordiality although

he was more or less unknown. Later he had been associated with a regiment closely identified with Perthshire, and he recollected that his first night as a soldier was spent within earshot of the murmuring Tay. Elected in 1922 as Member for the constituency, he was unsuccessful in 1923. During these years he had the privilege of their whole-hearted support and when Unionism was on the top of the wave in 1924 he had again been given their enthusiastic assistance. Surely, as he had said, he had the right to call Perthshire his spiritual home.

'Mr Skelton thus continues member for Perth,' observed the *Perthshire Advertiser*. 'He has done good service to the community and to the Conservative cause, and until the present poll, was generally regarded as "booked for promotion".'[110] But although Skelton was indeed 'booked for promotion', he had already resolved that this would be his last election campaign in the fair city of Perth.

'MY POLITICAL BOLT IS SHOT'
(1929-31)

The general election of 1929 was a disaster for the Conservative Party, several members of the YMCA[1] and, not least, Stanley Baldwin. Following the result he decided against meeting Parliament and resigned as Prime Minister on 4 June. 'The bold new initiative of 1924-25 had risen and receded like the tide,' judged John Ramsden, 'and it seemed that it all had to be done again.'[2] Baldwin also proved to be an ineffective leader of the opposition, and the following two years were to be fraught with political difficulty.

Skelton, meanwhile, decided almost immediately that he had contested Perth for the last time. At a meeting of his constituency association on 28 June, Skelton thanked everyone for their hard work at the recent poll, and (the minutes recorded)

> stated that the first duty they had to consider was who was to be their candidate at the next Election and he intimated with great regret that he had decided that he was not to stand at the next Election. He informed the Meeting that his decision was final and that he had already been asked to change his mind but that he could not see his way to do so. The Chairman, the Vice-Chairman and Mr Alexander Macduff voiced the feelings of themselves and all the Members of the Association at Mr Skelton's decision, but

with great regret, in the circumstance, they must simply fall in therewith.[3]

Lord Scone, the eldest son of the Earl of Mansfield and an active member of the association, was chosen as Skelton's successor. Ironically, Scone would hold the seat at the next general election two years later, and with an increased majority.[4]

The Scottish Unionist Party, meanwhile, was also engaged in a bout of soul-searching. At a conference in Edinburgh shortly after the election, Skelton influenced a motion (supported by a young candidate called Alec Dunglass) calling upon the party to abandon its Conservative name. It passed with only three delegates voting against, and asserted

> that this Conference of Scottish Unionists is of the opinion that the use of the word 'Conservative' to describe the Unionist Party and Policy is injurious to the interests of the Party, and, agreeing with Lord Balfour that the word 'Unionist' expresses better the things in which 'we most passionately believe', urges that the use of the term 'Conservative', whether in speeches or writings, be discontinued, and the term 'Unionist', which is the correct and official designation in Scotland, be always used.[5]

Skelton was obviously trying to protect what he saw as a distinct Unionist identity in Scotland,[6] while seeking explanations for the poor election result. His previously hard-line position against Scottish devolution also seemed to soften a little. Speaking in a debate on public buildings on 19 July, Skelton praised the 'incorporated Union', but added:

> My hon. Friend the Member for the Scottish Universities [John Buchan], while disclaiming the qualities of a prophet, suggested that there might be a time when further devolution might produce some qualification or alteration

of the present system. I, for one, am inclined to think that you cannot regard in the history of the nation any system as necessarily permanent or final, but be that as it may, should there be some devolution, some alteration in the present system, and if Scotland has to take up some part of the burden of parliamentary life for herself north of the Tweed, Scotland will come to that new duty and that new responsibility not as a minor member, not as inferior to England; she will come to it with a full knowledge of parliamentary life, and she will come because she is ready. At some future time it may be she will come to it, and then she will be ready to take up some part of the parliamentary burden which is now exclusively and, as I think, very onerously carried on within this chamber.[7]

That 'future time', of course, came seventy years later with the creation of a devolved Scottish Parliament. As the long summer recess approached, Skelton was clearly winding down. 'I have never held office,' he remarked melancholically during one exchange, 'and I do not suppose I ever shall.'[8] He did, however, believe there remained work to be done in order to safeguard democracy in the UK:

In an age when democracy is, in so many parts of the world, threatened, and in some parts threatened on account of its failure to be efficient, it appears to me that those who care for democracy must in the twentieth century carry out a different work from what they carried out in the nineteenth century. Their work in the nineteenth century was the extension of democracy, but the work of this twentieth century is the concentration and making more efficient of the democracy which we have; and it is from that point of view that I have always regarded our act as a step towards sounder democracy and not towards reaction, as is so often said.[9]

The summer recess gave Skelton the opportunity to rekindle his love affair with Katharine Tennant, and he wrote to her for the first time in several months on 4 July. 'I want to come to see you. May I?' he asked. 'The letter is the enemy of the goal: but shd not, I think, be allowed to kill it.'[10] She must have refused, for a few days later he wrote again, explaining that 'the only way we can meet often is by marriage & it is one of the advantages of marriage that it enables people who love each other and take comfort, in the difficulties & hollowness of life, in each other's security, to enjoy that comfort'. Skelton added that such intimacy would not be possible through social encounters. 'Let us, however, do it as an experiment. I'll begin by coming to tea with you tomorrow at 5 p.m.'[11]

Their meeting on 9 July, however, was clearly not a success. Katharine apparently tried to explain her rejection of his proposal. 'You said "Listen" as I said goodbye yesterday,' he wrote the following day. 'It wasn't that I didn't want to listen but nothing much could be said then. I am free tomorrow afternoon at tea-time. Shall I come to see you? I really want to help if I know how.'[12] Within a week, Tennant was reconsidering Skelton's proposal of marriage. 'Will it really do to think of marrying an old, useless . . . person like me?' he wrote. 'You must go warily, with such a danger as a possibility.'[13] And on 19 July, Skelton even broached the detail of their wedding plans.

> K, my dear, if we were to get married, when do you think it should be and where? I rather think that the 7th October . . . be a good date & that we should be married before the sheriff, (which equals the Registrar.) You might not like that perhaps, however, in which case I . . . suppose that it should be done from Birch & . . . most intimate friends (of which I have none) . . . My objection to Birch is that I want to spend our honeymoon in Colonsay, which in October must be divine, but of course we might go to Sicily instead. Honeymoons should always be spent on an island.

'Then, my dear, what do you think of [discussions] of that kind?' added Skelton. 'Do they frighten you, as they did last autumn or is there no rationally unpleasant reaction.'[14] He wrote again on 24 July: 'I am shallow & useless: but I shall try to be worthy of your love and affection however events may turn out: for I do believe that to have what I have of that is in truly a miracle & a blessing.'[15]

But having reconsidered his proposal, Katharine again decided not to go through with it. 'Really, really, my dear K, you mustn't make such violent love to me, as you do in your last letter!' Skelton wrote on 3 August. 'You have got to remember that you have refused to marry me (on excellent grounds) . . . and clearly don't want to: & to make it the subject of constant pointless talk is . . . to trivialise something that, whatever else it is shouldn't be trivial.' There was also obvious concern about their affair becoming public. 'I fear – don't you – that it will be quite impossible for us to meet when you are at North Berwick. It wd give the hounds of rumour & scandal . . . too hot a scent – but it will be nice to know that you are there.'[16]

The following month, Skelton explained at length his decision not to stand again in Perth, a decision Katharine appeared to think she had influenced.

> My dear, my decision not to contest Perth again has nothing in the world to do with you or anything you have or have not said or done.
>
> My decision was based on a variety of factors. First that I had been there long enough. I first contested it in Dec 1910! Secondly, that if I was ever going on in politics, the time had come when, if the party wants me, I must have an easier constituency. Rashly, but, in any case, I decided not to . . . stand again anywhere . . . I felt I had to clear my feet & see what happened. I clung to Perthshire, while I was passionately interested in clinging to politics. I have long since given up any desire to cling to politics & therefore it is no longer necessary or desirable to cling to Perthshire. There were lots of other elements in the situation, which I can't go through in a letter; but of this be sure, that you had nothing to do with my decision.[17]

Skelton's depressive streak was again to the fore. 'You are the only person, except my own family, who has ever really liked me at all,' he lamented on 26 August. 'But is a great blessing to me, whatever befalls.'[18] But not only had Tennant been causing him anguish; so too had his political career.

> There isn't much to say about my political doings. I have been getting bored with the H. of C. for some time: but this is the first such opportunity I have had of quitting the scene. In the spring of 1928 I very nearly decided not to stand again: but there was then no Labour Candidate for Perth & as in a straight fight I shd have been beaten most probably by the Lib. To have resigned then wd have looked like fright. But when I was, after everyone said I was going to be beaten, & when young Scone was . . . [selected] to take my place, the moment had [come] . . . If I had done well in Parliament, if I had felt that it was worth the practical difficulties . . . to stay, I wd have stayed perhaps: but nobody could say that I was a Parliamentary success: & for . . . I had said or written everything I wanted to say & without any sort of result or effect: so it was clearly time to be off. & off I am! . . . Politics is for the young and strong.[19]

And what was more, concluded Skelton, he did not want to spend 'a futile day by hanging around the H. of C. to pick up a baronetcy or a Peerage! Now let there be no more worrying, my dear K, or playing with ideas which will never come to fruition.'[20]

From September, their correspondence became less frequent, but as full of agonising and irritation.

> I asked you to marry me. You found you didn't want to & for perfectly sound reasons – although at the same time you rather liked me. But . . . It's not a story worth thinking about any more. The chances . . . are you have had a very lucky escape . . . Why cannot you accept your own decision when

you know you wd make it again, if necessary? I've accepted it.
To have also to persuade you to accept it, when you made it,
is really the strangest task anyone was ever called on to do.[21]

And on 29 October:

It's quite clear that since June we have been at cross-purposes
to some extent. But now we know the danger . . . of that &
we shall be warned in future . . . It is quite beside the point
to call yourself selfish. I see nothing selfish about it. You
either want to marry me or you do not . . . People marry
because they want to live with the other person always &
not just see them occasionally as a friend.[22]

Skelton's last letter of 1929 to Katharine was dated 17 December and
is incredibly poignant. 'The chances are that you will survive me by
many years,' he wrote. 'If there is any reason to suppose that say 20
years hence you take . . . any interest in me, I'll leave you a short
autobiography in my will. But I suspect that I shall . . . have become
the merest shadow of a name to you long before that.'[23]

The new session of Parliament began in November 1929, but
Skelton's heart clearly was not in it. The previous month he had
written to Harold Macmillan, expressing hope that 'amongst all
the conflicting ideas & talk that is going on about the future of
the Unionist party that you're exercising all your influence to get
Neville C. made Chairman', an appointment he believed would
demonstrate that the party was 'neither dead nor asleep'.[24]

Following that constructive suggestion, Skelton's mood
darkened. Although Macmillan recalled in his memoirs that
Skelton helped him and others 'to keep alive some of the ideas
which we had put forward in the last Parliament',[25] in another
letter dated 5 November Skelton praised a recent article written by
Macmillan, but warned him that 'the Unionist party is doomed'.
He continued:

Parties of the right are psychologically incapable of taking a long view or making sacrifices or taking risks to achieve it. We are now in the crisis of a Revolution (by legislation) which is exhibiting all the characteristics of a Revolution by force – and in particular the inevitable feature that the . . . mind of the right is quite powerless . . . I fear it must always be so: because until a Revolution is far advanced the left is united or the right divided between resistance or construction . . . Anyway, you'll get no response for thought and sacrifice from the present Unionist Party. The harrow will have to go over their backs again and again before they accept the hateful necessity of thinking.[26]

This, remarked Macmillan, 'was perhaps written in an unusually despondent mood, by a man who had given more constructive thought to politics than almost any other member of the party in or out of the House of Commons'.[27] Lady Tweedsmuir remembered:

Noel was the complete Parliamentarian, and he would never have been happy out of the House of Commons. Now and then he would get very tired of its trivialities, and talk about retiring to a chicken farm in Scotland. Upon which Walter Elliot observed drily [sic] that if Noel had a chicken farm he would have one pen for the 'Ayes' and another pen for the 'Noes'![28]

Despite this disillusion, Skelton entered the ballot for notices of motion, and signalled his intention to move a resolution on 'Profit Sharing and Industrial Co-partnership' three weeks hence.[29] Shortly after, he spoke during a debate on the Widows', Orphans', and Old Age Pensions Bill. He told the House:

It is essential for the welfare of this country that legislation as a whole, both remedial and social, should be founded on

the basic principle that it should be used as far as possible
to help people to help themselves . . . That is another reason
why we should have a means test, provided that it does not
exclude people who ought to be included, and provided
that it acts as a suitable dividing line and does not have a
crippling effect.[30]

Skelton ended 1929 with a familiar refrain.

I have ventured to say so in this House – one of the main
problems in this assembly is in every way to secure the
development of a property-owning democracy. The
wider and more extensive the relation of the bulk of your
people is to property-owning, the more secure are the
foundations of your State, and that kind of consideration
should not be absent in the financial administration of
the Treasury.[31]

Although Skelton's personal life was fraught and he had resolved
to quit politics, the spirit of his constructive Conservatism was still
alive and well.

The YMCA had effectively been destroyed, or at least heavily
neutered, by the 1929 election, and by early 1930 it had regrouped
in a different form. Anthony Eden recalled in his memoirs:

Early in the new year, 1930, half a dozen of us agreed to meet
at a weekly dinner and work as closely together as possible
in the life of that Parliament. Noel Skelton, Oliver Stanley,
William Ormsby-Gore,[32] Walter Elliot and W. S. Morrison[33]
made up our loose fraternity. We held the same views, our
domestic politics being to the left of centre in our own
party. With the exception of Skelton, who died young, all
the group were future Cabinet Ministers.

Skelton remained the group's guiding light, and also began to make a more profound impression on Eden in particular. He recalled:

> Stanley Baldwin was accessible and to members of our small group he was the most sympathetic, sharing our youthful ideas for a progressive Conservatism which would have positive aims, and knowing what we meant by such expressions as 'a property-owning democracy'. I believe that it was Noel Skelton, a thought-provoking young Scotsman and a close friend of mine, who first used this phrase in our talks together during this Parliament.[34]

More importantly, however, Skelton and the reconstituted YMCA were firmly wedded to Baldwin's leadership, largely because the reactionary elements in the party (and therefore the leadership alternatives) remained so unpalatable. Colin Coote, a former Tory MP who observed the Commons at that time from the Strangers' Gallery, reckoned the regrouped YMCA were

> people who had devoted the necessary thought as well as emotion to our new economic and political problems. In fact, though it would have been blasphemous to say so, their conclusions were not wholly different from those of some of the young Socialists, such as Oswald Mosley or John Strachey. But in neither party were the feet of the young men lifted high enough to kick out the old.[35]

One of those young men was Anthony Eden, whose main interests throughout the 1924–9 parliament had been defence and foreign affairs; it was only following the 1929 defeat that he began to address wider Conservative philosophy. With his matinee-idol looks, Eden cut a dashing figure in his immaculate suits and Homburg hats (soon known as the Eden hat), but this outward image as the Beau Brummell of British politics disguised a greater political depth. He had recently spoken of enabling all workers to become capitalists through industrial co-partnership schemes and, clearly spotting his progressive potential, Skelton encouraged Eden to use the phrase 'property-owning democracy'.

The pair shared some common ground. Like Skelton, Eden was a product of Christ Church, Oxford, while the First World War had left an indelible mark on both men. Both were also keen journalists. Eden's father-in-law, who was chairman of the *Yorkshire Post*, an influential Conservative newspaper in the north of England, had allowed his son-in-law to write regular articles on foreign affairs, while the connection also proved beneficial to Skelton.

'K, my dearest,' Skelton wrote on 16 January, 'my articles begin on Tuesday in the *Yorkshire Post*.' There would also be, he added, 'a leader about the views of the younger Conservatives (me "younger"!)'.[36] These four articles were essentially a restatement of the essays that had first appeared in *The Spectator* seven years before. 'Noel was an excellent writer,' recalled Lady Tweedsmuir. 'He wrote little, and he wrote laboriously, but the result was most vigorous and luminous prose.'[37] Skelton's quartet of articles for the *Yorkshire Post* demonstrated that his journalistic ability was still potent.

The first part of what was collectively called 'The Conservative Task' appeared in print on 21 January. In 'Leader or Looker-on?' Skelton said that 'surely it is not too much to expect that a great political party should know what its task is and what are the lines of advance and the objective which it has in view'. Writing, as he did, in the midst of Labour's second minority administration, Skelton observed:

> Socialism is to England merely a new acquaintance, lavish of promise and attractive in its novelty, its activity, the impression it diffuses that it has new lamps to give for old; Liberalism is an old friend – though senile and past work now: but Conservatism is blood of England's blood, and bone of her bone. If Socialism disappoints – well, new acquaintances are apt to do that; but if Conservatism fails her, if Conservative thought cannot grapple with the

problems of her life, England sustains a real inward shock and feels that the very pillars of the house are shaken.

It was typically lively Skeltonian prose and included a rebuke to the party's reactionary elements. 'Now large numbers of Conservatives think that the work of the Conservative party is merely to act as a brake on the wheel of change,' he wrote, 'to ensure that the life of the people is altered by gradual steps and not by sudden jerks and jolts.' Britain, therefore, was 'a complete democracy. Its development, its future, its existence depends in the most direct and definite way upon the decision of the men and women who make up the adult community – in the ultimate test, upon the character of its individual citizens.'

> More attractive, perhaps, but still quite inadequate, is the view that the task of the Conservative party is merely to keep the national atmosphere sweet and wholesome – to prevent strife and folly from interfering with or stunting the natural evolution and development of the British people. That is an easy creed; for it excuses the Conservative party from any close study, knowledge, or analysis of what is actually happening, and confines it to the congenial task of diffusing a mildly benevolent influence on anyone prepared to accept it . . . its fatal defect is that it affords no alternative to Socialist policy. And further, it is based on the perilous assumption that all will go well of itself and that the Conservative party can safely be a mere spectator of the national life, occasionally applauding the opposing teams or warning them to play the game. It is in fact looking on – not leading. Is the leadership of the nation, then, to be left to the Socialists? How many Conservatives would in fact like that?

Skelton concluded:

> To understand and grasp these problems, to show the

country their nature and importance, to point out where
their solution is to be found (whether it be through Acts
of Parliament or not), and to make clear to the democracy
where lies its true objective and the road by which it can be
reached – this, surely, and not to act as brake or looker-on
or deserter, is the task of the Conservative party.[38]

'I have today in the "Yorkshire Post" the first of 4 articles on the
"Conservative task",' Skelton reminded Katharine in another letter.
'I have said all of it before; but . . . [with] a new emphasis . . . in
any case I shd like you to read them, but I fear you will think them
dull.'[39]

The second instalment of 'The Conservative Task', 'Problem
and Clue', also repeated old themes with a new emphasis, but
was far from dull. Skelton asserted that 'the basic strength of any
community lies in the individual citizens: it stands or falls by their
character, outlook, energy, and stability'. But he lamented that
despite full political and educational status, the 'economic status
of the worker, his position in industrial life, has actually declined
since the early days of the Industrial Revolution and is immensely
below its level before that tremendous change'.

It is said by many politicians that, if the workers have steady
jobs for good wages and under good conditions, no more is
needed. Little, in their comfortable sheltered lives, do such
men realise how far we have left behind the placid mentality
and steady-going outlook of the nineteenth century. No
diffusion of a genial and friendly atmosphere can alter the
fact that in the modern industrial structure the workman's
economic position is, in essence, that of a machine.

And, continued Skelton, referring to the agricultural question,
'The fundamental rural problem lies deeper. It is the peril of the
almost total urbanisation of the community.' The balance, he
said, 'between town and country must be restored . . . Too many

politicians – and apparently most industrialists– harbour the dangerous delusion that Britain may safely become an almost exclusively urban community, leaving the Dominions to contain the rural population of the Empire.' But, claimed Skelton, 'a democracy not closely linked with and based on the soil is a democracy artificial, unstable and insecure'.

> And the individual? On nothing to-day in our national life is there greater apprehension than upon his position. Every tendency, it would seem, of the modern world combines to surround him with influences cramping his energies, narrowing his economic life, sapping his independence, putting his vigour in jeopardy. Strengthened though these influences are by Socialist thought and teaching, the Socialist himself is only moving along the line of least resistance and thereby developing, instead of countering, the elements of danger and weakness.

Skelton ended with his usual declaration about the importance of private property.

> The particular contribution which the Conservative mind makes to political thought is the special importance which it attaches from a personal, social, and political point of view, to private property. It used, indeed, to be jeered at by its enemies as 'the Party of Property'.
>
> It recognises in the possession of private property one of the greatest means of expression and of development for the character, outlook, and capacities of the individual human being. It sees in the effort to build up capital through thrift and energy one of the most potent influences in the development of character. It sees in a man's opportunity and capacity to control his own property – in his having something of his own to control – one of the most powerful aids in the growth of a sense of responsibility . . .

> Nor are these views recently adopted nor lightly held by
> Conservative thinkers; they are of the very core and essence
> of Conservative philosophy . . . It is by the development of
> the property sense and property opportunity that the life
> of the individual can be strengthened: the economic status
> of the industrial worker advanced to meet his political and
> educational status: a numerous rural population built up:
> British democracy underpinned and stabilised.

'The task of Conservatism,' concluded Skelton, 'urgent, vital, fundamental – is the development in Britain of a property-owning democracy.'[40]

Part three of the series, 'A Property-Owning Democracy', contained perhaps Skelton's most vivid exposition of his central contention. He began with a strangely detached critique of his own party's record on the policy of co-partnership in industry:

> As far back as June 1924, a statement of policy issued by
> its leaders declared that they 'will encourage the admission
> of the workers, by the application of the principle of
> co-partnership, to a direct share in the success of the
> undertakings in which they are employed'. Since these
> words were published, however, they have apparently
> been entirely forgotten, for during the life of the late
> Conservative Government no step was taken either by
> word or deed to indicate to the nation that any importance
> was to be attached to them. No attempt of any sort was
> made to inform the public mind. In the preoccupations of
> government, the whole topic was let slip. Perhaps to some
> extent timidity operated.

But, said Skelton, 'in seeking to develop an industrial property-owning democracy, the Conservative party will have the sympathy of the great mass of thinking and prudent working people in this country'. This, however, need not take the form of an Act of

Parliament. 'It is guidance and leadership from the Conservative party that is required. In no direction is this leadership more needed, nowhere can it be more fruitful, than in showing the world of urban industry how to reach, by the road of industrial co-partnership, the objective of a property-owning democracy.'[41]

In the fourth and final article, Skelton attempted to detail some 'Practical Applications' of his thinking.

> Co-partnership and profit-sharing are no mere humanitarian fad. They are the next stage in the journey to a higher industrial efficiency. The reason is that they influence the mind and spirit of the worker. It is surely a truth of universal application, that, until mind and spirit are engaged, the task, whatever it be, brings only partial satisfaction to the worker, and is itself, a weariness to the flesh. And where, as in modern life, education as well as the general stir and movement greatly stimulate the mind and spirit, and where, at the same time, the actual work for many is necessarily stereotyped and monotonous, the working hours become, both by contrast with the world outside and as the inevitable result of the extreme 'division of labour', dull and insipid to a degree undreamt of before modern industrial life had reached its present state of development and elaboration.

Again, Skelton drew upon personal experience to illustrate his point:

> To give, out of many, one example of each point. The present writer is well acquainted with a holding, only 9 acres in extent, almost within sight of a great Northern city [Perth], which through the cultivation of fruit, flowers and poultry, not only affords a livelihood to the holders themselves, but pays wages of nearly £550 a year.'

The time was ripe, argued Skelton, 'to call the rural world to restore
the balance of the urban'.

> But though 'individualism', as a school of economic or
> political thought, is dead and buried, the individual remains.
> Between those wider flights of modern economic thought,
> those larger economic problems and the creation of a
> property-owning democracy, there is no collision. They are,
> indeed, complimentary. For unless the economic structure
> of the future is based upon individuals, whose industrial
> status corresponds to their political and educational status,
> the fabric will fall, because – fatal defect – its foundations
> will be lopsided, off the true level, unstable.[42]

'Unstable' was a word that, in 1930, best described Baldwin's
leadership of the Conservative Party. Between 1929 and 1931 there
was much, often vehement, criticism of Baldwin's stewardship,
not exactly a helpful phenomenon in opposition. 'After a defeat, a
political party has often to endure a kneading process to consolidate
and toughen it,' observed Eden in his memoirs. 'So it was with the
Conservative Party in that period. We sloughed off some of the old
husk.' He also recalled:

> It was typical of the times that at a party meeting held to
> discuss the leadership, one of Stanley Baldwin's critics
> should complain: 'At every luncheon party you go to you
> hear criticism of him.' Noel Skelton cried out from the
> gallery: 'But what do you hear in the back streets?' We
> might not have known as much about back streets as we
> thought, but at least we knew it was their confidence we
> must win and their conditions we intended to improve.[43]

Throughout this period, Skelton constantly sought to keep the
party more in tune with the wavelength of the back streets than
the average luncheon party. But despite the support of the YMCA,

Baldwin was in difficulty. Although the party's Central Council meeting of 2 July 1929 passed a resolution of confidence in Baldwin's leadership, it did not disguise the fact that his moderate line had failed to keep the Conservatives in office. The 1929 losses had also tilted the balance of the parliamentary party towards the safer southern constituencies, and the Diehards soon began pushing for a change in policy, chiefly a full tariff programme including duties on food imports. But Baldwin wanted to recover seats in the urban Midlands and north, which were essential if the Conservatives were to win the next election, and therefore he considered any suggestion of 'food taxes' to be unthinkable in electoral terms.

Baldwin, therefore, resisted the pressure for tariffs, but as this ran counter to the mood in the party's strongholds, it prompted an internal crisis that seriously threatened his position in the summer and autumn of 1930. Not only was Baldwin forced to accept Neville Chamberlain instead of the unpopular J. C. Davidson as party chairman (as Skelton had wished the previous year), he also had to fend off three separate attacks on his leadership.

The most serious came in September 1930, when Baldwin's colleagues began to view his position as hopeless. But the impact of the economic slump and rising unemployment was changing the mood in the industrial regions, and on 9 October Baldwin announced that he would ask for a 'free hand' to introduce tariffs at the next election. Almost all of the party now rallied behind him, and his leadership was endorsed by a large margin at a second party meeting on 30 October 1930. Skelton recalled that gathering in the *Quarterly Review* some months later:

> Mysterious cloak-and-dagger colloguings took place. Three days before the meeting there was issued to the Press, late at night, the statement that forty-two Conservative members, whose names were given, had resolved that 'a change in the leadership was essential in the national interests'. Who issued it has never been definitely established. In any case

it blew the conspiracy sky-high. There was not a name, amongst those given, which carried the slightest weight.

'Colonel Gretton, plucky to the last, moved the resolution of censure,' continued Skelton.

> How flimsy that indictment was became clear to all when one of the main counts turned out to be the action of Mr Baldwin's Government at Han-kow. Still, a quarter of the meeting supported the resolution. It was not perhaps quite a full meeting of the party, for some of the left flankers found that they had business elsewhere. However, if not Trafalgar, it was at any rate Jutland.[44]

On the day of the meeting *The Times* also carried a letter from Skelton defending Baldwin's leadership. He listed four main points:

> (1) Mr Baldwin is trusted and respected by the country as a whole as no leading member of the Conservatives, or of any other party, is to-day. At a time when distrust and contempt for 'politicians' is growing apace, there is a steady, deep-seated confidence in the soundness of Mr Baldwin's judgement, character, and aims.
> (2) Mr Baldwin has satisfied the great mass of the electorate that, under his leadership, the Conservative Party is a national, not a class, party, and that its policy is directed to the general good, not to sectional advantage.
> (3) These two predominant features of Mr Baldwin's leadership would be at any time a very great asset to the Conservative Party. They are to-day of special and paramount importance. For the immediate task of the Conservative Party is to secure at the next election the substitution of a protective for a free trade system. Just because the electorate trusts and respects Mr Baldwin's judgement, character, and aims, and recognizes that, with

him, national interests, not class or sectional, come first, it will trust with him the making of this momentous change. To whom else would, in this matter, the country give – or be right to give – 'a free hand'? To jettison Mr Baldwin is to jeopardize the policy for which Conservatives stand.

(4) For what would the country think of the deed? Widespread suspicion would surely be roused that the Conservative Party wanted a leader more complacent to the private solicitations of sectional interests, of the Press, of 'big business'. In such an atmosphere, what chance would protection have of being accepted by the nation.

Skelton went on to ask:

And what would be the effect upon the general prestige and position of the Conservative Party if it discarded a leader who has given its policy and tone to a national, not a sectional or class, quality? Clearly the inference would be that at heart it was devoted to class and sectional interests. What a weapon for its enemies, what a fatal admission for itself! For it is as true to-day as when Disraeli used the phrase that 'if the Conservative Party is not a national party it is nothing'.

Skelton concluded his letter with a caustic rebuke: 'Many who read the statement attributed to the forty-four will feel that what is needed in the national interest is not a change in the leadership of the Conservative Party, but a change of some of its personnel in the House of Commons.'[45]

Otherwise, Skelton spent 1930 speaking only occasionally in the Commons, attempting to revive his love affair with Katharine Tennant, and keeping his hand in at the Faculty of Advocates in Edinburgh – presumably in preparation for a post-parliamentary career.

The summer recess, meanwhile, brought time for rest and relaxation. Skelton discovered the drooping lady's tresses orchid on the island of Colonsay while walking with Lady Strathcona,[46] continuing an interest in botany that went back to his schooldays at Glenalmond, while he once again resurrected his proposal of marriage to Katharine. 'You must know that the events of 1928 were . . . something of a shock to me,' he had written to her in January. 'You do know that you don't want to marry me & that the love I described isn't mine. It's mine perhaps in quality, but not in sufficient quantity. I know too that it wd be madness for you to marry me.'[47]

Clearly, though, Katharine had not completely ruled out the prospect. 'I am thinking of nothing but you; not thinking of you perhaps so much as trying to prepare my heart & soul . . . for the possibility that in a few months we may be married people,' Skelton wrote on 31 August. 'If I could be really with you I shouldn't [need] anything else. Meantime, the next chapter is drawing on when we shall meet either to unite or to meet no more . . . Bless you whatever the event & be happy.'[48]

And the following month Skelton wrote:

> It's quite clear to me that the situation isn't wholly clarified yet . . . Meantime, I refuse to take a serious view of life, except that, as I said in my last letter, my [main] preoccupation is to try to be, as a human being, not altogether unworthy of you, if it so happens that we marry.

Curiously, he even went on to suggest alternative potential partners. 'Cyril Radcliffe is the most probable husband. Or do you fancy Walter [Elliot]? Bless you, my dearest K; be good, like me, & something pleasant is sure to happen.'[49]

As 1930 drew to close, Skelton again revived his agricultural refrain, and spoke in support of the Labour government's Small Landholders, etc. (Scotland) Bill despite having talked out an earlier clause in May 1930. He also defied the party line over the Agricultural Land (Utilisation) Bill on 13 November.

Many of my Friends have argued, and argued powerfully,

that land settlement is a dangerous thing to encourage because it cannot be economic, and they point to the cost of the erection of houses and buildings.

If you apply that test to any farm, no farm upon which human beings live is economic. If you take the history of any British farm in the heyday of British agriculture, and put on one side the total expenditure laid out on building it up, and on the other side the total profits that you get from it, you will be able to say of it that it is not an economic proposition. The truth is that when we talk of agriculture and of rural life purely in terms of a balance sheet, and insist on getting a full economic return for the money expended, we are applying to the country principles that can be applied only to urban trade.

Skelton refused to support a delayed second reading, while his irritation with his reactionary opponents on the opposition benches also came to the fore. 'I do not like political phrases and I do not like personalities in politics,' he told the House, 'but there is a phrase which is going about the world of politicians just now – not a personal phrase but a psychological phrase, and it is "the old gang".' Skelton added that he did

not like to see on a great occasion, when we are facing a great problem, when this parliament if it is ever to be so, should be a council of state – I do not like to see this narrow, limited, out-of-date, paralysed, point of view being expressed. I do not like it and I do not propose to endure my dislike in complete silence.[50]

The 'old gang' also had to endure another Skeltonian broadside the following week, as the Commons debated raising the school-leaving age to sixteen.

There is a well-known figure which one can always

trace through political history from the time when men
were politicians at all, and that is the aristocrat turned
revolutionary. You can trace him in every history and in
every country. He has never done any good and he never
comes to any good. But he has one quality above all others –
I do not care to what century or to what country you go – he
exhibits this quality always, that he loses the trained sense
of the governing classes and does not get the instinctive
sense of the great mass of the people. For what he loses he
does not get anything in return.[51]

Unfortunately for Baldwin, the beginning of 1931 saw the 'old gang'
grow even more restless, and when they again attempted to force
him out the beleaguered Tory leader seemed almost relieved at
the prospect. The situation came to a head amid renewed attacks
from the Beaverbrook Press and unease over Baldwin's moderate
line on the future constitutional position of India. On 1 March,
Chamberlain presented him with a critical memo written by a
senior Tory official, and Baldwin decided to retire. This low mood
lasted only a few hours and, rallied by his wife and friends, he
instead decided to fight back.

This time, Baldwin's position was actually much stronger than
the previous year, and a powerful speech in the House on India,
together with a frank discussion at a meeting of the Shadow
Cabinet, restored his authority. Meanwhile a story began to
circulate that Baldwin would resign his seat to fight a by-election
in Westminster St George's, for which no pro-Baldwin candidate
could be found. In the event, a friend of Skelton's, Duff Cooper, was
summoned from Sweden to contest it. Baldwin spoke in Cooper's
support at the Queen's Hall on 17 March, and delivered his famous
denunciation of the press lords, who he said sought 'power without
responsibility – the prerogative of the harlot through the ages'.[52]
Two days later, Cooper won the contest with a majority of 5,000.

As a result, from the spring of 1931 the Conservative Party came to
its senses and united behind Baldwin; by-elections from then until

the summer even pointed to the party winning a large majority at the next general election. It is likely that at around this time Skelton began to reconsider his decision to leave Parliament. Between February and April he increased his journalistic output, delivering at least a couple of broadcast talks entitled 'The Month in Scotland' on the BBC, while in April he prepared a mini-pamphlet to send to his electors in Perth. 'As to my letter to the constituents,' Skelton told Katharine on 23 April, 'I enclose a copy – so you can judge it for yourself. I rather like its set-up . . . To me, it looks rather clean & stimulating, & as if it might make people read it. The propositions are, of course, elementary.'

A Note on the Situation, as the pamphlet was called, was, in truth, both elementary and rather simplistic. It asserted:

> The Socialist Government is doing no good for the country. It is a millstone round the neck of every trade and industry . . . It refuses to do anything to prevent the dumping of Russian goods, produced under awful conditions, by forced or terribly underpaid labour . . . The nation wants to see the last of the Socialist Government, and the sooner it goes the better for Britain.

Of the 2½ million persons then unemployed, Skelton said that 'so long as we allow the goods made by foreigners to come into our country unchecked and untaxed, our industries will remain in evil plight. Britain has clung to Free Trade as long as she could. It must be got rid of now.' To Skelton it was a basic case of giving home-grown products a domestic advantage by taxing foreign goods. He added: 'Almost every other manufacturing country has given up Free Trade in favour of Protection. And there is not a single country which, after having adopted Protection, has abandoned it.'

This Skelton also linked to the agricultural situation. 'Britain will never reach the full prosperity of which it is capable', he wrote, 'until there is a greater demand for our home agricultural products. When that comes, our country districts will carry a much larger population, who will afford the best market for the manufactured goods made in our towns.' Skelton went on to say that while Britain would never be able to grow enough wheat to feed itself, 'there are many kinds of food-stuffs of which we could produce all we need, if our country people were given a fair chance'. He concluded:

> It may be said that all this is obvious and not worth pointing out to you. But it is only the Unionist Party which has the common sense to appreciate these obvious things and the courage to lay them before the people. It is because I so profoundly believe that we must protect ourselves and our fellow-countrymen and women in their work both in factory and field that I have put this short statement before you.

The pamphlet ended with some patriotic quotes from Baldwin: 'I am tired of seeing men in England, Scotland and Wales thrown out of work by low-priced labour on the Continent' and 'I am for my own country first, last, and all the time'.[53]

By the summer of 1931, Baldwin's troubles appeared to have transferred to Ramsay MacDonald and his faltering Labour government. Skelton analysed the political balance in his last political essay, 'A Conservative Survey', which appeared in July's *Quarterly Review*. 'To the nation distraught with its individual troubles,' he wrote, 'when industry, finance, agriculture, labour do not know what the next day may bring forth, the politicians seem to be pirouetting and gyrating with the aimless detachment of gnats above a torrent.' The machine, he said, was 'falling to bits'.

And the Liberals, who for the past two years had been propping up the minority Labour government, did not escape Skelton's criticism: 'But self-preservation is the fundamental rule of political life, and it is in an effort to obtain the Alternative Vote that their energies are now concentrated. That is to be the prize which reconciles them to the huckstering and juggling of which they are at heart ashamed.'

But Skelton saved the meatier analysis for his own party:

> Much more important and far more dramatic has been
> the struggle which has gone on in the Conservative party.
> It has seldom spent a more uncomfortable year. It, too,
> has seen the attempt to form a new party, exacerbated
> by a bitter vendetta against its leader. The attacks on Mr
> Baldwin and their repulse have been the most significant
> and most crucial event in recent political history. It is an
> incident of which the importance extends far beyond the
> domestic concerns of party life. If Mr Baldwin had fallen,
> as at times it seemed he must, the effect upon public life
> and democratic politics would have been calamitous.
> The stage would have been set definitely for a political
> class-war. For those in the Conservative party who hated
> Mr Baldwin hate democracy. Their dislike spread to him,
> because he, Tory though he be, is making the only great
> political experiment which is being made in Britain to-day.
> He is treating democracy with consideration and respect.
> He neither fears nor hates it. Therefore, he does not flatter
> or abuse it, neither contempts nor cringes. That is why, of
> course, he has secured for himself a unique position. The
> people of this country know that Mr Baldwin trusts them.
> They therefore trust him as they trust no one else.
>   . . . Mr Baldwin has fairly and finally beaten them [his
> opponents]. As usual he does not seem to have reaped
> the full fruits of his victory, and more than he did for his
> handling of the General Strike. But his methods are not
> those of the sky-sign and the brass band; as a result, it has
> been all taken for granted.'

Time and again, Skelton said, Baldwin's opponents were

> confident that they had got him. His chances indeed seemed
> about as good as were Caesar's against the conspirators – for

throughout there has been the atmosphere not of a fight but of an assassination. And as in old Scottish history, a group of nobles, of essentially divergent interests, used to enter into a solemn 'band' with each other to destroy a common enemy, so against the Unionist leader the most diverse types of enemy were arrayed.

Skelton then moved on to the press barons.

Whatever their differences, the press attack upon Mr Baldwin, and through him the attempt to control the Unionist party, was in fact the greatest danger that democratic politics have run since the General Strike. The issue was fundamentally the same. 'By permission of the T.U.C.' was merely to be exchanged for 'By permission of Lord Rothermere'.

These are the men who have never ceased to complain that between 1924 and 1929 Mr Baldwin, 'in spite of his huge majority, did nothing.' What they mean is that he did nothing to relieve them of the spectre which is never absent from their minds. In short, the right wing of the party, the Diehards, and such industrialists as, engrossed at home in their business concerns, leave their politics to their Parliamentary jackals, found that all the worst they had ever felt or thought about Mr Baldwin was expressed by the press attack.

And that was not all. Behind the scenes some of the younger Parliamentarians were manoeuvring for position, against the time, which looked so near, when the leadership should be vacant. From the left flank, however, the attack never indeed fully developed. [They] had nothing in common with the Diehards; but might not the 'Forty Thieves' have their uses? For the most part they kept discreetly in the background. Even so, it was all very exciting. It offered endless opportunity for vague discussion about vague policies. It made one feel very clever and very important.

In essence, said Skelton, 'it was Fox and North all over again'.

Skelton then harked back to the aftermath of the October 1930 party crisis. 'There remained a final episode,' he wrote.

> Mr Churchill feels deeply but vaguely that there should be a different policy pursued towards India. When he made his views public he found himself a hero in the Conservative quarters where previously he had been least appreciated. His artistic temperament took fire. New prospects seemed to open before his vivid imagination. Had the great moment come? What did come was a debate on India in which Mr Baldwin spoke. It was enough. The Churchill rainbow faded. With that, peace has been declared in the Unionist party.

The result, said Skelton, was that the Conservative Party was 'preserved intact, that it is more in harmony with itself that at any time since the end of the General Strike'. Furthermore, Baldwin had

> shown himself to have the first indispensable quality of a party leader. For a leader who cannot hold his party together is wanting in the first qualification. Without it all others are mere sounding brass and tinkling cymbals.
>
> Thus the Conservative party remains united at a time when the others are in the melting-pot. Thanks to Mr Baldwin's victory, it is capable of being an adequate instrument of government, for the double reason that it is at one with itself again and that – what is essential if a party is to govern with success – its leader is now clearly master in his own house. Such a result has been more than worth the mutterings, grumblings, and uncertainties of the last two years.

Nevertheless, continued Skelton, the businessmen and Diehards 'instinctively feel the absence of any expression of Conservative principle in the Conservative programme'. What, therefore, was the ultimate objective of Conservative thought, he asked. 'Must it be to secure stability in the economic and social structure? And is not a stable condition in the national life exactly what the business classes are so anxious to secure?'

Slowly, said Skelton, the working people were beginning to realise the 'necessity of Protection', although they could not 'rid themselves of the belief that these classes will be the most immediate and assured gainers'. An industrial tariff would increase share prices, he said, although it would also 'check the fall in wages which is inevitable if the free import of manufactured goods continued . . . Moreover, Protection of itself does not solve the problem of the relations of Capital and Labour.'

Skelton then returned to his by now hackneyed personal political manifesto:

> Is there any way to do this except by profit-sharing, co-partnership, and share-owning by the wage-earners? Protection introduced without any attempt to secure equally full and equally rapid participation in advancing prosperity for employed as for employer will inevitably lead to a fresh period of social and industrial disturbance.
>
> But the politician has other functions besides passing acts of Parliament. A great party must form and lead opinion. The industrialist should know more about industry; the wage-earner about the problems of labour; these are their special provinces. The province of the politician is the body-politic, the community as a whole. And where the welfare of the body-politic is concerned, the politician, if he is properly to exercise his function, must speak with authority, because he speaks of what he knows. It is for the Unionist party frankly and clearly to tell the employing, investing classes that, if by a tariff they are to secure economic security, they must

make the necessary sacrifice, if sacrifice it be, in order that
fair dealing between all the partners in production should,
with the coming of prosperity, secure social stability.

Skelton then moved on to the economic threat posed by the
Soviet Union.[54]

> Every exporting success which Russia obtains will seem
> to the mind of labour another proof of the failure of the
> capitalist system. It is of no avail to say that slave labour
> is less efficient than free. However strong and remorseless
> be the compulsion applied to the Russian population, it is
> clear that the Bolshevik system is vitally different from the
> easy-going unorganised slipshod slave systems of the past.'

The Soviet leaders, said Skelton, had 'created a new economic
weapon; they are prepared, with this new weapon, to wage an
economic war, remorseless and bitter'.

The Conservative Party, he continued, 'must look at this
question from the ground, not the air. Its principles have always
recognised that contribution brings with it a status which mere
public assistance does not.' And that distinction 'must not be lost
sight of in a flurry of economy. Contribution must be given its full
weight, and however sharp a distinction it may be necessary to
draw between those who are in truth insured and those who are
not, drawn that distinction must be.'

'The reduction of income tax is imperative,' declared Skelton.
'None the less, it will be to the direct and immediate advantage
of all the investing classes.' And he still had not given up on
agricultural reform.

> Is land settlement, the development of small independent
> cultivators, to be or not to be one of its major objectives?
> At present, the attitude is that it is useless to put men on
> the land 'when agriculture does not pay'. But what when it

does pay? [Unless] land settlement is definitely accepted by
the Conservative party, at the moment when the remedial
measures for agriculture are to be put into operation, it is
most unlikely that it will be accepted later on.

But Skelton realised that his polemic would not make comfortable
reading for many of his colleagues. 'Of Conservatives who may read
these paragraphs many may find them inconvenient and untimely,'
he admitted. 'Let them survey the situation for themselves. They
hope, and with justification, that we are on the verge of exchanging
Free Trade for Protection—in their view an essential revolution, if
the economic life of Britain is to be saved.' They knew very well, he
continued, 'that the attack on capitalism, which is the attack on
the principle of the private ownership of property and of private
enterprise, is gathering force and, with the growing economic
menace of Bolshevik Russia, is now knocking loudly at our doors'.

It surely puts no undue strain on powers either of vision
or of reason to appreciate the fact that if property-owning
is to be made secure, or even to survive, the classes which
at present in their work have no property–interest must
be enlisted in its support, that on the land a new army of
property-owners must be created, that in a democracy,
property-owning must be widely spread, so that it becomes a
national not a class attribute, and that the cause of stability,
order, security is for our country inseparably bound up with
its development into a property-owning democracy.[55]

This was to be the last time that Skelton's potent phrase appeared
in print under his byline.

Meanwhile, Skelton's relationship with the Liberal socialite
Katharine Tennant remained volatile. The year had begun on a
slightly more upbeat note, with Skelton writing to Katharine that
'I hope you are happy. I am not at all happy! but I am beginning
to feel real, which is much better form than being happy.'[56] He

was, however, almost resigned to the fact that marriage was not an imminent possibility. 'Even if you don't want to marry me,' Skelton wrote on 13 February, 'we shall always be friends – & real friends – & play golf & go to concerts & see each other & love each other & you shall not have the dangers or the possible horrors of marrying me.'[57]

Skelton also began hatching plans for fact-finding trips, one of which anticipated George Orwell's surveys of working-class life:

> If we ever get married – which I am bound to say is beginning to look not only improbable but impossible – how would you like a . . . tour amongst the industrial towns . . . with visits to unemployed men & women . . . to see what they actually looked like etc. It might be rather interesting [because] most of the people who talk about the unemployed have never seen one in the flesh. Or a tour through rural England looking at small holding settlements in the early summer – that wd be – or rather would have been – quite good fun, wouldn't it? . . . I'm afraid I'd have given you too much to do, as my wife, however. If you had married me, I believe I might have had the energy to start in on that serious book on modern Toryism wh. is so much needed & which I believe I might, with your help, [have] been able to do. You, of course, would have been kept busy looking up facts & collecting all this information which I have always been too lazy to try to amass. Still, it wouldn't have been much fun for you.[58]

Alas, Skelton's tome on 'modern Toryism' remained unwritten. He continued to write while Katharine holidayed in Munich in April–May 1931. He described how much it would delight him to relocate to Germany for the summer, but 'I shall almost certainly have to spend it in long work . . . [at] the courts in Edinburgh'.[59] That he did, although Skelton kept Tennant informed of both his reading – which included a biography of Lord Salisbury – and current political gossip. 'The Govt is in "for keeps" . . . so it seems,' he wrote on 25 April. 'Coal will bring them a pack of troubles & complete the internal disintegration of the Labour movement.' He speculated that there would be an 'August election, when Conservatives will be holiday-making. It might very well save them some seats: but the British Electorate is a wonderful thing. It means always doing the right thing.'[60] In May, Skelton started reading *Places in the Sun* by Anthony Eden. 'I must say I found it very heavy going,'[61] he noted, adding a few days later: 'Eden and I had a long talk about his book . . . His style is not partial – only poor; but it is always readable enough.'

It still seemed to be Skelton's intention to quit politics at the next election. He wrote to Katharine in May predicting that 'this autumn there will be an Election after which I shall be able to retire to some . . . solitude'.[62] Meanwhile, he told K that he was writing 1,000 words 'for a new 2/6 publication',[63] and by July 1931 (the relationship always seemed to recover in the summer) the prospects of marriage, at least from Skelton's point of view, were looking rosier. 'However,' wrote Skelton on 11 July, 'you seem to be prepared for the gamble of marrying me & . . . if only you find when you live with me that you do really like my company & that I make life pleasant . . . for you, it may be a gamble worth making.' But, he added, 'it's a queer business life; when I felt [like] . . . a drowning man & shouted to you for help, you stood on the bank, telling me how much you liked me . . . now that I have [said] I am a drowned man, you leap into the water & try to drag the corpse to land . . . At least, however, . . . if anyone can resuscitate me, it is you.'[64]

More anxiety about his career also cropped up in letters at around this time. On 21 July he wrote:

> I increasingly feel that my political bolt is shot & that I must reconcile myself to that slightly irritating fact. I have so long felt that my . . . claim to any sort of consideration at all depends on such political efforts as I have made, that it is almost impossible to realise that anyone, least of all

you, can like me as a human being. You were looking quite delicious at lunch. Bless you. How hellish it is that you are going away for 7 weeks.[65]

But still there was no decision. 'It is a bad business that you would marry anyone of 51. I felt so very much younger & more vibrant three years [ago] but I hardly recognise myself as the same person . . . I was in 1928,' he wrote in July. 'I think it's all very difficult, far far more difficult than it was three years ago.'[66] But on 25 July he joked: 'I, of course, am quite cheerful: I am so glad to be done with Parliament & London.'[67]

Indeed, in a biography of her husband, John Buchan, Lady Tweedsmuir recalled that Skelton could enliven a meal with his cheerful sense of humour, and that he was particularly fond of Tiptree jam.

> I have seen a jar of the famous 'Little Scarlet Strawberry' in front of him on the table empty itself in the twinkling of an eye . . . I did not see him again for some years [after the early 1920s]. When we did meet he had become stouter and had jettisoned all his earlier gravity.'[68]

Skelton's weight appears to have bothered him. Holidaying at Colonsay House in late July, he wrote: 'I wish to Heaven you were here. It would be too lovely. But alas I get fatter and fatter! Which shocks me.'[69] But two weeks later he had moved on to Dundonnell Lodge for some walking and fishing ('I don't know which I like best'[70]) and reported that 'even my weight is down a few pounds & I feel distinctly slimmer. But better still, I feel magnificently idle-minded.'[71]

Skelton continued to feed Katharine political tit-bits. 'I shouldn't be alarmed about Germany,' he wrote on 28 July from Edinburgh. 'I am satisfied that nothing alarming or disastrous is going to happen there – but then, of course, I am permanently pro-French. The Huns have merely over-reacted.'[72] He also continued to dwell on his unsuitability as a husband. On 14 August he wrote:

> When I asked you to marry me I saw a fair [prospect] of an active political life ahead of me. I felt that that was a life you wd like . . . Since the time when I gave up the idea I was doing anything serious in politics, I have always . . . told you again and again that I have no life & activities to offer you . . . and I have never really varied in that opinion. [But] I still wish you wd . . . marry me. If I . . . go on in politics . . . then I think you wd be slightly less mad . . . [although] it looks increasingly unlikely that I shall be in the next Parliament.

And besides, Skelton explained,

> I should not [be] marrying an active wife 23 years younger than I – far from it. But she would hate, in a very short time, being married to a lazy [man] . . . 23 years older than she! . . . I have told you again & again that . . . it became obvious you didn't want to [marry me], when I had something of a life to share with you, [so] it was folly to go on thinking of it, when I had no life worth considering to offer you.'

The age difference was, for 1931, unusual. Skelton had turned fifty-one in July, and Katharine was a mere twenty-eight, younger than he had been when he first stood for Parliament in 1910.

> What in the world wd you make of life, and what opportunities would it offer – if you were tied up to a derelict man of 51 or six years hence, when you will be 34, to a still more derelict man of 57 – it's got nothing to do with selfishness or unselfishness . . . 'it has nothing to do with love'.

Also, he joked, 'I am an exceptionally bad golfer – what fun is that for you & so on & so on'.

Again, Skelton began suggesting alternative suitors. On 13 August he wrote:

My dear, it's a hard business perhaps: but it seems to me that you should face the facts. A man like W[alter]. Elliot is the proper kind of husband for you, having character, career, energy, immense zest for life . . . Besides, marrying such a man say, for instance Walter, wd not . . . be marrying beneath you. In his [case] ability is everything. When he is leader or one of the leaders of the Conservative Party.[73]

Three days later he wrote:

I don't quite know why you dislike so much the idea of marrying someone much older than yourself, but it is clear that that remains the basic feeling . . . From every rational point of view you are well out of matrimony with me. The people who think you are wrong know nothing about me. I am not first-rate or anything like it. I am & always have been a very mediocre second-rate.

And, he added, 'I should never have asked you to marry me: for then you wd have been spared a great deal of heart burning'.[74]

Skelton penned another, similarly lengthy, letter to Katharine the following day:

It is as clear as day that, as I said, your basic feeling is that you don't want to marry anyone so much older than yourself . . . So I feel now as I have never felt quite definitely before, the finality of your decision. For myself I shall try to put this whole subject . . . out of my mind & I recommend you . . . to do the same. It's no use hanging suspended between two wants – the want to marry me & the want not to! You have made your [decision] for the second time exactly as you did the first. I am sure it wd be exactly the same if you had to face up to the question for a third time – although so far as I am concerned, I promise you you will not have to do . . . However, when the real Mr

K comes along, I suspect that you will know your mind at once & without difficulty.

Katharine then sent Skelton a 'delicious' telegram, to which he replied: 'I am having a hell of a time indeed: I am not sleeping much; but . . . I am . . . trying, for once in my life, to know what is the right course of action . . . So much of life is one's own fault.' But, as he added in another letter written the same evening, he had at least given her 'an insight into loving & being loved. That, you know, is usually rather a privilege for an old man like me! I love you so much that I don't want you to loathe or despise me . . . I really would find it hard to bear if you started hating me.'[75]

It seems that Katharine did not respond. Two days later he complained:

> I can't understand this absence of letters. I [expect] you have had plenty by this time. It is rather curious your saying that when you write to me you feel as if did not exist & were only a [figment] of your . . . imagination. I too feel as if I didn't exist very much. I suppose it is this sense of supreme uselessness & aimlessness which . . . makes me feel as if I didn't exist: for I have always existed through what I wanted to be, not [through] what I was. Now I don't want to be anything & so exist any longer. Even you can't save me. The best thing you can do is to escape while this is not true.[76]

A few days earlier, Skelton had given Katharine his assessment of the political situation.

> I can't tell you anything about politics, because I've seen or heard from nobody. But it is . . . clear that Ramsay is going to have a shot at being a 'statesman' . . . If he pulls it off it may alter the face of politics for some time – indeed it will in any case – for if he fails, there will be a terrific crash in his Labour party.[77]

It had not been a good year for the Labour government. In early 1931 the enigmatic MP Oswald Mosley had left the Labour Party and formed a 'New Party' constituted along fascist lines,[78] while in March the government had appointed a committee chaired by Sir George May which proposed spending cuts totalling £96 million. The UK was not the only European country to suffer from the depression; across the Continent, particularly in central Europe, banks collapsed, and as the crisis worsened, Baldwin concentrated on attacking the tottering Labour government.

The burden of unemployment payments had unbalanced the budget, and Conservatives were determined that this should be dealt with through spending reductions rather than increases in taxation. The need for 'economy' and preserving the 'free hand' on tariffs, therefore, were Baldwin's priorities during the financial crisis that overwhelmed the Labour government in August 1931.

'I feel, in my bones, that it will end in a Labour–Liberal Coalition', Skelton told Katharine on 23 August, '& yet it is difficult to see how that wd last more than a few weeks. We shall know, I suppose, by Tuesday & Wednesday at latest what is going to happen.' It was, he said, a 'chance for Ramsay MacDonald. I have always thought that he had statesmanlike instincts. If he can educate his party now, democracy may even yet be made safe for Britain.'[79]

The following day Baldwin was summoned to Buckingham Palace and reluctantly compelled to join an emergency all-party Cabinet. He had expected to become the Prime Minister with some Liberal support, but instead the King implored him to serve under Ramsay MacDonald, who had consented to remain as premier until the crisis was resolved. In reality, Baldwin had little choice, and the arrangement did at least save a Conservative-led government from implementing unpopular spending cuts. Publicly, Baldwin stressed that the 'National Government' was a temporary arrangement, and that once the UK's currency had been stabilised there would be an election in which the Conservatives would seek a mandate for the promised 'free hand'. Little did Baldwin know that this temporary arrangement would, in fact, last (in various guises) until the end of the Second World War. Having made his name engineering the downfall of one coalition administration, Baldwin spent the rest of his political career as the central figure in another. 'If God succeeds in making Ramsay do Baldwin's economy for him,' quipped Walter Elliot, 'I really shall believe in a personal Deity – with one motto "This is my beloved son Stanley".'[80]

'The Govt has resigned,' Skelton declared to Katharine. 'Ramsay Mac is to form a National Govt with S.B. . . . No doubt it will incur an election this late autumn, after the Tariff issue. It will mean very little future for me, I'm afraid.' Had there been 'a Conservative Govt with Liberal support,' he added, 'that wd have [suited] me better; but this Parliament can't live long & then we'll see where we are.'[81]

Skelton, meanwhile, continued to urge Katharine to consider Elliot as a possible husband. 'If you marry anyone else,' he wrote on 27 August, 'it would be quite essential that we shall not meet again; or at least for many years.'[82] Physically craggy, intelligent and articulate, Elliot had been for much of the 1920s the sole under-secretary at the Scottish Office. Like Skelton, he had been a member of the YMCA and a regular visitor to Katharine's Lord North Street home, although he had first encountered her during the 1924 election. Skelton listed Elliot's selling points in another letter on 28 August:

> He's 8 years younger than I am & what a difference that is. I am a mere looker-on at life, he is a most active participant. I belong to the past. He belongs, most emphatically, to the future. You'd be safe with him: whereas I am so uncertain in character, in moods, in temper . . . You are having in Walter a second chance of an interesting life & a husband . . . You don't have second chances at 51 and I don't expect it.

'You failed me at this critical moment,' Skelton concluded. 'Don't fail Walter. It wasn't your fault: it was your inexperience and your good luck. Walter is a man who deserves a wife like you. I deserve nothing.'[83]

Meanwhile, Baldwin set about appointing four Conservatives to the ten-man crisis Cabinet. (In a government of forty-six, Conservatives occupied twenty-one ministerial posts.) 'Walter is to be Financial Secretary to the Treasury – one of the most important posts,' Skelton told Katharine on 29 August, 'but I'd rather have seen him Minister of Labour . . . Walter is, I'm afraid, one of the [people] . . . who will always be called on to bear his heart and burden of the day.'[84]

Skelton wrote again a few days later with some surprising news. 'Of course we're delighted at Archie [Sinclair] being Secretary for Scotland,' he wrote, adding excitedly that 'yesterday afternoon Baldwin asked me to be Under Secretary for Scotland, which I accepted! So I am to be in the [government] too.'[85]

After a disappointing year, both personally and politically, Noel Skelton was a minister for the first time in his decade-long political career. Two tasks awaited him: getting to grips with the administration of Scottish affairs during a difficult economic period and, more importantly, finding himself a new constituency to ensure that he remained in Parliament. For someone who had written just weeks before that his 'political bolt [was] shot', it was a remarkable reversal of fortunes. Yet still Skelton suffered from self-doubt. 'Thank you very much for your kind congratulations,' he replied to Harold Macmillan, who had offered his regards in a short letter. 'It will be a short life and not a very merry one.'[86]

'A SHORT LIFE AND NOT A VERY MERRY ONE' (1931–5)

The Scottish Office in 1931 was just forty-six years old and the sole territorial department in Whitehall.[1] The secretary of state was the dashing Samuelite Liberal politician and future Liberal leader Sir Archibald Sinclair,[2] and his sole under-secretary was Skelton, although the department also had the support of two law officers, the Lord Advocate and the solicitor-general for Scotland. Skelton was in charge of an eclectic mix of duties, mainly health, education, agriculture and, especially pertinent for someone who had introduced the phrase 'property-owning democracy' to the political lexicon, housing.

It was probably the consistency of Skelton's support for Stanley Baldwin that was key to his belated promotion, albeit under the National Government and covert Baldwin leadership; but in truth Skelton must hardly have found a broad coalition of centrist ministers difficult to support. Other YMCAers also joined the government: Robert Hudson became parliamentary secretary to the Ministry of Labour; Oliver Stanley an under-secretary at the Home Office; Walter Elliot was already Financial Secretary to the Treasury and, most importantly, Anthony Eden became an under-secretary at the Foreign Office.[3] But the YMCA, in spirit, was essentially a busted flush, although its successors revolved around Harold Macmillan and, to a lesser extent, Bob Boothby.

'What did intrigue me was the appearance of a new type of young Conservative,' observed Colin Coote in his memoirs. 'Noël Skelton – to my mind the most brilliant of all. He actually got the job of Scottish Under-Secretary, and used it to study the principles with which Britain could be dragged out of the Slough of Despond.'[4]

Unfortunately, however, Skelton's promotion to junior office demonstrated the difficulty of translating political ideals into legislative or administrative action. His four years at the Scottish Office did not see a bold new dawn of home ownership, industrial co-partnership or agricultural smallholdings; instead Skelton helped two Scottish secretaries manage decline during an economic depression, an unenviable situation for any politician, and particularly one of Skelton's imagination and administrative ability. Even a cross-party National Government found it could do no more about unemployment than its predecessors.

Skelton also began to suffer, almost immediately, from the ill health that was to dog him throughout the twilight of his career. He managed to appoint Major David John Colville (a future Scottish secretary and governor of Bombay) as his parliamentary private secretary, but came down with a temperature soon after and checked in to the Empire Nursing Home in Vincent Square, Westminster, in order to recover. His indisposition meant he missed a speaking engagement at the annual dinner of the Incorporation of Weavers in Glasgow, but he had left the nursing home by the following week. 'It was learned later that Mr Skelton's condition is not regarded as serious,' reported *The Times*, 'and that he hopes to resume his Parliamentary duties by about Tuesday.'[5]

No sooner had Skelton returned to his desk at Dover House than the government was forced to abandon the Gold Standard on 21 September. The National Government's very existence became a key factor in restoring financial stability and maintaining foreign confidence, so the need to secure a mandate became imperative. Baldwin and the Conservatives were willing to support a national appeal under Ramsay MacDonald, provided that this did not restrict them from seeking the outstanding commitment to a 'free hand' on tariffs. After a struggle with the free-traders in the Cabinet, Baldwin secured the best position for the Conservatives under the circumstances: each party would campaign under its own manifesto, and the government as a whole would simply ask for 'a doctor's mandate' to implement whatever remedies it felt necessary. But, as the Conservatives provided most of the new government's parliamentary support, this meant, in effect, the introduction of tariffs.

Skelton, of course, was without a candidacy having abandoned Perth two years previously, but in the run-up to the general election of 1931 his good luck continued to hold. In early October the standing Unionist joint committee of the Combined Scottish Universities constituency[6] gathered, appropriately enough, in Perth to adopt John Buchan as a National Unionist. And, 'in view of Sir George Berry desiring not to seek reelection, the Committee adopted as second Unionist candidate, Mr A. Noel Skelton, the Parliamentary Under Secretary for Scotland'. During his career, added the report, 'Mr Skelton has made a special study of Scottish questions, and has distinguished himself by his vigilant advocacy of Scottish interests.'[7]

There had been speculation in the *Glasgow Herald* that Skelton 'may be persuaded to stand for one of the Glasgow or Lanarkshire Divisions',[8] but Berry's decision to retire presented not only a safer platform, but also one free from the burdens of constituency business. Together with the Liberal candidate, D. M. Cowan, Skelton and Buchan did not even have to face an electoral contest.

The three nominations were lodged in the Upper Library of Edinburgh University on 13 October, with Sir Thomas Holland, principal and vice-chancellor of the university, acting as returning officer. 'After the prescribed time for lodging nominations had expired', reported *The Scotsman*, 'Sir Thomas Holland said that, as not more than three nominations had been received for the three seats, he had therefore, in accordance with the provisions of the Representation of the People Act, to declare Mr Buchan, Mr Cowan, and Mr Skelton elected members of Parliament'. Skelton, 'in seconding the vote of thanks, said he could not imagine any position that a Scotsman who cared for the life of Scotland would more wish to fill honourably and well than that of member of Parliament for the Scottish Universities'. Holland spoke of his duty as 'a very pleasant one' and promised that the deposits of £150 would be returned to them as soon as they took up their duties in Parliament. He joked: 'In case there is any possible change of Government for good or bad, I have taken care that the actual notes deposited will be those notes returned. So what you have given you will get in currency that you yourselves approve of.'[9]

The trio, therefore, became the first three members elected to the 1931 Parliament, and before polling day had actually taken place. Skelton, however, continued to campaign. Speaking in Bo'ness Town Hall on behalf of Sir Andrew Baillie, Skelton endured heavy heckling as he defended the National Government's short record. He said that 'for every 1s. a man had in his pocket, at least the value of 6d. was owed to the National Government. It was due to the courage of Mr Ramsay MacDonald, Mr Snowden, and Mr Thomas.'[10] This was greeted by loud cries of dissent, to which Skelton retorted: 'A month or two ago you would have cheered the mention of those names, and why is it, when they have performed an act of courage which has saved this country, you do not cheer them now?' What about the cuts in unemployment benefits, another heckler cried. 'I am not afraid to touch on the question of cuts,' replied Skelton. 'The basis of democracy is free speech, and the man who fears free speech is no democrat.' He added that 'there was no sacrifice that was being made to-day which was more valuable to the nation than the cut in that benefit, because it did away with the necessity of borrowing £1,000,000 a week to pay the benefit'. Our duty, proclaimed Skelton, 'was to see that the policy of this nation was so framed that our people would be restored to work'.[11] Skelton's career had begun with the dramatic rejection of one coalition government; it drew to a close with the spirited defence of another.

MacDonald, however, could not count on mirroring Skelton's

hassle-free return to the green benches. It was reported in the *Glasgow Evening Times* on 20 October that if MacDonald was not returned for his Seaham constituency, Skelton would stand down in his favour. 'Mr Skelton is anxious to resign from politics for business reasons,' speculated the report. 'He recently withdrew from Perth, which he represented in the last Parliament, and surprisingly accepted nomination for the Scottish Universities.'[12]

Such a noble act of self-sacrifice, however, proved unnecessary when MacDonald held on in Seaham. Labour, meanwhile, was obliterated from the political map, losing 225 of its MPs. The Conservatives, or rather the National Conservatives, took 473 of the government's total of 554 seats when polls closed on 27 October 1931.[13] The overwhelming majority in Parliament was now in favour of tariffs, and the Conservatives took eleven out of twenty Cabinet seats. Baldwin effectively became the dominant figure in the government, occupying the prestigious non-departmental post of Lord President of the Council (and also Lord Privy Seal from 29 September 1932). He moved into 11 Downing Street, chaired the Cabinet in MacDonald's absences and deputised for him in the Commons as leader of the House.

At the Scottish Office, Skelton proved to be a stimulating, if unremarkable, junior minister. He worked well with Sinclair, whom Skelton respected a great deal, although circumstance meant that the Scottish secretary did not exactly have a productive year in office. Soon after his appointment, Sinclair asked Skelton to make a point of examining the Scottish education estimates. His under-secretary replied at once, agreeing that he wanted to take 'a careful look at Education administration – not because I have any reason to think it faulty, but because I don't believe that any of your immediate predecessors, or of mine, have ever devoted much attention to it, and certainly in my time in the House no Scottish member ever seems to have taken much interest'.[14]

Skelton also found time to devote attention to another bright young MP, the recently elected member for Lanark, Alec Dunglass.

The eldest son of the Earl of Home, Dunglass had read Skelton's
Constructive Conservatism at Oxford and had contacted both its
author and the then Scottish secretary, Sir John Gilmour, in the
run up to the 1929 general election saying he would like to be a
candidate. Skelton encouraged him to fight Coatbridge, a mining
town 10 miles east of Glasgow.

An uncertain public speaker, Dunglass endured a rough ride from
hecklers and lost decisively, but was not deterred. Almost at once
the more promising (although marginally Labour) constituency of
Lanark lost its Conservative candidate, and Dunglass was adopted.
He was swept into the House of Commons in the landslide of 1931
on a National Unionist ticket and was immediately asked by Skelton
to replace Colville (who had become parliamentary secretary at the
Overseas Trade Department)[15] as his unpaid parliamentary private
secretary. Coote later observed that together with giving Eden the
'property-owning democracy' slogan, another shrewd move was
making Dunglass his PPS. 'So Noël did a good turn to two future
Prime Ministers.'[16]

Dunglass thought Skelton was 'a very able, thoughtful
Conservative' whose work he continued to study carefully. 'It was a
good start to one's political philosophy,' he later told a biographer,
although he complained that Skelton had 'a bee in his bonnet
about referenda. He was always keen on the idea! . . . Skelton never
convinced me.'[17] Dunglass spent the next four years working with
Skelton at the Scottish Office and from 1931 to 1933 worked closely
with William Murrie and Charles Cunningham,[18] successive private
secretaries to Skelton. Skelton believed in the practice of political
master and civil servant meeting informally to seek acceptable
solutions to difficult problems, and when Skelton was ill, Dunglass
reported directly to Sir Godfrey Collins (Sinclair's successor as
secretary of state from 1932). Just like Harold Macmillan and
Anthony Eden in the 1920s, another future Prime Minister was
drawn into Skelton's circle and left with an indelible political
impression.

Dunglass was also a frequent guest at Katharine Tennant's

gatherings at her home in Westminster, although he would probably have been unaware that Skelton's affair with his lively hostess was finally drawing to a close. 'My dear,' Skelton wrote to K on 14 January 1932, 'if I thought I had anything real to give you . . . a real determination to lead life as it should be led; even at this eleventh hour – I should . . . but I am afraid of the risks you would incur if you married me – whereas if you married, say, Walter, within its own limits, it would be a safe & certain living.'[19]

On 20 January Skelton wrote again, this time at greater length.

> You may take it as fundamental but to marry you wd be for me to save myself or to save the remains of myself. It would give meaning, reality to life . . . But that is, I know, a view of quite terrific selfishness. For what is the situation? Here are you, young, of immense physical and spiritual energy, capable – I, 51, tired, bored, incompetent . . . moody . . . critical . . . It's about all I can do to keep going as a lonely wanderer on the face of the waters. What use would I be to you if we sailed in company?
>
> You say you love me . . . but if love failed & if disillusionment came, the absence of any material advantage . . . would leave you in a situation which would have no merits at all. You talked today of giving up your career if you married – but I am not worth giving up your career for . . . Everything that has happened seems to make it more difficult for me to marry you, just as it seems to have made it easier for you to marry me . . . Compared with the situation now, that of 1928 seems so simple, clear & straightforward. Perhaps alas we were both simpler people then. You say that I shirk from doing the pleasant easy thing. My dear, it would be a deep profound joy to have again the days of last summer; but I fear I have no right to them . . . It is clear, I think, that no tragedy is involved for you if you don't marry me. You have taken that in your stride – as you take everything else. The right course is for me to stand aside. Then there can be no

disillusionment or a sense of wasted life for you – or . . . remorse for me.

. . . I fear, in short, it is too late. I have learnt a sort of 'technique' – to use your favourite word – by which I can make my own life almost tolerable. This, at any rate, is clear that you [are] a great & wonderful woman & I am . . . a miserable specimen of a man.[20]

Skelton wrote only twice more to Katharine, at least at any length. On 8 April he wrote:

I know that I am very much to blame in many ways you do not understand. But it cannot be helped. You must feel, I am sure, that I have failed you – that is true – but I know that I will fail you more if I married you now . . . You felt then [in 1928] the difficulty of marrying anyone 23 years older than yourself [and I] of marrying anyone 23 years younger than myself. And that is all there is to it . . . It is exceedingly hard. But life is hard & it is impossible to get away from it. The real difficulty is to accept the fact in one's own case.'[21]

And on 26 June, Skelton wrote that 'it is for you to consider whether the "dreams" you write of are dreams . . . but you and I are friends'.[22]

Relations between senior Coalition ministers were somewhat more harmonious. The unity of the government had been preserved by the pre-election agreement that ministers could, so to speak, 'agree to disagree' on the tariff issue. Baldwin also got on well with MacDonald and saw the value in retaining him as Prime Minister. In fact, the Conservative leader did much to reassure MacDonald that he was not seen simply as a Tory puppet. He also had the trust of the other non-Conservative ministers, and his non-partisan image was strengthened by his willingness to allow a generous (i.e. disproportionate) share of Cabinet posts while pursuing policies with clear bipartisan aspects, for example on agriculture, housing, education and, later, over India. Baldwin, therefore, remained the safety valve which prevented 'Diehard' Conservatives calling the shots.

One curious side effect of this new political consensus was a marked shift in industrial relations. From 1931 onwards the trade unions worked closely with the National Government, ushering in an unprecedented period of industrial calm. This obviously devalued Skelton's argument that industrial co-partnership remained essential to achieve 'peace in industry', although he showed no let-up in his campaign. In March 1932 he was reunited with Harold Macmillan (who was not in the government) when he spoke at an Industrial Co-partnership Association luncheon at the Holborn Restaurant in London, over which Macmillan presided.

Skelton said he remained 'a profound believer' in the application of co-partnership principles wherever possible, and that the 'correct method of arriving at the remuneration of capital and labour respectively was that, after dividends and wages had been deducted, the remainder should be treated as the real, profits of the undertaking'. He 'deplored' the popular impression that only gas companies were suitable for co-partnership, and pointed to a Board of Trade return on the subject, which showed that co-partnership arrangements existed in such diverse industries as agriculture, glass and chemicals, metal, engineering, textiles, food and drink manufacture, printing and paper-making. Skelton said he regretted that a proper inquiry had never been made into the view of workers already in co-partnership schemes. Such an inquiry, he believed, would help develop public opinion.

Skelton then regurgitated portions of *Constructive Conservatism*, saying that 'work people had now full educational opportunities and a full political status', and that 'if their economic powers and activities were ever to be developed to the full, they must have an economic status commensurate with their educational and political status, otherwise social and industrial life would be lopsided'. The current government's new fiscal regime had contributed to this, he continued, but added that 'the battle of industrial revival was not only a politicians' battle or a generals' battle; it was a soldiers' battle', and he 'did not think the principles of co-partnership could be made effective by acts of Parliament. It was only people of good intent and wise mind in industry itself who could do it, but those whose interests were public and political could assist.'

Trade unions, added Skelton, were not 'altogether unfavourable' to these ideas, and he thought it 'was also pretty clear that the rank and file of the working people were determined to be the masters and not the servants of Trade Unionism, and that, if they were satisfied that co-partnership was sound, they would not allow its development to be interfered with by suspicions and hostilities of that sort'.[23] Skelton's defence was not altogether convincing, especially when talking of the scheme's 'progress'. He estimated that 205,000 'workpeople' had, by 1932, direct experience of co-partnership and should be interviewed for an inquiry. But in reality, Skelton's dream of industrial co-partnership was, ten years after the publication of *Constructive Conservatism*, little closer to becoming a reality.

A property-owning democracy also failed to progress. On housing, Skelton stressed its financial burden on the state, saying that in his opinion 'people were determined to go on with housing, determined to clear away slums, and determined that the State money was to be used properly'. He added that if any occupant of an Addison house[24] was financially able to buy a house it was his 'duty to do so, and relieve the State of £40 per year for the next sixty years'.

Turning to Scotland, Skelton said the question before the country

> was whether her new vitality was to disappear in a narrow, shallow, sterile nationalism in which she cut herself off from England and the British Empire, and paddled her own canoe, or was Scotland going to take part in the great work which she commenced in 1603 to help England in the domination of the world in everything that was wise and good. He himself had no doubt regarding the answer which the people of Scotland would give.[25]

To Skelton's frustration, whereas in England private enterprise involvement in house building continued apace, in Scotland it did not. 'I believe that there is no matter more important,' he told the House in June, 'in connection with housing in Scotland, than to restore private enterprise to its function. How to do it I do not know. No one has yet agreed as to the causes of its decline.'[26]

Baldwin, meanwhile, led the British delegation to the Imperial Conference at Ottawa in July and August, and successfully negotiated preferential tariff arrangements with the dominions. This proved too much for Labour's Philip Snowden and the Samuelite Liberal ministers (one of whom was Sir Archibald Sinclair) to swallow, and they left the government in September 1932, although sufficient Labour and Liberal ministers remained for the government's national status to be credible. Skelton fully supported the government's tariff policy, and thought 'the foolish Liberals who left the work they were doing in order to scramble round the country preaching about Free Trade were barking up the wrong tree'.[27]

A reshuffle followed, in which the Liberal publisher and Greenock MP, Sir Godfrey Collins, replaced Sinclair at the Scottish Office, much to his and, it seems, everyone else's, surprise. Collins, although well intentioned, was not exactly a political heavyweight,[28] and Skelton's remaining three years in office saw him shouldering a heavier proportion of the Scottish administrative burden.[29] The shake-up also meant that, for the first time, Walter Elliot joined the Cabinet as Minister of Agriculture and Fisheries. By this time, the ebullient Elliot had replaced Skelton as the object of Katharine Tennant's affections.

Collins's arrival at Dover House coincided with a periodic upsurge in Scottish national sentiment. The typical Unionist reaction to this had always been to tinker with the machinery of government, and it remained the case in 1932. Skelton was instinctively cynical, particularly when it came to suggestions that Scotland should seek its own version of Irish home rule. Addressing the issue at a meeting in Adam Smith Hall, Kirkcaldy, on 4 November, Skelton said he did not believe that a separate Scottish parliament would do anything to help Scotland's larger industries, depending as they did upon export trade. On the contrary, he said, a parliament in Edinburgh 'would only accentuate the difference between the two countries and would at least bring about a risk of friction between them'. Skelton added that the Union had been a success for both countries. *The Scotsman* reported him thus:

> An attempt had been made to arouse some public interest in the question, but in the municipal elections it had been shown by results that this was merely superficial. He considered that those who wanted a separate Parliament for Scotland were quitters. So long as all was going well, and there was prosperity for both countries, they had not bothered very much about Home Rule, but now that they were faced with difficult times they said, 'Let us try cutting the painter between us and England.' That, he contended, was quitting.

Skelton said that the world

> depended wholly upon the strength and union of the British Empire, which in turn depended upon the strength and union of the United Kingdom. To separate Scotland and England would be to diminish that strength and union, and, in the interests of the two countries, the United Kingdom, and indeed the whole world, they should fight through the difficult times until they reached more prosperous times.[30]

Scottish Office thinking, however, was moving towards an administrative response. Previous Scottish secretaries, most notably Skelton's old sparring partner Sir John Gilmour, had worked hard to consolidate all Scotland's governing boards and departments onto one central site in Edinburgh, freeing up

Dover House in London to act 'as a clearing-house or embassy for parliamentary and liaison work and for the service of the Secretary of State when he is in London'. Skelton also instructed an official to 'further explore the question of "administrative devolution"'. 'The result of some thought on the subject is shown in the enclosed Memo,' scribbled the functionary on a Scottish Office file, 'the substance of which I have already briefly outlined to Mr Skelton.'

This memo, entitled 'Administrative Devolution', built upon a previous memo written by Walter Elliot, and explained the practical arguments against political devolution. It suggested:

> The clean method of overcoming all these difficulties is to make one fold as there is one shepherd, by a general transfer of the powers and duties of departments to the Secretary of State, so that all the departments concerned would be in effect, 'The Scottish Office' or 'The Department of the Secretary of State for Scotland'.

This was, in itself, attractive, as Scottish government was at that time far from cohesive. The Scottish Board of Health was semi-autonomous but answerable to the Scottish secretary, its president, and Skelton, its vice-president. Skelton also had to deal with the Scottish Education Department directly, as it had no 'officer of high status residing in London'. 'The Scottish Board of Health method either throws far too much influence and responsibility on the Private Secretaries', commented the memo, 'or alternatively unnecessarily burdens Ministers. Also the higher officials in the Scottish Office are often imperfectly aware of what is going on.' As for the Board of Agriculture for Scotland, 'it is only by a miracle of grace that it works at all . . . In fact the whole thing was a muddle and often a source of friction or misunderstanding between the Board and the Scottish Office.'

The memo also floated the possibility of creating a new 'Scottish Department of Home Affairs'. It also suggested reviving 'only more whole-heartedly – the experiment of having a branch of the Scottish Office in Edinburgh'. There were, however,

> two serious objections at least to this scheme. In the first place, while getting round the difficulty of a General Headquarters in London cumbered with administrative detail, it does not fit in to the theory of planets revolving round a central sun, since one of the planets would be a bit of the sun hanging loose! How would it and the other planets work together, and would not their prestige suffer?[31]

Collins outlined his response to Parliament during a debate on the address on 24 November, just after a speech from Sir Robert Horne, who had written the introduction to Skelton's 1924 pamphlet. Horne said far too much of the departmental work of Scotland was done in Whitehall, and that there 'should be concentrated in Edinburgh – I say boldly "in Edinburgh" – all the main work of the Departments which look after the business of Scotland'.[32] Collins agreed, recalling:

> During my first official visit there [Edinburgh] it was apparent to me, as it had been to my predecessors, that the existing arrangement, whereby ten different departments are scattered in twenty-two different buildings throughout the city, is neither conducive to economy or efficiency . . . A centralised building in Edinburgh to which all sections of public life could come for the transaction of business with responsible heads would have real and obvious advantages, and I feel that sooner or later, such a building must be provided.[33]

Skelton spoke later in the same debate, and again drew upon childhood memories in explaining his position.

> I am not convinced that there is any force in the suggestion that because you develop the administration north of the

Tweed you must develop a separate parliament. I have had administrative connection with the affairs of Scotland only for a year, but I have an hereditary connection with Scottish administration and have been brought up in the atmosphere of administration, and to some extent that interest is in my blood.

. . . In my ten years' experience of the House of Commons I have formed the view that the duties and positions of a Scottish member of Parliament in this united Parliament are not precisely the same as those of an English member. We are a minority. We are out of Scotland, and we have a special duty while we are here to pay attention to the needs of Scotland . . . Further, I have always thought and have said it on public platforms and elsewhere that the test for Scotsmen as to whether the Union ought to be continued or not, is whether it has been successful from a Scottish point of view or not. If, as Scotsmen, we were satisfied that the Union had been a failure, then as Scotsmen it would be necessary for us to review the situation and see what ought to take its place.

This was essentially a pragmatic Unionist position. Skelton added:

Unless you have better arguments than to say, in a time like this, that you are going to devote your national thought to constitutional rather than to economic problems, 'or that there are certain things you can do without grievous damage, then I think the question is blown sky high.

. . . It is my firm conviction that if you were to set Scotland on the path of separation, however tentative and hesitating were the steps taken to begin with, you would be rousing ancient fires, you would be putting in motion centrifugal forces which, once set in motion, you could not control . . . take it long or take it short, if you give up the Union between England and Scotland, you are taking a course of action which leads you to complete separation.

Skelton had always believed in the sanctity of the Union, and more particularly, the sanctity of its place within the British Empire.

> The House has to recollect that Scotland has played a considerable part in the development of this great imperial structure, and not only that, but I think no member, not a Scotsman, will disagree or think I am blowing the national trumpet when I say that the Scottish people do add a definite flavour and strength to the imperial centre, namely, the United Kingdom.

Skelton concluded with an analysis of Scottish devolution that stands up even eighty years later:

> Even a Parliament of local affairs only would necessarily have the result that there could be no secretary of state in the British Cabinet. He would have no function. All the local affairs would be done by the Scottish parliament and the Scottish government in Scotland. All other affairs would have in the British Cabinet a minister of their own, and if there were to be a Scottish secretary of state in the British Cabinet and a Scottish government and parliament in Edinburgh, the secretary of state could take no step without treading upon the toes of another minister because he would have no department and no sphere of action of his own. The result would be that in the general affairs of the United Kingdom, in all the larger questions, there would be in the Cabinet nobody definitely representing the Scottish point of view.[34]

Speaking at a Unionist fete in Nairn two years later, Skelton's thinking had hardly changed. *The Scotsman* recorded his boast that

> the Secretary of State for Scotland and himself were bringing to Scotland a great deal more of the administrative work than had been done in the past.

Offices were presently going to be brought to Edinburgh, and he believed that thereby they would make the work of government – and particularly of that side of government where the central authority had to be in close touch with the Local Authorities – much easier for the Local Authorities. That would be a benefit to Scotland, and Scotland in many other ways would benefit from having some of her own government done at home.[35]

Throughout the remainder of 1932, all of 1933 and a substantial part of 1934, Skelton's main role was to defend the government's record, while propping up an increasingly frail Scottish secretary in the narrower field of Scottish affairs. In December 1932 he said that after twelve months of hard work on behalf of agriculture, he 'did not think it was asking too much that . . . the Government might have a little recognition of what had been done'. Skelton was by now involved with the successful Empire Marketing Board, which contrived ingenious schemes for selling British produce to the dominions, and he 'ventured to say that in 1933 there would come to fruition a large number of schemes dealing with the internal organisation of marketing'.[36]

Skelton also spoke of the need for strict economy in public expenditure, not just by the government, but also by individual citizens 'so as to help towards the restoration of our own trade'. He was, essentially, engaged in government propaganda. '"Buy British" must be most rigorously maintained,' explained Skelton. 'It was the public duty of every citizen to "Buy British".'[37]

Addressing the Peebles and South Midlothian Unionist Association in July 1933, Skelton was on evangelical form, proclaiming that

in August, 1931, Britain was trembling on the edge of the abyss – currency, credit, and savings were in danger. Everything which had been done for the welfare of the people was placed in jeopardy. July, 1933, was reached with much of the road still to travel, but Britain was now nearly on the road towards prosperity again, and, quite clearly, with a larger degree of sunshine shining upon her than upon any other country in the world to-day.[38]

But despite the circumstances, Skelton's pursuit of a property-owning democracy was not quite moribund. Sir Godfrey Collins shared his deputy's interest in housing conditions and in February 1933 introduced the Housing (Scotland) Bill, which aimed quixotically to eradicate slum housing in Scotland within a few years. While in England a subsidy for private house-building had been removed, in Scotland it was to be retained. 'The housing legislation of the National Government', Skelton pointed out in May, 'was an interesting example of how a united Cabinet, representing both England and Scotland, could provide in detail for the different requirements of the two parts of the country.' Meanwhile, Skelton fought to keep building costs low, while praising social housing schemes such as a stretch of new dwellings built by the Edinburgh Welfare Housing Trust.

In terms of agricultural smallholdings, there was also progress of a sort. The Scottish secretary initiated an experimental scheme whereby unemployed miners were provided with a small piece of ground which they could cultivate near their homes. 'There was absolutely no need for anyone to fear that if he took up this business', reported *The Scotsman*, 'which [Skelton] believed would be of great interest and great value – he would lose his right to benefit relief until the moment came when his operations showed a net profit for the year.'[39] Skelton also hoped that the scheme would allow applicants to occupy larger, self-supporting, holdings if it later became possible for the government to supply those too. Skelton visited one such scheme just outside Edinburgh, where 1,400 acres had provided a range of holdings. 'I recommend any Scottish member who finds himself in West Lothian or near Edinburgh in the course of the recess', said Skelton in July the following year, 'to visit the plots at Oakbank where a piece of rough field has been converted into what looks like a model poultry farm, almost entirely by unemployed men. If I still use the word "experiment" it is to hold in check my own hopes and beliefs.'[40]

As a political thinker and practitioner, however, Skelton was growing increasingly detached. He had ceased his journalistic activities just before he joined the government in 1931, and as a result of his promotion he had also quit his work at the Scottish Bar. Indeed, during his few years as a junior minister, much of his output became almost frivolous. Addressing the British Colour Council's annual dinner in February 1934, he said that when 'he looked back to a Victorian childhood he saw an extraordinary increase in taste, in sense of colour, and enjoyment of beauty'. When he was young, he recalled, 'gardens were ugly, and nothing had improved more than the general taste in gardening and the colours of flowers'. Skelton also remembered that 'as a very young man Lord Rosebery [said] to him that England had never recovered its sense of joy since the time of the Puritans'.[41]

There also came further heartache in 1934. 'One of the problems which he supposed bachelors would never solve', quipped Skelton in January, 'was whether it was the dressmaker or the public who decided new fashions.'[42] Skelton's letters to Katharine Tennant had reduced to a trickle throughout 1933, and lacked the warmth and vitality of their earlier correspondence. So a bachelor he would remain for the rest of his life.

'The two peak moments in the life of a human being', Skelton observed at the beginning of 1934, '[are] the day of his marriage and the day he made his first investment.'[43] Walter Elliot experienced that first 'peak moment' when, in January 1934, he and Katharine announced their engagement. Skelton had long urged Tennant to consider marrying Elliot, but the actual announcement must still have come as a shock. In March the Prime Minister presented a wedding gift from the Cabinet to Elliot, joking that 'it was the ambition of every true Scot to win the K.T., and the Minister of Agriculture had now achieved that ambition'.[44]

The couple were married at St Baldred's Church, North Berwick, on 2 April. Katharine wore a long-sleeved gown of cream satin and was given away by her half-brother, Peter Lubbock. As newsreel commentary of the wedding punned, the 'staunch' Conservative Elliot had wed the 'equally staunch Liberal' Tennant.[45] Katharine's brother-in-law, Captain Thomas Dugdale MP, was the best man, while the reception was held at Hyndford House. A wedding photograph shows both Katharine and Walter beaming with happiness. Goodness knows what emotions rushed through Skelton's head during the ceremony, as he sat in the church alongside his spinster sister Evelyn.[46]

The rest of 1934 was dominated by the deteriorating situation in Europe, and closer to home by the government's 'special areas' policy and reforms to the Poor Law. Skelton had wound up the second reading of the Poor Law (Scotland) Bill on 27 March, once again on a personal note.

> It so happens that the work of carrying on the Poor Law in Scotland, by administrative machinery only and with practically no statutory foundation to guide the administration, was for the last third of the nineteenth century conducted by my own father. The House will understand, now that I am asking it to give a second reading to this bill, why I recall the famous phrase: 'The roots of the present are deep in the past.'[47]

The bill worked its way through the Scottish Grand Committee from the end of May, with Skelton deftly handling a number of amendments. In October the buzzwords for tackling industrial depression and unemployment were 'special areas', whereby the government designated certain areas across the UK as deserving of special economic attention. The Scottish Office initially took little interest in the policy, until Percy Rose, an assistant under-secretary, alerted Skelton, who immediately 'reserved' the Scottish

position. Another pressing concern was whether Scotland was to
have her own separate commissioner. Both Skelton and Collins
made it clear to Neville Chamberlain that public opinion and local
authority demand required one, and the government eventually
agreed. Interestingly, Skelton 'emphasised the importance of the
different administrative system in Scotland'.[48]

The limited nature of his ministerial duties, meanwhile, clearly
depressed Skelton. 'Noel, rather to my surprise, seems to be tired
of his job,' noted Cuthbert Headlam in his diary on 12 April 1934,
'whether because he is tiring of the HofC or not I could not gather
– or whether because like me he feels he is too old to be relegated
to a subordinate position.'[49]

Stanley Baldwin, meanwhile, occupied far from a subordinate
position. Following the election of Adolf Hitler as the German
Chancellor in 1933, rearmament became a growing concern. In
July 1934 Baldwin warned Parliament that Britain's defensive
frontier was no longer the White Cliffs of Dover, but instead lay
on the Rhine. The same month, he announced the first of several
expansion plans for the Royal Air Force.

The collapse of a conference on disarmament also led to
Germany's withdrawal from the League of Nations, an organisation
that would provide Skelton with his only direct foray into foreign
affairs. Most likely at Anthony Eden's request, his old political
mentor joined the British delegation to the fifteenth ordinary
session of the assembly in Geneva from 10–27 September 1934.[50] A
Scotsman correspondent reported:

> I am told by a friend who has just come back from Geneva that
> Mr Noel Skelton, the Under Secretary for Scotland, who is
> acting for the first time as a member of the British delegation,
> and Mr Geoffrey Shakespeare, of the Ministry of Health, also
> a newcomer, have created an excellent impression both by
> their thorough grasp of the questions upon which they have
> had occasion to speak, and by their personality.[51]

Skelton also acted as reporter for the sixth committee, which submitted a report on slavery to the assembly.

The League, however, was by then in terminal decline. Just a month after Skelton's trip to Geneva, both King Alexander of Yugoslavia and the French foreign minister, Louis Barthou, were assassinated. Eden acted as a mediator for the League of Nations in the ensuing Balkan crisis, and the acceptance of his proposals added greatly to his international reputation.

Speaking at an event in November, Skelton said he

> did not believe himself there was a public man, whatever his political faith and outlook might be, who did not feel that it was a prime object of statesmanship to ensure peace, and to ensure that never again would the lives, the treasures and the hopes of the world be destroyed by such a catastrophe as occurred in 1914.

He emphasised that the National Government was

> ceaseless and unwearying in [its] effort . . . to ensure that the nations would be brought together, that every form of international agreement and understanding would be pursued in order that good-fellowship should remain amongst the peoples and that there should never spring into existence even the temperament, the outlook, and the mood which might result in war.

Clearly delving into his own experience of the First World War, Skelton said it was his audience's duty

> never to forget those who survived the war; never to forget those who bore the brunt of the struggle and never to forget them whether they suffered from wounds or physical disability or from, what sometimes was even worse, the economic disability of unemployment and despair'.[52]

Just five years later, the world would again be at war, but Skelton was firmly in the appeasement camp.[53]

Yet at the beginning of 1935 Skelton was still addressing the issue of what the Conservative Party should stand for in the new era. He told the Federation of University Conservative and Unionist Associations in Edinburgh that

> if there was one defect in the public life of our country, it was that the great mass of people thought that the work of political and public life and of government was purely an empirical day-to-day business anybody could try his hand at; whereas, in fact, it was one of the most profound and difficult of human activities, and led inevitably to nonsense and folly unless it were based upon real thought and deeply worked-out principles.

Skelton said they should take the long view: 'Let them realise that a party was worth nothing unless it was based upon real principles, which applied not only to the conduct of government, but which had their roots in an inner outlook and point of view about life, and let them draw this lesson from the past.'[54] Skelton's 'view of life', therefore, remained intact.

Beyond this rhetoric, Skelton continued his propaganda tour on behalf of the National Government. In London he said he did not 'want Scotland to become a museum piece', rather he wanted 'it to do what no other part of the Empire is better fitted to do, take its full share of the industrial and commercial life of the world'.[55] He also started encouraging Scots to use their savings for the development of new Scottish industries. 'There is more quiet money put away in quiet pockets in Edinburgh than in any other town I know,' he said.[56] Those who had saved from Scotland's prosperity in the past had a duty to do something to help their country in the future.

Back in the Commons, the Housing (Scotland) Bill continued its progress through Parliament. 'We must in social legislation see that we do not put pressure, hardship and injustice upon a few or many,' Skelton told the House. 'Such criticism cannot be made of this bill, and echoes of it still remain in this debate as an aftermath.' He sketched the historical background to the relatively poor state of housing in Scotland as compared with England.

> Most of Scotland was terribly impoverished until the Industrial Revolution. The Industrial Revolution is not so far back, and a standard of housing is something of very slow growth, and it is not surprising that the Scottish population on the whole finds itself worse housed and overcrowded – and, indeed, endures those conditions more readily – than a population which has far greater traditions of wealth behind it.
>
> But let us make no mistake. At this time, when progress moves upon such rapid feet, when the idiosyncrasies and the points of view of one district are obliterated in the general quickening of transport and the speed with which news travels from one part of the world to another, we cannot allow the present housing conditions to continue . . . if we want to attract new industries to our country we must bring them to a country where the workers are well housed, where their inner spirits are filled with that sense of content for which good housing is essential, and though that is not our motive for dealing with a crying social need, I believe that when this bill is operated and this appalling proportion of overcrowding – 15 out of every 100 living more than three to a room – is steadily decreasing, we shall have a factor in Scottish life which will be of direct assistance towards its future industrial and general prosperity.

Housing was, of course, an important issue to Skelton, although it is important to note that a decade on from his first public espousals of a 'property-owning democracy', as a minister he was preoccupied with practicality rather than theory.

> The suggestion has been made from time to time – not

in this House, but I have seen it elsewhere – that there is something revolutionary in a government which contains Tories dealing with overcrowding. May I read one sentence from what was said by a Tory statesman – I will tell the House who it was in a moment: 'After all, whatever political arrangements we may adopt, whatever the political constitution of our state may be, the foundation of all its prosperity and welfare must be the mass of the people shall be honest and manly and shall have common sense. How can you expect that those conditions will exist among people subjected to the frightful influences which the present overcrowding of our poor produces?'

That is not a revolutionary proposition of an under-secretary in 1935. That was the great Lord Salisbury, speaking in the year 1884; and I do not think that even those among us who are Tories and have the greatest respect and belief for tradition – and I myself am not wanting in that respect – will feel that a step which is going to remedy a grievance pointed out in 1884 by one of the greatest of Tory leaders can, from a Unionist point of view, be regarded as an unjustifiable revolution.[57]

Skelton's eloquent invocation of the spirit of Lord Salisbury proved to be his Commons oratorical swansong. He answered questions in the House on 5 March, and dealt with the Housing (Scotland) Bill in the Scottish Grand Committee two days later, but thereafter he was absent from Parliament through illness, which he must already have known to be cancer. 'I am sorry to learn that Mr Noel Skelton, the Scottish Under Secretary of State, who has been off duty owing to illness, will not be able to return to duty for some weeks,' noted a *Scotsman* correspondent. 'His absence is all the more unfortunate since his Departmental colleagues are at present busy with the Scottish Housing Bill, in addition to their normal work and Mr Skelton's intimate knowledge of the measure is greatly missed.'[58]

In April he underwent an operation, and appeared to be recovering well.

On 7 June 1935 Ramsay MacDonald finally retired as Prime Minister and Stanley Baldwin – aged sixty-seven – began his third and final term as Prime Minister. There was a Cabinet reshuffle, which saw Sir Samuel Hoare promoted to Foreign Secretary, while Anthony Eden also joined the Cabinet as Minister for League of Nations Affairs (without portfolio). It was a rich and terrible year for political events overseas. Mussolini invaded Abyssinia, while Hitler consolidated his grip on Germany, reoccupying the Rhineland within months. Baldwin had deliberately sought to promote younger men – another was Oliver Stanley – to give the National Government a fresher look. Had Skelton been in better health, it is not difficult to imagine him having been among those elevated. Alec Dunglass, Skelton's PPS since 1931, also moved on, transferring to the same role at the Ministry of Labour. The indisposed Skelton, meanwhile, remained at the Scottish Office.

Skelton returned to front-line politics on 18 June, accompanying Sir Godfrey Collins and officials from the Scottish Department of Health to a meeting with Scottish local authorities, but he was clearly seriously ill. Photographs from this period show Skelton looking much heavier, his face tired with baggy eyes. The following day, he also returned to the House of Commons. 'He was welcomed with great cordiality by both sides of the House,' reported *The Scotsman*, 'whose sympathy with colleagues who have been off duty through illness no political differences can impair. That is especially true in the case of members who, like Mr Skelton, are held in high personal esteem.'[59]

On 24 July Skelton answered questions in the House, and the following day he made his final appearance in the Commons, answering questions on Scottish education. His last major appearance in Parliament had been to report on the activities of the special commissioner for the Scottish Depressed Areas on 4 July 1935, including his progress in establishing something close to Skelton's heart, smallholdings in certain regions, which included Dunglass's constituency.

Shortly after the House rose for the summer, Skelton embarked on one of the more mundane duties expected of Scottish Office ministers – an annual tour of the Western Isles. He departed on the fisheries cruiser *Minna* at Oban on 5 August, accompanied by his friend John Loder, the Marquis of Titchfield (MP for Newark) and officials from the Department of Agriculture for Scotland. This little group spent the next ten days touring the Western Isles, ostensibly to investigate infrastructure and agricultural problems in the Inner and Outer Hebrides. Skelton took particular interest in the MacAulay Demonstration Farm on the Isle of Lewis, while he also observed crofters at Portnalong (on Skye) who had reclaimed moorland by hand (at the MacAulay farm it was achieved mechanically).

Skelton finished the tour on 15 August and left Oban by train the following morning. 'Mr Skelton,' *The Scotsman* informed its readers, 'it is understood, is to pay a visit to Orkney.'[60] There, Skelton met with the business committee of Orkney County Council and George Hogarth, chairman of the Fisheries Board for Scotland, to discuss roads, piers and illegal trawling in or around the island. 'Mr Skelton's visit to Orkney was his first for forty years,' reported *The Scotsman*. 'His father for a number of years tenanted shootings and fishings at Melsetter, when the present Under Secretary of State was at school, and Mr Skelton then visited Orkney regularly.'[61]

Skelton spent the rest of summer resting, but resumed his ministerial duties that autumn. On 6 October he accompanied the Scottish secretary to receive deputations of Scottish teachers and the Scottish Farm Servants' Section of the Transport and General Workers' Union. Two weeks later Sir Godfrey Collins reviewed the recent work of the Scottish Office during a speech in Greenock. At the outset he 'acknowledged the invaluable and active support he had received from his able colleague and friend, Mr Noel Skelton, Under Secretary of State for Scotland'.[62]

During the past three years Collins and Skelton had opened a new Scottish Office headquarters in Edinburgh and transferred Scottish Education Department officials to the Scottish capital, meaning that more than 96 per cent of Scottish administration was now conducted north of the border. Collins also boasted of his and Skelton's progress on abolishing slum housing, reiterating his belief that it would disappear completely by 1938. Exports of Scottish coal were up, while Skelton's land settlement programme had grown from 100 experimental smallholdings in 1933 to a much larger scheme designed to establish up to 1,000. In fisheries, the new Herring Industry Board had been a great success, while the Scottish secretary also boasted of his achievement (together with Skelton) in having secured a separate special areas commissioner for Scotland.

At around the same time, Baldwin called a general election. Once again, and despite being seriously ill, Skelton was nominated to stand as the National Unionist candidate for the Combined Scottish Universities constituency. The National Liberal MP, D. M. Cowan, had died in 1934, prompting a by-election won by Dr G. A. Morrison, also a National Liberal, while J. Graham Kerr had replaced John Buchan (who had been appointed governor-general of Canada) earlier that year. This time, however, a Scottish National Party candidate entered the fray, the writer and academic Professor Andrew Dewar Gibb. Dewar Gibb's presence ensured that there would be an electoral contest, which had not been the case in 1931.

Skelton, however, was by then terminally ill. On 19 November he slipped into a coma and three days later, at an Edinburgh nursing home in Belgrave Crescent, he died aged just fifty-five. His elder brother, John Henry Skelton, signed his death certificate. Interestingly, Skelton had passed away after the general election poll, but before the declaration of the result – creating the first modern case of a posthumous election. Archibald Noel Skelton, who had contributed so much to Conservative thought and politics, had rendered one final, and curious, effect on public life.

7

'A MAN OF IDEALS, AND A MAN OF VISION' (1935)

Polling for the general election of 1935 had closed just a few hours before Skelton's death became known publicly, creating an unusual constitutional situation. The 1918 Representation of the People Act included the provision that

> if one of the candidates nominated dies after he has been nominated and before the commencement of the poll, the returning officer shall countermand the poll and other proceedings for the election, and commence the same again as if the writ had been received by him on the day on which he was satisfied of the fact that death took place.[1]

That, however, did not cover the situation in question, as the poll had already concluded when Skelton's death took place.

So under the legislation, the count for the Combined Scottish Universities seat was set to proceed as normal at Edinburgh University on Monday 25 November (Skelton having died the previous Friday). Complicating matters further was the fact that the election was by proportional representation, which meant that the count took much longer than a regular first-past-the-post poll. 'The unusual situation', noted *The Scotsman*, 'was the subject of a good deal of question and speculation yesterday.' Four candidates had put their names forward for three seats, but one of them was now dead.

Immediately, Unionist Party legal experts set to work to consider the matter. 'The election goes on as if nothing has happened,' a Unionist Central Office official told reporters. 'If Mr Skelton happens to be elected, his name will be declared on Monday as duly elected, and then the Speaker will be advised that a vacancy has occurred through death, and a new writ will be issued.' Sir Thomas Holland, vice-chancellor of Edinburgh University and returning officer for the Combined Scottish Universities constituency, confirmed that he could not interfere with the normal proceedings of the election. 'If Mr Skelton receives a sufficient number of votes,' he said, 'I shall have to declare him elected.'[2]

Meanwhile, Saturday morning's newspapers were full of glowing tributes. Sir Godfrey Collins, Skelton's senior minister at the Scottish Office, said:

> It is with the greatest regret that I have heard of the untimely death of Noel Skelton. At the Scottish Office he has been to me in all matters affecting Scotland a wise counsellor, a loyal and able colleague, and a true friend. Of the services which he has given to Scotland, and of his zeal for improving the lot of his less fortunate fellows, I cannot speak too highly. Scotland has always been fortunate in producing men who are willing to spend themselves on her behalf, and Noel Skelton was such a man. For his personal character, his qualities of mind and heart, his enthusiasm, his courage, and his modesty, all who knew him felt the deepest admiration. We shall miss him more than I care to think: but the memory of his work and personality will long remain as an inspiration to the many friends who mourn him.[3]

Little under a year later Collins also departed prematurely from the political stage, dying from septicaemia following a minor nose operation in Zurich.

The Scotsman commented:

> Profound regret has been excited by the news of Mr Noel Skelton's death. When he re-appeared in the House of Commons last summer after his severe illness it was evident, in spite of his cheerfulness, that he had not made a full recovery, but his friends hoped that his fine physique would enable him to regain his health during the leisure of the recess.

The newspaper went on to pay tribute to his work at the Scottish Office:

> His post as Under-Secretary was highly congenial, for the reason, among others, that it gave scope to his enthusiasm for land settlement, a cause which he had at heart long before he had any thought of Ministerial responsibility for it ... His only defect in debate arose from the tendency, which is common to members of his profession, to underrate the alertness of mind of the House of Commons. He was thus prone to make his explanations more detailed and profuse than they need have been, such was his anxiety to ensure that he was being thoroughly understood.
>
> ... In his pre-official days Mr Skelton wielded a graceful and witty pen, generally anonymously, but a pamphlet he issued under his name about ten years ago showed that he had a forward-looking mind not trammelled by party convention. By his death public life has lost an attractive figure.[4]

The Times noted that

> it was known to his friends that he was very ill, but the news

of his death came as a painful shock in Edinburgh. The possibility of his being unable to take his seat if elected for the Scottish Universities had been discussed, and there had been speculation as to the situation that would then arise.[5]

In London, there was already speculation that Skelton's place could be taken by either Ramsay MacDonald or his son Malcolm, both of whom had lost their seats in the election.

Another lengthy appreciation also appeared in that day's edition of *The Scotsman*:

> No one ever spent any time with him without realising that the world was rather a jollier place than he had been inclined to think, and fuller of good things, alike for mind and body and spirit. If I were asked to name his outstanding quality I should not hesitate at once to say generosity. The word is used in its widest sense primarily, of course, as an attribute of the mind and not of the purse, although in the latter sense too he was as liberal and as careless of the morrow as could well be imagined. No man ever suffered less than Noel Skelton from little-mindedness and his appreciation of good qualities in others never faltered. He never grudged anyone else any success great or little, and many of his brethren in both law and politics must gratefully remember to-day occasions on which Skelton not only applauded their successes but contributed to them, and helped to bring them about by gratuitous and unobtrusive acts of kindness.

'His true metier,' continued the tribute of one who could only have been a close friend, 'of course, was politics and public life, and on the political platform and in the House of Commons he found audiences more to his mind than in the law courts.'

> From early years he had a passion for the affairs of State, and throughout his life he was a convinced and enlightened

Tory, whose faith found reasoned and articulate shape in a number of admirable articles in the *Quarterly Review* and elsewhere. His years in Parliament came as the fulfilment of a long apprenticeship and few men can have entered with such zest on official life as he did on being appointed Under Secretary of State for Scotland four years ago. He brought to the discharge of his many duties in that office the full force of his invigorating zeal.

The appreciation ended on a moving note.

The tragedy is that he should have been struck down just when he was on the verge of entering his rightful kingdom. He had a good life, he lived it fully and he enjoyed it. Like most men, he had his rough luck and his disappointments. He never showed his consciousness of them, either in word or in deed.

'I consume my own smoke,' he would say if questioned and would turn with a laugh to plunge into conversation again. It was in conversation that he was best of all. Avowedly he 'talked for victory'; but his talk brought out the best in other people's, and he appreciated their sallies as much as they (and he) appreciated his own. It will be long before, his many intimates, in every walk of life, forget 'one dear dead friend's remembered tones'.[6]

Indeed, friends seemed to mourn deeply Skelton's passing. 'Noel Skelton I can never think of', wrote Lady Tweedsmuir several years later, 'without a pang of regret that he is no longer here to laugh with, or to make ironic comments on the state of the world.' She added:

Since Noel's death his friends have felt a smarting sense of loss. The world without the sauce of Noel's wit is like a dish of cold veal . . . his descriptions of people and their

behaviour cut clean into the consciousness of his hearers
. . . But his summings up of points of character had so much
fun and fancy in them that those who were mocked could
not fail to smile (if ruefully) at his epitaph on their living
selves.[7]

In the *Times* of 25 November, meanwhile, 'One of his Friends'
provided a more insightful tribute to Skelton's political contribution:

> We knew well enough what he had done, between the
> University and the War years, to make Toryism a live creed
> in Scotland and to shake the rooted Scottish political
> traditions; hopeless though it seemed at the time . . .
> He did not reach his full measure in public life, but he
> accomplished much. He proved again to our days how to
> combine a European outlook and culture with a personality
> purely and intensely Scots in peace and war, in Parliament
> and out. He gave us all a lesson in ungrudging fulfilment of
> the second part. He gave salt and savour and a heightened
> tension to any company where he found himself; and he
> was a true friend.[8]

And locally, the *Perthshire Advertiser* carried an appreciation 'by
One of his former Constituents' on 27 November:

> He was big in mind and spirit, all mean things were alien to
> him, and the petty and hypocritical he would brush aside
> with a laughing contempt. When he came into a room there
> was a brightening and freshening of the atmosphere, and
> none who has attended a City Hall meeting will forget his
> infinite patience and courtesy under a stream of questions.
>
> It is perhaps typical of Noel Skelton that after his death
> he should still have won a fight; for not only in Perthshire
> did he light a fire that will not be easily extinguished.[9]

Beyond the vacancy created by Skelton's death, the general election produced 429 National Government MPs (of whom 387 were Conservatives) to Labour's 154. The results of the Combined Scottish Universities constituency, meanwhile, were the last to be declared, on 25 November. The electorate of 52,981 (all of whom were graduates of the four ancient Scottish universities) had voted by postal ballot and the result was announced shortly after one o'clock:

J. Graham Kerr (Unionist)	8,252
Dr G. A. Morrison (Nat Lib)	7,529
A. Noel Skelton (Unionist)	7,479
Prof. A. D. Gibb (Scot Nat)	3,865

There was no second count, as three of the candidates, including Skelton, had received more than their required quota on the first round. Professor Dewar Gibb, the SNP candidate (who had known Skelton both from the Bar and from the Great War), made a statement through his election agent in which he contended that owing to Skelton's death he was de jure member of Parliament but announced that, should the returning officer decide otherwise, he would not press his claim. *The Scotsman* reported that Dewar Gibb had taken legal advice, 'and while the statute made no provision for the present situation, he considered that, as a matter of law, since a vote for a dead candidate and a declaration of his election could not be otherwise than totally ineffectual, he was entitled to be declared elected'.

The returning officer, however, was having none of it. Sir Thomas Holland declared that as the number of effective votes cast was 27,125, and the number of seats available was three, then the quota necessary for successful election was 6,781 + 1 or 6,782. Since Dewar Gibb, with 3,865 votes, did not meet the threshold, he could not claim to have been elected, even taking into account the death of Skelton.

Dr Morrison then spoke. 'The tragedy', he said, 'was that of a man who after years of successful labour, had found something which he could do and which he could do well, and who was enjoying great and increasing success and widening appreciation of his labours.' Dewar Gibb also remarked that Skelton 'and he had had a certain tie of which he liked to think. They were educated at the same school.'[10] Some of those present at the count wore mourning colours.

Skelton's name was then inscribed on the roll of new members. When Parliament met, notice of his death was intimated to the Speaker, who then issued a writ for a by-election. It was customary for each of the Combined Scottish Universities MPs to be nominated by the universities of Edinburgh, Glasgow and Aberdeen and St Andrews respectively, and since Edinburgh had put forward Skelton, a movement quickly grew for it to nominate Ramsay MacDonald as the late MP's successor.

MacDonald's supporters feared he might be challenged in the Combined Scottish Universities by-election and defeated, which would have humiliated him further, but a group of students finally nominated the former prime minister and he was elected – despite a challenge from Dewar Gibb – in February 1936. There was a certain irony to this series of events. Skelton and MacDonald had clashed during the former's maiden speech back in 1923; now the death of one had provided a political comeback for the other.

Skelton had left everything, including his books and manuscripts, to his sister Evelyn, who supervised the funeral arrangements.[11] He was buried at the Kinross Kirkgate burial ground, Kinross-shire, next to his parents, while his name was also added to his mother's gravestone in Edinburgh's Dean Cemetery. Skelton's total estate came to more than £14,687, which included a myriad of stocks and bonds in the Caledonian Trust, the Commercial Bank of Scotland, the Ceylon government, the Kingdom of Belgium Stabilisation Loan, the imperial Japanese government, and even Baldwins Ltd, the family firm of the incumbent Prime Minister. No one could have accused Skelton of failing to practise what he preached in terms of promoting a property-owning democracy.

Perhaps the most substantial tribute paid to Skelton came from Stanley Baldwin towards the end of November, in his first public speech since the election. 'There was something in the early days of the Labour Party that they had, and at that time we had not,' Baldwin recalled during a rally at Dundee's Caird Hall.

> There was a spiritual force moving among the men who first preached socialism in our country . . . I felt that it was essential, if our party was to fight a party of that nature, it must have some spiritual ideal to fight for, and incidentally I don't think any man felt that more than Mr Noel Skelton for I have talked to him many a time about it.
>
> I certainly have done my best at various times to try to inculcate some spirit of that kind into our younger men, and I think not without some success. Noel Skelton was cut off before he had fully proved what he might have done in the House of Commons, but to those who knew him, and to you in Scotland who knew him, there shines out another fine character, a type of cultivated Scots gentleman – and there is no finer type in these islands – a man of culture, a man of ideals, and a man of vision, so far as our own party was concerned, and we cannot say how much he might not have accomplished not only in speech but in writing, for he had a ready pen, on these causes which were near to his heart and near ours.

'I can think of no individual in the ranks, as he was for so long,' concluded the Prime Minister, 'who has contributed more in his work to make our party in Scotland what it is, and make it an integral party of Scottish life and Scottish thought.'[12] Loud cheers greeted Baldwin's closing words.

8

'A PROPERTY-OWNING DEMOCRACY IS THE AIM'

So what of Noel Skelton's legacy? Although considerable, it is easy to overstate. As Nick Lee observed in his MA dissertation on the impact of the 'property-owning democracy', 'it would be a mistake to assume that Noel Skelton was the sole, or even principal, architect of Conservative strategy' during the 1920s and 1930s. Even in 1923, most of the policies outlined by Skelton were not new. His significance, however, assessed Lee, was fourfold:

> Firstly, he articulated these ideas in an explicitly democratic manner, and recognised the need to widen the opportunities for ownership where possible. Secondly, the phrase 'property-owning democracy' became inextricably associated with the values of ownership, citizenship and individualism for which he was concerned. Thirdly, he influenced key individuals such as Macmillan and Eden, and his vision was central to their attitude to state welfare and nationalisation in the 1940s. Most fundamentally, however, Skelton was among the first to recognise the need for Conservatives to move beyond their traditional association with privilege and wealth.[1]

Harold Macmillan and Anthony Eden would certainly have agreed.

'His early death was a grievous loss,' wrote Macmillan of Skelton in his memoirs. 'Had he lived, it is hard to say what would have been his career in politics. But his influence on politics and political thinking must have grown steadily year by year.'[2] So what would have become of Skelton had he lived? 'Skelton . . . is one of the largely forgotten figures of Conservatism,' observed D. R. Thorpe in his biography of Anthony Eden, 'but had he not died prematurely of cancer in 1935, he could well have been one of the great figures of the party, even a possible future leader.'[3]

This, however, seems unlikely. Skelton was fifty-five when he died, and given the ensuing war and the rise of Churchill, the top job would probably have passed him by, although he could perhaps have succeeded Sir Godfrey Collins as Scottish secretary in 1936. What is remarkable, however, is that three of Skelton's political protégés – Eden, Douglas-Home and Macmillan – all went on to lead the Conservatives and become Prime Minister. It is safer to say, therefore, that had Skelton lived, he would probably have been a leading figure alongside Eden, R. A. Butler and Macmillan in the post-war renaissance of the Conservative Party.

Above all others, it was Anthony Eden who most retained the Skeltonian ethos, his former mentor having what Thorpe described as a 'Disraeli-like influence' over him. He never forgot that it was Skelton who had first encouraged him to use the phrase 'property-owning democracy' in his speeches. 'After our defeat, many years later, in the general election of 1945,' recalled Eden in his memoirs, 'I was able to revive it and keep it as the central theme of our policy.'[4]

Eden did so on 3 October 1946 at the Conservative Party's annual conference in Blackpool. 'We believe', he declared, 'that it is desirable to elaborate schemes whereby the private citizen and the returned soldier should be in a position not only to rent a house but to own one.' Conservatives believed, he added,

> that the tenant farmer should be assisted and encouraged
> to become an owner-occupier. We would welcome schemes
> designed to enable the workers in industry to participate

in its development and in the ownership of industry to a greater degree than they do at present.

In a socialist state, where ownership is the monopoly of the government, where everyone must rely on the state for his job, his roof, his livelihood, individual responsibility and individual liberty must wither and die. And so it is that we of the Conservative Party must maintain that the ownership of property is not a crime or a sin, but a reward, a right and a responsibility that must be shared as equitably as possible among all our citizens.

There is one principle underlying our approach to all these problems, a principle on which we stand in fundamental opposition to socialism. The objective of socialism is state ownership of all the means of production, distribution and exchange. Our objective is a nationwide property-owning democracy. These objectives are fundamentally opposed. Whereas the socialist purpose is the concentration of ownership in the hands of the state, ours is the distribution of ownership over the widest practicable number of individuals.

We must not be content that the workpeople in our industries should be mere units of labour. We must regard them as individuals who have a right to share in the knowledge of the common purpose of the industry in which they are working. If capital and labour are to be partners, they must be full partners, and labour is entitled to expect full information as to the achievements and the purposes of industry and the distribution of its fruits. Nothing less than this matches up to the needs of human personality.

In tone and language Eden's famous speech was richly imbued with all that Noel Skelton had taught him. Although he made no mention of a referendum, Eden expanded on the means by which Skelton's property-owning democracy might be achieved by focusing on 'a great increase in the production of wealth in the country and in particular in the productivity of industry'. Only when the average individual, he argued, had a 'sufficient margin of income over the requirements of day-to-day consumption'[5] could home ownership be achieved.

Unfortunately, however, little corresponding work was done to define what Eden's renewed use of the phrase 'property-owning democracy' actually meant. A fortnight after the 1946 conference, James Stuart (a future Scottish secretary) reported that 'from conversations overheard among not unintelligent citizens, it would appear that there is some confusion as to the exact meaning . . . Some are misled into thinking that ownership of the mines, Bank of England and so on by the nation is a step in the direction of a "property-owning democracy"'. The publicity director at Conservative Central Office, meanwhile, was pleased Eden was taking up a popular theme, but warned him:

> It takes an immense amount of reiteration to get a thing of this sort across to the public. The position at the moment is that they have become aware of the phrase and are asking 'What is this "Property-owning democracy" idea that Anthony Eden is talking about?' The next stage is to get them to understand it![6]

Lord Woolton, the architect of post-war Conservative Party modernisation, understood it to mean home ownership. A 'lot of people liked to own their own houses,' he remarked on the eve of the 1948 Conservative conference. 'That was what Conservatives meant when they talked about property-owning democracy.'[7]

Even a former YMCA member and Skelton protégé, Bob Boothby, urged a rethink. He wrote to *The Times* in 1949 saying that although the phrase had 'done good service for the Conservative Party during the past twenty-five years . . . like patriotism, it is not enough'.[8] Responding directly to Boothby's letter, a Mr A. R. Harvie asked what 'a property-owning democracy' had 'done for the people, for whose advantage it was presumably designed'.[9] Even more scathing was the future Cabinet minister Angus Maude, who warned that the 'Conservatives had failed to explain their long-term policy to the people. What was the good of talking about a property-owning democracy when Conservative local councils served compulsory purchase orders on small householders whenever an official advised it?'[10]

Nevertheless, during a 1950 speech in Edinburgh, Sir Winston Churchill declared that it constituted an essential part of Conservative policy. He quoted Attlee, who had said that the 'nation was much more a property-owning democracy than when Labour came into power. They own the railways, the Bank of England, and the coal mines, and there are a lot more things the nation will own presently.' But, added Churchill,

> I doubt if it gives very much pleasure to the average socialist when he wakes up in the morning to say to himself, 'Oh, I own the Bank of England, I own the railways, I own the coal mines.'
>
> The truth is that Mr Attlee and his friends feel the force of our Conservative theme, a property-owning democracy, and are trying to avoid it by talking nonsense about it. They know perfectly well that what we mean is a personal property-owning democracy. Households which have possessions which they prize and cherish because they are their own, or even a house and garden of their own, the savings certificates that their thrift has bought, a little money put by for a rainy day, or an insurance policy, the result of forethought and self-denial which will be a help in old age or infirmity, or after their death or those they love and leave behind – that is what the Conservatives mean by a property-owning democracy.[11]

The chance to make it a reality finally came in October 1951 when the Conservatives returned to government. Fittingly, Harold

Macmillan chose to become Minister of Housing and Local Government. It was a risky choice, for at the 1950 party conference the Conservatives had pledged to build 300,000 houses a year on returning to office, a feat which in the context of post-war British austerity seemed highly unlikely. We must 'try to increase the property holding of the people', Macmillan wrote in his diary on 28 October 1951. 'The only way I can think of it to get more of them to own their own houses. This really ought to be seriously studied at once.'[12] Macmillan set about the task with relish, setting up regional housing boards, reducing the mandatory proportion of new private (as opposed to municipal) houses from one in ten to one in two, and introducing the sale of council houses. In Macmillan's first public statement as Minister for Housing he had also asserted that 'no property was more suitable for the creation of a property-owning democracy than house property'.[13] A triumphant Macmillan reached the 300,000 target in December 1953. Later, he looked back on this period as 'in many ways the happiest and most rewarding of my time as a Minister'.[14]

The revived post-war commitment to a 'property-owning democracy', however, was still some way off. Although Macmillan's reforms liberalised the housing market, they failed to provide enough private housing that the working classes could actually afford. He had tried to find a middle way by encouraging alternative forms of private ownership in the form of co-operative societies, but it did not take root. In short, Macmillan found himself constrained by the dominance of the status quo, chiefly state-built and state-owned housing. The basic problem was that it was cheaper and easier for people to rent rather than to buy or build, and local authorities much preferred constructing their own housing. Owner-occupation, however, did increase from 32 per cent of the available housing stock in 1938 to 44 per cent in 1960.

Meanwhile the One Nation group, which included the future chancellor Iain Macleod (who later promoted what he called a 'capital-owning democracy') continued the progressive tradition of the YMCA, while over at the Conservative Research Department

R. A. Butler urged bright young activists to read Skelton's 1924 pamphlet, *Constructive Conservatism*. The influence of that tract also continued to be felt in other, more surprising, political spheres. In his seminal work, *The Future of Socialism*, the Labour MP Tony Crosland examined property ownership together with industrial profit-sharing.

> The 'risk' on a really good ordinary share . . . is on balance a positive risk. Indeed . . . writers not only admit the decline in risk, but make it the basis of their contention that the ordinary share is now a suitable vehicle for those small savings which will gradually convert us into a 'property-owning democracy'.

Elsewhere, Crosland maintained that the property-owning democracy was a 'socialist rather than a conservative ideal', as long as 'the property is well distributed'.[15] Skelton would no doubt have been amused to read those words by a leading social democrat.

As Prime Minister from 1955, meanwhile, Anthony Eden, like Skelton, found that political power did not make the creation of a property-owning democracy any easier. 'There is evidence from a number of quarters that the Government are now making a serious study of how to widen share ownership,' stated *The Times* in November 1958. 'It is believed that the Prime Minister himself is taking a close interest in this subject.'[16] Eden had first suggested employee shareholding schemes at the 1956 Conservative conference, but the idea stagnated. Eden's government was also plagued by industrial action. Although trade union leaders agreed to a voluntary three-week 'cooling-off' period between a decision to strike and industrial action, little came of Eden's desire to reconcile the two, often conflicting, sides of industry.

Harold Macmillan, who became Prime Minister following Eden's resignation in 1957, was not much more successful. As Lord Hailsham (Quintin Hogg) and Butler battled to succeed him in late 1963, he even fretted to his diary about 'the underlying struggle.

It is really the old one, I feel. Hogg . . . represents what [Oliver] Stanley, and John Loder, and Boothby, and Noel Skelton and I tried to represent from 1924 onwards.'[17] Fittingly, the task of continuing the 'underlying struggle' actually fell to the 14th Earl of Home, Skelton's former PPS. 'He was a man of ideas,' said Home of Skelton in his memoirs. 'He would have gone a long way in politics had he not died in his early fifties.'[18]

Shortly before the 1964 election, which the Conservatives narrowly lost, Eden sent Home a letter reminding him that 'a property-owning democracy is the aim'.[19] Indeed, Skelton's Disraeli-like hold over Eden remained undiminished. 'Never a year', wrote Robert Carr in 1976, 'and scarcely ever a month has gone by over these last twenty years without Anthony writing to me or telephoning me urging the Conservative Party to awaken from its apparent disinterest in this basic theme.'[20] Eden clearly hoped his old chief whip, Ted Heath, would revive it during his 1970–74 government, but in the event it was taken up by Heath's radical successor as Conservative Party leader, Margaret Thatcher.

Although Thatcher had almost certainly never heard of Noel Skelton, the first Conservative Party conference she had attended was in 1946, when she heard Eden call for a 'nationwide property-owning democracy'. She began using the phrase in speeches in 1949, and also recalled Eden's rallying cry in her own first conference speech as Conservative Party leader. 'You will understand, I know,' said Thatcher, 'the humility I feel at following in the footsteps of great men like our leader that year [1946], Winston Churchill . . . In the footsteps of Anthony Eden, who set us the goal of a property-owning democracy – a goal we still pursue today.'[21]

In August 1975 Thatcher told the magazine *Crossbow* that she had been studying the contributions of Disraeli and Lord Salisbury to Conservative philosophy. She observed:

> More recently the only memorable phrase illustrating our philosophy was 'property-owning democracy', which was Anthony Eden's. And one has to applaud Harold Macmillan

for the practical way in which he made Conservative philosophy a reality for the average person in Britain. He brought within the reach of the average person things which hitherto had been the prerogative of a comparative few.[22]

And so in 1975 Skelton's phrase had been revived once again. Thatcher told audiences that Labour's Community Land Bill 'pierces the heart of a property-owning democracy'[23] while her housing policy slowly began to take shape. In a speech to the Conservative Women's Conference in 1976, Thatcher boasted that in 1972 'under a Conservative government and Conservative councils, we sold over 60,000 council houses in a year'. 'When it comes to the crunch,' she added, 'state control is more important to socialism than the property-owning democracy which the people want.'[24] The party's first female leader had given Skeltonian philosophy a modern, populist, revival.

Shortly after becoming Prime Minister in 1979, Thatcher declared:

> We will give to every council tenant the right to purchase his own home at a substantial discount on the market price and with 100 per cent mortgages for those who need them. This will be a giant stride towards making a reality of Anthony Eden's dream of a property-owning democracy.[25]

The so-called 'right to buy', together with a raft of other measures to boost home ownership, was arguably one of the biggest success stories of Thatcher's Conservative governments. It had taken more than forty years, but for the first time Skelton's dream of a property-owning democracy was finally being vigorously, and successfully, implemented. If Margaret Thatcher provided the hard-nosed political will, Noel Skelton had supplied the intellectual guidance.

Two years into Thatcher's first government and the property-owning map of Britain had been transformed. Whereas in 1914, only 10 per cent of householders owned their own homes, by 1981 the figure was 60 per cent. Writing in *The Times* in 1982, the Tory MP Peter Hordern linked this achievement directly to Eden's pronouncements after the war. 'Our democracy does not own property in the terms that Anthony Eden meant,' he said. 'To make his vision come true, there has to be a fundamental and irreversible shift of resources to the worker.'

Hordern suggested that the government apply the principle behind council house sales

> so that workers can buy shares in the public companies for which they work, that is at a substantial discount, as of right . . . If he chose to do so, a worker could build up a significant capital sum in his firm by this means, and the consequence of doing so must be to strengthen his commitment to the business which provides his livelihood.

This was as close to a restatement of Skeltonian belief a politician could come to in 1982. Hordern continued:

> If we are to keep the market system, it is imperative that the worker should have the right to join it, rather than be treated as a factor in the market equation. That is the practical argument. But there is also a moral argument . . . I think that is what Anthony Eden meant, and I think it is time we brought his 'property-owning democracy' to reality.[26]

The great privatisations of the 1980s (likened to selling off the family silver by Harold Macmillan, later Lord Stockton) – Cable & Wireless, Rolls Royce, British Airways, British Steel, British Telecommunications (BT), and the public utilities, gas, water and electricity – saw an expansion from three million shareholders in 1979 to eleven million in 1992. Indeed, during a House of Lords debate on privatisation and wealth creation in 1985, Lord Renton said this increase in share ownership, 'coupled with the sale of council houses and the encouragement of owner-occupying, takes us a big further step towards making us into a property-owning democracy'.[27] Renton went on to attribute the phrase to Lord Stockton, prompting an intervention from Lord Boothby, who reminded their Lordships that the phrase was, in fact, Skelton's.

Thatcher's successors, however, did not share her love of Skelton's phrase. It was not until David Cameron became Conservative leader in 2005 that it was again revived. Outlining his own brand of constructive Conservatism in one of his first major speeches, Cameron harked back to the days of industrial strife that pitched worker against employer. Praising Thatcher, he said 'she gave to millions of union members and their families the chance for the first time to participate in a property-owning democracy'. But, Cameron added, 'Margaret Thatcher herself became increasingly worried that not everyone was participating in her property-owning democracy. She became increasingly worried that the new, open economy was not tackling problems of family breakdown, crime, poor schooling, drug dependency and the decline of respect in parts of our inner cities.' His analysis of the political realities produced by three successive New Labour governments also contained shades of Skelton's survey of the 'new era' more than eighty years before.

> Embracing a 'new politics' and accepting that in many areas New Labour was closer to the Conservative Party was a difficult thing to do. But nevertheless it was the right thing to do. Not least because it's true. And make no mistake – I will stick to this path. The alternative to fighting for the centre ground is irrelevance, defeat and failure. We are not facing a spiral of economic decline. We are no longer a country divided by battles between 'us and them'. And, as a Conservative Party changed by those recognitions begins to build a better Britain, we will be fulfilling, not betraying, our inheritance. We will be showing that we have understood our past, and that we can see the way to our future.[28]

And even Gordon Brown revived Skelton's phrase in his 2003 Budget. 'Our country faces a great challenge,' he declared: 'to overcome inequalities of income and wealth and to build a Britain that is not just a property-owning democracy but a wealth-owning, asset-owning democracy open to all.'[29] Shortly before becoming Prime Minister in 2007 he was at it again, saying, 'We are a home-owning, asset-owning, wealth-owning democracy. This is in the interests of our country because everybody would have a stake in the country.'[30] Not to be outdone, in September 2007 the Conservatives pledged to roll out the 'home-owning democracy'[31] by giving council tenants 10 per cent of the value of their home to buy a house in the private sector. Even the Scottish National Party, no fan of Thatcher's right-to-buy policy, pledged in 2007 (but did not implement) to give first-time home buyers £2,000 grants. Skeltonian thinking was once again in the political mainstream.

This consensus reached its apex in late 2009, when Labour and the Conservatives vied for intellectual control of the co-partnership, or 'mutual ownership', model. In December Labour's minister for the Cabinet Office, Tessa Jowell, launched an independent commission on ownership while suggesting that 'enterprises owned by staff or communities should deliver more public services'.[32] This sentiment built upon an idea already sketched out by David Cameron, and in February 2010 the Conservative leader promised to unleash 'a new culture of public sector enterprise and innovation'[33] by allowing state employees to run their own co-operatives, funded by the state as long as they met certain standards.

The architect of the Tory plan to place co-operative ideals at the centre of all public services was the so-called 'Red Tory' Phillip Blond, whose paper 'The Ownership State'[34] had been widely read within the Tory high command. Skelton's political thought was even acknowledged by Blond as a strong influence. Responding to criticism that he was simply reviving an ugly Tory tradition, Blond said that charge ignored 'the fact that both Chesterton and Belloc were not Conservatives but Edwardian Liberals, whose thesis on a property-owning democracy inspired Tory MP Noel Skelton in

1923, Anthony Eden in 1946, Mrs Thatcher in 1979 and me today.'[35]

And with Cameron's Conservatives in power after the 2010 general election, it looks as if Skelton's old party will be best placed to implement Blond's proposals. 'By offering public sector workers the opportunity to own and run the services which they provide,' judged the historian Matthew Francis, 'David Cameron could arguably come closer than any previous Conservative leader to fulfilling Skelton's vision.'[36]

One is reminded of John Ramsden's observation as applied to Stanley Baldwin:

> Baldwin's contribution to Conservative thought was made neither in policy nor underlying philosophy. Like most refurbishings of Conservatism, Baldwin's was concerned with attitudes and responses rather than with either abstract theory or concrete policy. Such had been Peel's basic achievement in the 1830s and Disraeli's in the 1870s; such was to be the basis for success after 1945.[37]

And, it can safely be added, the basis too for the Cameronian Conservatism of the twenty-first century. More than seventy-five years after his untimely death, Archibald Noel Skelton, one of the most unjustly forgotten figures in twentieth-century British politics, had – and has – helped to refashion constructive Conservative thinking – and perhaps continues to do so.

Appendix A

'CONSTRUCTIVE CONSERVATISM – THE OPPORTUNITY'

The Spectator, 28 April 1923

The fate of Conservatism and Unionism hangs in the balance. It must lead or perish. The issue is quite plain: is the body of political principle inherent in the words Conservatism and Unionism to be the main creative and moulding influence in the new era we are entering to-day? A moulding and creative force in politics there must be. Free nations do not live by caretakers and policemen alone; and if the Conservative Party were to redefine itself to a caretaker's job and make *per viltate il gran rifiuto* when faced with the architect's, it would itself be the bar to its principles – principles which are the point of attraction for all those better and braver elements of the nation that instinctively abhor the political mentality and morality of the Socialist. If so, it will have no second chance in our generation; but in its place will arise a hybrid organization of opinion, with compromise at the root of its thought, and for that reason presenting, in place of the massive and impressive simplicity of a homogeneous structure, the blurred and meaningless outlines of a composite photograph. Such a hybrid organization will neither have the will nor the power to apply the principles nor expound the faith which, despite much neglect and some misuse, still animate the Conservatism of the people.

Every practical man knows, of course, that between the pure political principle which lies at the core of any living Party and the expression of it in legislation or otherwise by a Government there must be some loss of quality. The wine cannot be poured from the golden to the silver cup without parting with some of its fragrance. That is one of the inevitable features of the translation of thought into action, and only a pedant would deny that if compromise has any legitimate place in men's affairs it is there. But the compromise of thought, the hybridization of underlying principles, is in quite another category. It produces sterility of action; it turns the organic into the mechanical.

Failure of the Conservative Party to realize and express the vital elements in its faith would produce a wave of disillusionment and disgust sufficient to overwhelm utterly the ship and its precious cargo. It does not help at all to recall how often, in the past, the Conservative Party has failed, when in power, to realize and express its principles, has mumbled instead of speaking out, has drawn back instead of moving on, and how, despite it all, confidence in the essential truth of these principles remains one of the deepest-rooted political instincts of Britain. But let there be no such failure this time; for one of these opportunities has arisen, for which a Party has often to wait for a generation, when the whole set and habit of its principles seem to 'jump' with the dangers and the special requirements of the time. To-day Conservatism, rightly understood and widely applied, can bring something like a real solution of our problems. It is, most certainly, more fitted to express the hopes and aims of the British people than any other set of political principles. It is only when we try to analyse the opportunity, the situation and the problem that we can realize how deep would be the ignominy and how poignant the irony of a Conservative failure. What, then, is the opportunity of the situation, the problem? The opportunity is this: Conservatism is in control of the national destiny at the very beginning of a new political era. For a new era it is; one of these times when old values have lost their meaning, old prejudices their force, old axioms their sanctity; when opinion, ideas, the minds of men are plastic. Nor is that all. Conservatism is a control by the people's choice – a highly significant fact. All beginnings are moments of instinct, and the election of November, 1922 (that national miracle which turned the water of the Carlton Club meeting into wine), was, in essence, an instinctive gesture on the part of the nation, an intuitive, subconscious recognition and reaffirmation of its trust and confidence in Conservatism.

On the writer recently expressing this view to a political friend he was met with the reply: 'But the Coalitionists thought in November, 1918, that they were the accepted heirs of the new era.' No doubt they did so think; but only because they never understood the character of their own election. They hoped it was a prologue; it was really an epilogue. The Coalition was, in fact, a War product. It could never rid itself of the smell of blood and antiseptics. It had a hospital outlook, and, regarding the nation as its patient, characteristically spent its last breath in urging it to remain 'under treatment.' But, with the callous ingratitude of the convalescent:–

> "The boy his nurse forgot
> And bore a mortal lot,"

preferring to shut the hospital doors behind him and to look the new era in the face. And the election bore the characteristic marks of a new era. The curiously simple outlook, the absence of elaborate views, the obsoleteness of old methods of controversy, the reliance on first instincts were all visible there, as they are in any form of intellectual or emotional renaissance. But the Conservative opportunity does not consist merely in being the party in power at the opening of this new era. It has, in a very special sense, a fair field.

On only one great branch of political thought and action has the country, from time to time, felt doubtful of the wisdom of the Conservative attitude. No franchise question can now arise to bring with it the risk that the country may suspect Conservatism of being the foe of popular political rights. A real danger is thus eliminated, and what has proved, again and again, the easiest avenue of attack upon Conservatism is closed. It is a remarkable paradox, of course, that the party which is instinctively trusted and understood by the people should at times, it would seem, have feared the people and therefore misunderstood them. And naturally enough, conversely, the period when the people's instinctive confidence became a deeply-reasoned and strongly-felt support was really ushered in by the Conservative Reform Act of 1867, that great act of faith in the people of this country to which the Conservative Party was led by Disraeli. It is perhaps not irrelevant to recall that the Act of 1918, which has produced a similar freedom from purely franchise questions, was passed with the support of the Conservative and Unionist Party led by a Cabinet predominantly Unionist.

So much, then, for the opportunity. It is unique: that Conservatism should have been thus preserved and approved by the people at the opening of a new era, that it should have been given the opportunity of drawing the plans and laying the foundations, that at such a moment the Conservative Party can speak as one having authority, and have a fair field for the exposition and application of its principles should surely, if anything can, fire the imagination and mobilize the best qualities of any political organism. Has the Conservative Party the imagination, the will, the courage to seize the opportunity and do an architect's work?

NOEL SKELTON.

Appendix B

CONSTRUCTIVE CONSERVATISM (1924)

PREFACE

The following chapters, with the exception of the first, appeared as three articles in *The Spectator* during May 1923. I am greatly indebted to Sir Robert Horne for adding an Introduction to them; and to Mr St Loe Strachey, both for their publication last year and for his permission to republish them now. They were then prefaced by a first article dealing with 'The Opportunity' which office gave for the development of a constructive Conservatism.

With the loss of the initiative resulting from last year's electoral defeat, that particular opportunity has passed. Yet defeat has been no unmixed evil. 1922 preserved Conservatism: 1923 consolidated it. It may well be that 1925 will see it engaged on its task of laying the foundations of a national future consonant with the traditions and the character of the race.

N.S.

September 1924.

INTRODUCTION

BY THE RIGHT HON. SIR ROBERT HORNE, G.B.E., K.C., M.P.

In a time of political unsettlement like the present it is well to review our principles and test our creeds. We have been the witnesses of a political revolution in Britain without fully realising it. The results, however, are now here for men to see. No longer do Conservatives and Liberals face each other in serried ranks, monopolising almost the whole field of party conflict. The once powerful Liberal Party has shrunk to exiguous dimensions, and a formidable Socialist group has snatched from it pride of place amongst the political sects which appeal for the suffrages of the people. Nor are the issues which divide political camps the same. The old party war-cries have for the most part died away, as a new set of problems have clamoured insistently for solution. In these circumstances we may well ask ourselves – as does the author of this admirable essay – whether the Conservative faith provides the elector with adequate guidance in our present difficulties; whether its gospel contains such a message of inspiration as will make men fight for it with conviction? All generalisations are dangerous, and they all break down in places: but if I may be permitted a very wide generalisation as to the politics of the last century, I should say that the Tory in the main was a person who was actively trying to pass measures for improving the conditions of the mass of the people, but was distinctly reluctant to enlarge the electorate: the Liberal, on the other hand, busied himself chiefly with extending the franchise, but thought it unwise to interfere with the natural play of economic laws. Now that the franchise has received the widest possible extension, the main business of the Liberal as such is gone. In social and constitutional matters he was generally a theorist in contrast to the practical character of the Tory, and the tragedy which has befallen him is that the people who like to follow theorists in politics find more will-o'-the-wisps to chase in the Promised Land of the Socialists than in the enclosed garden of Liberal doctrine. In the result the Liberal party has lost much of its strength, and it requires very little courage in prophesying to adventure the prediction that before very long we shall have in this country two main schools of thought – one preaching the practical principles of progress founded upon the maintenance of the immemorial constitution of this country, and the preservation of the utmost freedom for individual initiative; the other holding dogmas subversive and destructive of our ancient free institutions, and inculcating a policy of State restraint upon the enterprise of individual citizens as a mechanical method of achieving the millennium.

It is obvious that those who have hitherto called themselves Conservatives and Unionists will form the major portion of the first of the two schools to which I have referred. Will their faith and their conviction be adequate to the needs of these tremendous times, so fateful to our future? Mr Skelton has provided in this brief essay both a philosophy to sustain faith and a policy to inspire conviction. But he has also dwelt with some insistence upon a besetting sin of which Conservatives have need to beware. Stagnation must not be allowed to masquerade as stability. An exaggeration of a virtue may very easily become a vice, and we shall be signally lacking in our duty if we fail to put into action practical remedies for our present distresses which will commend themselves to the common-sense of the people. The reader will find in these pages a sketch of some of the practical proposals which the author commends to his Conservative comrades. Of these not the least important is that which he mentions last – namely, the institution of the Referendum. I would venture to add my own plea to Mr Skelton's argument in favour of this reform. It is in line with our democratic development – for what in a moment of doubt could be more democratic than a clear and unambiguous reference to the people? At the same time it is a safeguard which none who have reflected upon the usurpation of power in recent times by tyrannical minorities would readily forgo.

I. ARCHITECT OR CARETAKER.

Is Conservatism prepared to supply, in the new era we are entering, the main creative and moulding influence in the national life?

Liberalism cannot. Its thought is barren: its fires are cold: it sees no objective: even if it did, its energies are too exhausted to let it reach it.

Socialism, on the other hand, has force, fire, energy indeed; but its objective, if attained, spells economic disaster and moral despair; it can neither increase wealth nor develop character. The omnipotent State, the kept citizen, responsibility checked, initiative crippled, character in cold-storage, wealth squandered – towards such a goal, Britain, it may be said, will never consent to be led very far; but every step taken is a step wasted, and if a safer road with a better ending be not found for the people – if the alternatives are to be between Socialism and stagnation – the national choice will not fall on stagnation.

For a moulding and creative force there must be, since free nations do not live by caretakers and policemen alone. It is Conservatism which must do the architect's work. Nothing else is worth its while. From time to time, no doubt, there will be a demand for intervals of repose, when even the most stationary party might fulfil a useful function. But any party can 'mark time'. That calls for neither principles nor vision. It is in action that principles come into play. The caretaker's job is for those who are past work.

And, in fact, the principles of Conservatism are not only unexhausted but are exactly fitted to lead the country along the next stage of its journey. To adopt the caretaker's attitude now and refuse the architect's task would be to deprive the country of the benefits of a constructive Conservatism at the very time when most it needs it; for a positive, active alternative must be presented to the mass of the people, who are unceasingly urged to believe that in Socialism alone does there lie, for the rank and file, any hope of reaching and enjoying 'an ampler ether, a diviner air'.

Yet faith in Conservatism – subconscious, intuitive – remains to-day, as ever, the deepest-rooted political instinct of Britain. It has been a tragedy too often repeated, indeed, that the broad, sound, living national Conservatism has found itself reflected, in the purely political sphere, by a bloodless, rigid, paralysed habit of mind, which has traded on that subconscious, intuitive faith, and has often imposed what would have proved an intolerable strain on any loyalty less patient and less profound than is that of the people of Britain to the underlying truths of Conservatism.

Yet it is only by the Conservative party that the best energies of the country can be released; for it is the character of the race which feels the appeal of Conservatism; and it is only when its character is touched, that these higher energies can be liberated. Therefore, there is a work for Conservatism to-day which no other party in the State can do. If Conservatism will not do it, it will remain undone. Heavy, then, is its responsibility, if the Conservative party refuse to apply it active principles to the deeper troubles of the new era; for in these principles alone can a cure be found.

Britain, unlike France, achieved political democracy without the disaster of revolution. Whether or not a similar success can be achieved in the economic sphere, depends first and mainly upon the ability of a constructive Conservatism to apply its own principles to the problem.

Private property, in the Conservative view, is the basis of civilisation, for on it rest the character and the economic freedom of the individual citizen. To Conservatism, therefore, the way lies open to expound the greatest of all social truths – that the success and the stability of a civilisation depend upon the widest possible extension amongst its citizens of the private ownership of property.

And round private property the political combats of the future will rage: their issue will decide whether wholesale pauperisation is in store for the people, or an advance to new levels of character and responsibility: the issue itself depends upon the vision, the courage, the resource of Conservatism.

It is only when the new era is analysed, its problems stated,

Conservative principles recalled, their appropriate application suggested, that the full need for a constructive Conservatism can be realised. And whether the analysis, the statement, the application, in these pages attempted, be correct or not, this much is certain – that the battles ahead cannot be won, or the moulding, creative influence exercised, by the use of a caretaker's mop.

II. THE NEW ERA.

What then, are the main, the special features of the new era, in which Conservatism must play a constructive part, or perish? There are two on which attention must be concentrated, because in importance, in their reach and power, they stand in a class by themselves.

First, Britain is now, electorally, a complete democracy. A new and tremendous element is this in the situation, particularly because the acquisition of political rights by women has flung into the seething pot of our political life a fresh and distinctive ingredient, has brought into the general pool, and given opportunity for the expression of a mental and moral outlook, a temperament and a tradition which are different (though to what extent and even in what respects might be a matter of controversy) from those of the previous exclusively male electorate. However that may be, Conservatism, now and for the future, is face to face with democracy. Democratic electoral rights are, in a word, no longer a plank in political programmes, they are the medium in which the statesmanship of the future must work. This feature of the new era at last opens the way to the full operation of Conservative principles and, incidentally, makes it unnecessary even to mention Liberalism as a school of thought: for Liberalism, which had in the past so much to say about political freedom, has nothing to do in our era, when complete political freedom has been attained.

Secondly, the new era is one not merely of democracy, but of an educated democracy. Education is so gradual a process that its growth is easily overlooked. Yet, as in all continuous processes of growth, there are decisive moments when change is apparent. Last week the cherry was in bud, to-day it is 'hung with snow'.

Such a decisive moment was the War. In a flash, the distance which Britain had gone along the road of education was revealed. The technical ability, the rapidity in acquiring new kinds of knowledge and in mastering new duties, the self-reliance, the self-respect, the power to accept responsibility, the spontaneous facing of sacrifice, the large grasp of the issues at stake, the firmness and fineness of temper, the general spaciousness of character and outlook displayed by the men and women of Britain meant, and could only mean, that the influences of education had penetrated deeply and strongly into their minds and character. The present writer, who on four fronts saw men under the most varying conditions of danger and of dulness, has never wavered in his conviction that it was largely to the extent to which the mass of the people has absorbed the benefits of some forty years of strenuous education that we owed our achievements in the War.

And the more the temper and psychology of our people are seen and studied, the more apparent becomes the fact that ours is an educated democracy. A habit of mind, alert, sensitive, receptive, has replaced one traditionally prone to be sluggish and prejudiced. And if alertness has brought with it a wholesome inquisitiveness into the validity of traditional points of view, sensitiveness has produced a rapid appreciation of principle; and receptiveness, particularly marked in all the qualities which may be grouped under the phrase 'the social conscience', has given a remarkable power of appreciating what lawyers call 'the merits' of a question.

The change is so profound that only by a severe mental effort can the new situation it has produced be envisaged. The Conservative Party must make that mental effort, and the even greater one necessary to think out all the reactions which must follow in the political life of the people. If it does not, how can it meet the instinctive trust of the people with a view of politics fitted for the new era?

Meantime, upon this educated democracy – alert, sensitive, receptive, plastic – another Party in the State plays unceasingly, feeding the newly aroused intellectual appetites, the highly responsive social conscience, with wide and glowing general principles – comprehensive, challenging, alluring. It is to no purpose to reply that Socialism finds its strength in appeals to cupidity, envy and hatred. That may be true also: but it is the least part of the truth, and to emphasise it – much more, to treat it as fundamental – is entirely to misread the true appeal of Socialism. For the real strength of Socialism lies in the fact that it is making an intellectual appeal at the very moment when the craving for mental nourishment is so universal. It is presenting a 'view of life' to the nation in a method admirably suited to the mood and atmosphere of the new era. The Socialist finds a welcome because he comes disguised as an educator and teacher.

And just because it is presenting a comprehensive view of life, Socialism has very greatly extended the boundaries of politics. It is, of course, easy for Socialism to draw into the traditional territory of politics the whole structure of national life, for politics in its accepted meaning deals with the actions of the State and, in the Socialist ideal, the action of the State is co-extensive with the life of the nation. This widening of the territory of politics is, indeed, a reaction of the new situation, which even in the most general survey cannot be passed by unnoticed.

The battles between Whig and Tory, Unionist and Liberal, were, like those of an earlier stage of armed warfare, fought on a narrow front and by small armies of professionals, whose passage through the life of the nation affected it hardly more than a charabanc disturbs the countryside to-day – some vapour and much noise, a rut left in the highway, a film of dust on the hedgerow.

But Socialism fights on the broadest of fronts, and this breadth of front must dominate the strategy and tactics of the new era; for envelopment and the crushing defeat which successful envelopment achieves form the danger against which Conservatism must guard in the great battles ahead.

A view of life, a statement of fundamental principles, can only be met by the presentation of a truer view and of principles more fundamental. If Conservatives are not to fight with one hand tied behind their backs, the active principles of Conservatism must be felt anew, thought anew, promulgated anew. The whole intellectual content of Conservatism, its moral and economic foundations, its practical applications, must, whatever 'the mental strife' involved, be made plain to educated democracy. Conservatism must expound its 'view of life'.

Clearly this implies an extension of the functions of the Conservative politician, a new meaning, so far as he is concerned, of the word 'politics'. Conservatism believes in a restricted field for the action of the State, and most emphatically the view of life, the ideal of advance, it must present to the nation cannot be exhaustively embodied in Acts of Parliament. In the new era we must step outside the old limits and depart from the view that politics mean only public affairs, and that public affairs mean only public business. No doubt this makes politics more difficult, for it is easier to explain the provisions of a Bill than to present a 'view of life'.

But the older, narrower view is a caretaker's only: it confuses the function of the politician with that of the policeman. Historically, it is the survival into the era of educated democracy of methods which were successfully practised in the period of the triumphant bourgeoisie. But in the new era it will not serve: for it is to abandon the intellectual and moral leadership of the community: it is to withdraw from the duty of moulding and shaping public opinion. It may look like ruling: it is really abdicating.

One further word must be added. The prosperous, peach-fed classes do not readily understand the angle from which the mass of the people approach political life. To the former, politics is not a medium of education, of general culture. That side of life they have an infinite number of other means of enjoying – fastidious living, beautiful homes, the enjoyment of literature, art, travel, the closeness and variety of their points of contact with human culture and civilisation. Because their general interests are wider, the intellectual area they allot to politics is correspondingly narrower. And for those who are the heirs of 'the governing classes' of the past, politics naturally means, above all, administration.

To the mass of the people the opposite is the case. Politics is their main point of contact with general ideas; the paramount expression of the life of the community; the chief, if not the only means of satisfying their *goût des grandes choses*. But their attitude towards politics it is which makes true the definition of man as 'a political animal'; for the mass of the people feel the reality, the life, the organic, as opposed to the mechanical, quality of politics. To them political deliberation is a high function, as the gravity and sincerity of a 'popular audience' testify. If the British people do not now take their pleasures sadly, they certainly take their politics seriously.

Such, then, is the situation. A people at the dawn of a new era, equipped with full political power, educated, and still more, highly sensitive to educative influences, presented by a powerful and devoted Socialist Party with a view of politics which is really a comprehensive 'view of life', and yet instinctively trusting to their natural Conservative instincts: a Conservative Party, inclined perhaps, in common with other parties in the past, to regard politics with only a caretaker's eye, and yet, obviously, from the wider point of view, charged with the duty of expounding the Conservative 'view of life', since in it lies embedded the true solution of the fundamental problem the new era presents.

III. PROBLEM AND PRINCIPLE.

And the fundamental problem of this new era – what of it? Beneath the tangle of immediate anxieties – unemployment, the housing of the people, the agricultural emergency, the financial burdens of the State – it is possible to detect a master-problem which, while it remains unsolved, exercises a profound and malign influence upon the mental outlook and the material condition of the people?

If the analysis of the new era which has been attempted is in any degree correct, such a master-problem is not far to seek. For the mass of the people – those who mainly live by the wages of industry – political status and educational status have outstripped economic status.

The structure has become lop-sided. It is therefore unstable.

Until our educated and politically minded democracy has become predominantly a property-owning democracy, neither the national equilibrium nor the balance of the life of the individual will be restored.

To restore that balance is the master-problem of the new era.

The wage-earner has for long been attempting to solve the problem for himself. In the Co-operative movement, the Friendly Societies, the Savings Banks, and on their benefits side the Trade Unions, he has made a most determined effort to build up for himself (either by way of income to meet illness, unemployment, old age or by way of capital) 'something of his own' behind him, and the large amounts of wealth thus accumulated show how strong and persistent the impulse has been. These organizations are, indeed, the outstanding economic and social achievement of the wage-earner; they have at once exhibited, developed and tested his business capacity and his social sense, and in the steady devotion, hard work and unostentatious self-sacrifice shown in their management they have made a splendid contribution to the public life of the community. But the most remarkable proof of the wage-earner's determination to become a property-owner is to be found in the success of the War Savings Certificates scheme. Despite the fact that unemployment insurance, health insurance, and old-age pensions were in either partial or full operation when it was introduced, the steady flow of his savings, in good times and bad, into War Savings Certificates shows how fully the wage-earner appreciates the security and economic freedom which the possession of private property gives.

Yet the effort, large and fruitful as it has been, has not in itself solved the problem. And it is not difficult to see why. In the first place, it has been made by the wage-earners as a separate, isolated class. Its national importance has been overlooked. The Liberal, concentrating his attention on political rights, has passed it by. The Conservative, though he has aided it, has certainly not considered it in its full bearing upon the social structure; while the Socialist has seized the opportunity thus given him to pervert the impulse behind it into an element in the view of life which he presents; he declares, that is, that ownership by the State is ownership by the people, implying that that means a property-owing democracy. In fact, of course, it does not. What everybody owns, nobody owns; and far from expressing the wage-earner's ideal, Socialism makes it unattainable, while communal ownership, when obtained, neither interests nor influences a single human being. We have yet to hear of a man who, in the Great War, rushed to arms to preserve his share in the London County Council Tramways or in Battersea Park.

And the effort has been isolated in another sense. It has had no direct relation with the wage-earner's life as a worker. It has had nothing to do with his work. His thrift effort and his work have, moreover, not only been carried on independently, but in two opposite moods. His mood is 'Capitalist' when he saves; it is 'Labour' while he works. And the mental confusion resulting from that opposition of moods has had startling results, of which the most amazing example is the large application of the funds of the Co-operative Societies to assist and support the Socialist movement.

But more vital of all, these intense and prolonged efforts have not altered the industrial status of the wage-earner. Whatever his savings may be in the Co-operative Society, or in War Savings Certificates, the wage-earner, as industrialist, has only the economic status of a machine; for his wages, as such, are, and can only be, part of the costs of production, occupying the same position as the expenses of running the machine of the factory or workshop in which he is employed. Small wonder, then, if the wage-earner's isolated and barely recognised effort to become a property-owner has left, at the beginning of the new era, his own life and the whole social structure lop-sided and unstable.

It is these very efforts, however, which are largely responsible for the instinctive sympathy between the main body of the nation and Conservatism. Can it be doubted that the mass of the people feel that the only school of political thought which understands and is capable of solving the problem is the Conservative, and that it is for this very purpose (intuitively felt, indeed, rather than logically reasoned out) that the country preserves and approves Conservatism to-day?

For what are the principles of Conservatism, these leading ideas and ideals which are the essence of its view of life?

The first of these is the stability of the social structure. A stable condition of society is the main preoccupation of Conservatism. This is the real clue to its whole political philosophy. If change has been resisted, it has been because the Conservative has feared that it would produce confusion and instability. When it has been clear that only by change can stability be re-established, no party has been more fearless in making the most drastic changes. And similarly, the situations which have given Conservatism its moments of intense anxiety have been those when 'marginal cases' have arisen in which the problem has been whether stability is best secured by the existing conditions of by the proposed change.

And this insistence upon stability is no fad or catchword, for, as the generations come and go, the opportunity for full employment and full development to each individual during his little span of consciousness depends upon the society and community which surrounds and contains him being stable – at peace with its self, not at war.

But stability is not stagnation. Stability is as much the condition of steady progress for a society as it is for a ship. Stagnation, since life is movement, means necessarily that atrophy is at work; that tissues are dying which should be living; that dead matter is accumulating which must, by more of less violent means, be cast out. To confuse stability with stagnation is, however, from the nature of things, a special danger for Conservatism, for it is the natural defect of its real guardian of stability in the community – the school of thought which alone gives stable conditions their just valuation – it has a special duty constantly to search out the means by which stability threatened can be saved, stability lost can be recovered.

The second fundamental Conservative principle is that the character of the individual citizen being the greatest asset of the State, the primary object and best test of all legislation which deals with the individual is its influence upon his character.

Everything that weakens individual character and lessens individual effort and initiative is anathema to the Conservative. Everything that strengthens and increases these is very near to his heart. The consequences flowing from this principle are so manifold that they cannot be elaborated here. The main and most essential one is the insistence by Conservatism on the necessity of limiting the action of the State as far as possible to 'helping the individual help himself'. Further, it follows that the best kind of social legislation is that which gives to the citizens a better chance of helping themselves during their working lives, and that only second best (though admittedly essential in many cases) is direct State intervention to sustain, shelter, and support those who have failed in health or occupation. For these failures only touch the fringe of the life of the nation. It is improvement in conditions during the working life which marks the real advance.

These two leading ideas, moreover, are what give to the permanent relations existing between the British people and Conservatism their specially intimate quality; for the stability of the State and the value of character are not only the fundamental beliefs of Conservatism: they are the fundamental beliefs of the race. And these fundamental principles of Conservatism, which form the basis of its whole view of life, lead inevitably to the development of the political, the educated democracy into a property-owning democracy.

The beneficent effect upon human character both of the effort to acquire private property and of the opportunity, after it has been acquired, for its wise or foolish use, can hardly be over-estimated. For what is the effect of property, its proverbial 'magic'? In the getting, the exercise of thrift, or control, of all the qualities which 'the rolling-stone' knows nothing of; in its use, an increased sense of responsibility, a wider economic outlook, a practical medium for the expression of moral and intellectual qualities.

It is for Conservatism to see to it that this pathway to the development of character is opened wide to the people; and to expound to the nation – what no one else apparently dares or cares to – the vital inter-relation between character and private possessions.

Equally clear, equally fundamental, is the relation between the possession of private property by the people and the stability of the State. This, too, has been left for the Conservative to expound. So deeply, indeed, has Conservatism felt the importance of this relation, that in the past it was wont to maintain that only those who possessed private property should exercise political functions. That doctrine has now this new and pregnant application – that since, to-day, practically all citizens have political rights, all should possess something of their own. Mocked and jeered at in the past as 'the Party of Property', it is precisely as such, now that the wheel has turned full circle, that Conservatism in the new era holds in its keeping the key to the problem.

To make democracy stable and four-square; to give the wage-earner property and status; to bridge the economic gulf set between Labour and Capital; to present a view of life in which private property, instead of being reckoned, as the Socialist reckons it, a shameful thing, will be recognised to be an essential vehicle for the moral and economic progress of the individual; these are the tasks which the opportunity, the problem, and its own principles alike call Conservatism to perform in the new era.

IV. DEMOCRACY STABILISED.

In the proceeding pages an attempt has been made to sketch the main features of the new era, and to indicate the opportunity which opens to a constructive Conservatism to solve the problem it presents. It remains to state as clearly as may be some of the means which lie ready to develop a property-owning democracy, to bring the industrial and economic status of the wage-earner abreast of his political and educational, to make democracy stable and four-square.

These (to mention only subjects of the widest importance) are, it is submitted, four: (1) for the wage-earner, whether in factory or in field, industrial co-partnery, or its halfway house, profit-sharing; (2) for the agriculturist, who seeks to become completely his own master, small ownership; (3) for the rural world as a whole, agricultural co-operation; (4) for the community, to secure it against sudden assault, the Referendum.

One common principle underlies these proposals, making them a practical and accurate expression of the Conservative 'view of life', for each, in its own way and in its own sphere, at once develops the character of the individual, and the stability of the social structure. It may be objected that, of these, co-partnery and profit-sharing cannot successfully be brought into operation by Act of Parliament, but must grow as the nation's understanding of them grows. So be it – though the extent to which the State can induce the adoption of profit-sharing by legislation has never been zealously or exhaustively explored. All the more natural and essential it is that Conservatism should make this great topic its own: for it offers a means of economic, social and national progress which the State cannot dole out with a spoon. And if Conservatism fails to show the nation an alternative line of advance, it would have to bear the blame should the people come to the conclusion that the only way forward lay along the Socialist path, however desperate and perilous that might be.

(1) First, then, as to industrial co-partnery. It rests on a firm basis of principle. Capital and Labour by it are to the full recognised as partners in the work of the production of wealth, for each shares in the true profits of that production, arrived at after each, the one by way of a fair rate of interest, the other by way of a fair wage, has been paid the price for its services in the common work. And further, the wage-earner's proportion of the profits is paid to him partly in cash, partly invested for him in the concern, while, as the workers become capitalists, 'seats on the Board', either for the domestic internal government of the concern, or for its general direction, very naturally follow.

Thus status and property-owning grow together; the wage-earner, as industrialist, from a machine becomes a man. Nor is this all. To the wage-earner, co-partnery brings a new incentive and a new kind of interest in his work, arising out of his new relation to it; a union of his thrift effort and his work effort; a wider industrial outlook, since, as his savings in the business increase, so does his interest in its general prosperity, for that prosperity affects him directly as a shareholder.

To the community it brings all the results that flow from a real identification of interest between Capital and Labour – reduction of the number of strikes, with their waste of the national wealth and dislocation of the national life; the elimination of such crazy doctrines as that of 'ca' canny' [being cautious]; improvement in the standard of both management and work, since the wage-earner will not readily submit to his own work being neutralised by the slackness of his neighbour, or the incompetence of his manager.

Moreover, co-partnery is clearly on the broad highway of economic evolution, for it is the next available incentive to increased productivity. Increase of wages and reduction of the hours of labour have both contributed largely in the last hundred years to this result. But it is more than doubtful whether both of these factors have not exhausted their impetus, and from a purely economic point of view are not now 'squeezed oranges'.

And finally, the development of co-partnery and profit-sharing is the natural and obvious concomitant of any system of protecting British industry. For it has told against Tariff Reform that it has seemed to many to be the sole constructive suggestion which Conservatism had to make, and it has, perhaps in consequence, acquired almost the character of a substitute for, instead of a part of, a general policy of improving the status of the wage-earner. Certainly many opponents have made haste to point out to the working classes that, in the existing industrial system, the lion's share of any advantage would, in their opinion, fall to Capital rather than Labour.

Such a criticism would be of no avail under a system in which employer and employee clearly shared alike in the increased prosperity.

Yet there are objections. It is said, 'Some industries are not suited to the system.' Possibly not. But has there yet been any determined effort to work out in practice the modifications necessary to make it suit the special circumstances of particular trades? The overcoming of practical difficulties is a matter for resource and will-power, once the value of the underlying principle is realised. Conservatism in the new era must refute Anatole France's mocking remark that moderate men are those who have only a moderate belief in moderate opinions.

And again, 'The Trade Unions are against it.' Perhaps their Socialist leaders are, but battle has to be joined with them in any case. That the great mass of the wage-earners is hostile can hardly be maintained, since the fact is that no political party has yet seriously addressed itself to the exposition of co-partnery in all its bearings. In any case, co-partnery is the ideal ground on which to fight Socialism, for it emphasizes the distinction, fundamental but neglected, between a property-owning democracy and the Socialist ideal, and if the Trade Union leaders hide from their followers the more excellent way, so much the worse, when the truth is discovered, for them and for their leadership.

If, therefore, the master-problem in our highly industrialised country be how to bring the economic status of the wage-earner abreast of his political and educational, the master-key to that problem is clearly industrial co-partnery.

(2) Of small ownership in land, only a word can be said. In principle, generally recognised to be a most powerful factor in the stability of the State and in the development of a rural democracy of character and intelligence, the policy of small holdings has greatly suffered in Great Britain from the methods which have been adopted. Extravagant expenditure on equipment and administration by Government departments or County Councils has been combined with demands for payments from the holder, based upon the principle of making him pay rent for the land, and in addition interest on the full cost of erecting the buildings. No private landowner gets an annual return if he lets his land, or a purchase price if he sells it, calculated in this way. The result has been that our State-constituted buildings have imposed on their cultivators burdens which no other agriculturists in Britain have to bear. The resettlement of the land of England and Scotland, the development of intensive cultivation, the reconstitution of the rural community, are matters so vital that every effort to devise sounder methods of instituting small holdings than those presently in operation must be made by Conservatism. And this is pre-eminently a problem which Conservative knowledge and resource can solve. Let it not be forgotten that the Wyndham Land Act was the last and greatest constructive work which Unionism did for Ireland.

(3) And agricultural co-operation. The foundation of modern agricultural throughout the world, the way to prosperity for the small cultivator and large farmer alike, it is inextricably bound up with the Conservative view of life, because it is essentially the means whereby in the cultivation of the soil the individual can be helped to help himself. On this there can safely be neither silence nor indifference. All that the State can do, all that the politicians can say, should be said and done to spread knowledge and assist the development of agricultural co-operation, if in the new era Conservatism is prepared to give of its best to the nation.

And if it be here objected that apparently all parties in the State are alive to the importance of agricultural co-operation, it must be said, in rejoinder, that so preponderating is the influence of Conservative thought on at least two out of the three great agricultural classes, that without active and ardent Conservative support and exposition, confidence in co-operative principles in agriculture would advance only at a snail's pace, since distrust of Liberalism is complete in rural England, and is rapidly increasing in rural Scotland, while the country populations of both nations agree in their contempt for the town-bred fallacies of Socialism.

(4) But to pass to the Referendum – crown and apex of a constructive Conservatism in the new era. Accepted by Conservatives in the Constitutional crisis of 1910–1911, its value and necessity are infinitely more obvious now. It was called for then to save the House of Lords; it is needed now to protect democracy. For if democracy, faced in the new era by Socialism as its scarcely disguised enemy, is, from a constitutional point of view, to be made stable and safe, if its property and liberty are to be preserved, the people, in the last resort, must directly and for themselves develop their own fate. And for this duty they are ripe. Meantime, it needs only a blunder or two on the part of a Cabinet, a General Election dominated by passion or prejudice, and the flank of the Constitution is turned. The task of Conservatism in the new era would be only half done if the British democracy were to be denied a means of protection the value of which has been amply proved elsewhere.

And, in conclusion, whatever means be taken to stabilise democracy, this much is clear – that the Conservative Party cannot leave it a matter of guesswork what its outlook is. 'Democracy', Lord Balfour once said, 'is government by explanation.' The mass of the people are profoundly perplexed by the paradox that Conservatism, in which they have so deep an instinctive belief, is apparently content to leave its view of life unexplained, its principles unstated, while Socialism, which they distrust exceedingly, is fearless and untiring in setting out its aims and ideals. Liberalism is dying because its principles are dead. It will fare ill with Conservatism unless it breaks its silence and makes clear to the nation that it, too, has a vision of the future – of a property-owning democracy, master of its own life, made foursquare and secure, and able therefore to withstand the shrill and angry gales which, in the new era's uneasy dawn, sweep across the world of men.

BIBLIOGRAPHY

ARCHIVES

Earl of Avon (Sir Anthony Eden) (University of Birmingham)
Stanley Baldwin (University of Cambridge)
BFI National Library
Conservative & Unionist Associations & Clubs (Perth Archives)
Baroness Elliot of Harwood (Private collection at Crathorne House)
Walter and Katharine Elliot Papers (National Library of Scotland)
Sir Cuthbert Headlam (Durham County Record Office)
Harold Macmillan (Bodleian Library, Oxford)
National Union Gleanings and Continuations 1893–1968 (British Library)
Scotland's Record (National Library of Scotland)
Scottish Office (National Archives of Scotland)
Scottish Universities' Unionist Association (University of Glasgow)
Speculative Society
John St Loe Strachey (Parliamentary Archives)
Baron Wakehurst (John de Vere Loder) (Parliamentary Archives)
World War I officer files (National Archives, Kew)

PUBLISHED SOURCES

Atholl, Duchess of, *Working Partnership: Being the Lives of John George 8th Duke of Atholl and of His Wife Katharine Marjory Ramsay* (London: Arthur Barker, 1958)
Ball, Stuart, ed., *Parliament and Politics in the Age of Baldwin and MacDonald: The Headlam Diaries 1923–1935* (London: Historians' Press, 1992)
Boothby, Robert, *I Fight to Live* (London: Victor Gollancz, 1947)
Boothby, Robert, *My Yesterday, Your Tomorrow* (London: Hutchinson, 1962)
Boothby, Robert et al., *Industry and the State: A Conservative View* (London: Macmillan, 1927)

Butler, Lord, *The Art of the Possible: The Memoirs of Lord Butler, KG, CH* (London: Hamish Hamilton, 1971)

Coote, Colin, *A Companion of Honour: The Story of Walter Elliot* (London: Collins, 1965)

Coote, Colin R., *Editorial: The Memoirs of Colin R. Coote* (London: Eyre & Spottiswoode, 1965)

Crosland, Anthony, *The Future of Socialism*, new ed. (London: Constable, 2006)

David Dutton, *Anthony Eden: A Life and Reputation* (London: Hodder Arnold, 1996)

Eden, Anthony, *Memoirs, vol. I: Facing the Dictators* (London: Cassell, 1962)

Fraser, Sir Hugh, *The Representation of the People Act, 1918: With Explanatory Notes* (London: Sweet & Maxwell, 1918)

Green, E. H. H., *Ideologies of Conservatism: Conservative Political Ideas in the Twentieth Century* (Oxford: Oxford University Press, 2002)

Home, Lord, *The Way the Wind Blows: An Autobiography* (London: Collins, 1976)

Horne, Alistair, *Macmillan, vol. II: 1957–1986* (London: Macmillan, 1988)

James, Robert Rhodes, *Bob Boothby: A Portrait* (London: Hodder & Stoughton, 1991)

Levitt, Ian, *The Scottish Office: Depression and Reconstruction 1919–1959* (Edinburgh: Scottish History Society, 1992)

Macmillan, Harold, *Winds of Change 1914–1939* (London: Macmillan, 1966)

Macmillan, Harold, *Tides of Fortune 1945–1955* (London: Macmillan, 1969)

National Union Gleanings and Continuations 1893–1968 (Hassocks: Harvester, 1973)

Nicolson, Harold, *King George the Fifth: His Life and Reign* (London: Constable, 1952)

Norwich, John Julius, ed., *The Duff Cooper Diaries 1915–1951* (London: Weidenfeld & Nicolson, 2005)

Pottinger, George, *The Secretaries of State for Scotland 1926–76: Fifty Years of the Scottish Office* (Edinburgh: Scottish Academic Press, 1979)

Ramsden, John, *The Age of Churchill and Eden 1940–1957* (London: Longman, 1995)

Ramsden, John, *A History of the Conservative Party, vol. III: The Age of Balfour and Baldwin 1902–1940* (London: Longman, 1978)

Ridley, Jane, 'The Unionist Social Reform Committee, 1911–14: Wets Before the Deluge', *Historical Journal* (1987), vol. 30, pp. 391–413

Roberts, Andrew, *Salisbury: Victorian Titan* (London: Weidenfeld & Nicolson, 1999)

Sanders, Robert, *Real Old Tory Politics: The Political Diaries of Sir Robert Sanders, Lord Bayford, 1910–35*, ed. John Ramsden (London: Historians' Press, 1984)

Self, Robert, ed., *The Neville Chamberlain Diary Letters, vol. II: The Reform Years 1921–27* (Aldershot: Ashgate, 2000)

Skelton, John, *The Table-Talk of Shirley: Reminiscences of, and Letters from,
    Froude, Thackeray, Disraeli, Browning, Rossetti, Kingsley, Baynes, Huxley,
    Tyndall, and Others* (Edinburgh: William Blackwood, 1895)

Skelton, Noel, *Constructive Conservatism* (Edinburgh: William Blackwood, 1924)

Skelton, Noel, *A Note on the Situation* (Perth 1931)

Smith, F. E., *'Unionist Policy' and Other Essays* (London: Williams & Norgate, 1913)

Strachey, John St Loe, *The Referendum: A Handbook to the Poll of the People,
    Referendum, or Democratic Right of Veto on Legislation* (London: T. Fisher
    Unwin, 1924)

Thorpe, D. R., *Alec Douglas-Home* (London: Sinclair-Stevenson, 1996)

Thorpe, D. R., *Eden: The Life and Times of Anthony Eden, First Earl of Avon, 1897–
    1977* (London: Chatto & Windus, 2003)

Tweedsmuir, Susan, *John Buchan, by His Wife and Friends* (London: Hodder &
    Stoughton, 1947)

Warner, Gerald, *The Scottish Tory Party: A History* (London: Weidenfeld &
    Nicolson, 1988)

Woolton, Earl of, *The Memoirs of the Rt. Hon. the Earl of Woolton CH, PC, DL, LlD*
    (London: Cassell, 1959)

Young, Kenneth, *Sir Alec Douglas-Home* (London: J. M. Dent, 1970)

Unpublished sources

Gatland, Paul Gordon, 'The "YMCA" and the Search for a Constructive
    Conservatism in Britain 1924–1929', PhD dissertation, University of London
    (1990)

Lee, Nick, 'Creating a "Property-owning Democracy": the Conservative Party and
    Popular Capitalism 1918–1951', MA dissertation, University of Durham (2007)

Wakehurst, Lord, 'A Look at the Century', unpublished memoirs (c. 1950)

NOTES

Acknowledgements
1. www.politicos.co.uk/pages/Aspects_of_Political_Biography.htm?g

Introduction
1. E. H. H. Green, *Ideologies of Conservatism: Conservative Political Ideas in the Twentieth Century* (Oxford: Oxford University Press, 2002), pp. 2–3.
2. *The Times*, 18 February 1926.
3. *The Scotsman*, 29 June 1933.
4. *The Times*, 4 April 1949.
5. *The Times*, 11 February 1950.
6. *The Times*, 13 February 1950.
7. *The Scotsman*, 14 February 1950.
8. *The Times*, 20 February 1950.
9. *The Times*, 31 August 1974.
10. *The Times*, 22 April 1955.
11. *The Times*, 13 September 1963.
12. *The Times*, 4 March 1964.
13. *The Times*, 17 October 1981.
14. *Sunday AM*, BBC One, 13 May 2005.

Chapter 1: 'The hero of a Disraeli novel come to life'
1. Susan Tweedsmuir, John Buchan, *by His Wife and Friends* (London: Hodder & Stoughton, 1947), p. 204.
2. Anon., 'Skelton, Sir John (1831–1897)', rev. Sayoni Basu, in H. C. G. Matthew and Brian Harrison (eds), *Oxford Dictionary of National Biography* (Oxford: Oxford University Press, 2004).
3. Sir John Skelton, *The Table-Talk of Shirley: Reminiscences of and Letters from Froude, Thackeray, Disraeli, Browning, Rossetti, Kingsley, Baynes, Huxley, Tyndall and Others* (Edinburgh: William Blackwood, 1895), p. 184.
4. Hansard, HC Deb, 5 March 1928, vol. 214, col. 865.

5. Lady Skelton continued to live at the Hermitage until 1922, where her son was also resident immediately before and after the First World War.

6. Details of Skelton's schooldays are recorded in copies of the college magazine, the *Glenalmond Chronicle*.

7. 'I could not have afforded to have gone to Oxford', Skelton told the House during a 1934 debate, 'had I not been fortunate enough to be successful in a competitive scholarship examination at Christchurch' (Hansard, HC Deb, 19 December 1934, vol. 296, cols 1160–61).

8. Minutes of the Speculative Society from 1896 to 1909.

9. The Conservative Party at this time was known as the 'Unionists' as a result of an informal alliance with Liberal Unionists, who were opposed to home rule in Ireland. Both names are used hereafter in the text, together with the more informal nomenclature of 'Tory' and 'Tories'.

10. *The Scotsman*, 5 November 1910.

11. *The Scotsman*, 24 November 1910. The preamble to the Parliament Act of 1911 indicated that the House of Lords would become an elected, rather than an hereditary, body.

12. *The Scotsman*, 25 November 1910.

13. *The Scotsman*, 30 November 1910.

14. *The Scotsman*, 7 December 1910.

15. *The Scotsman*, 9 December 1910.

16. *The Scotsman*, 15 December 1910.

17. *Perthshire Advertiser*, 14 December 1910.

18. *The Scotsman*, 9 February 1911.

19. *The Scotsman*, 25 February 1911.

20. *The Scotsman*, 10 July 1911.

21. *The Scotsman*, 22 July 1911.

22. *The Scotsman*, 5 August 1911.

23. The Primrose League, named after Disraeli's favourite flower, was an organisation that promoted Conservative principles.

24. *The Scotsman*, 9 October 1911. Skelton also claimed that creating a Home Rule Parliament would simply provide 'a little cockpit for Irish Catholics and Protestants to fight in' (*The Scotsman*, 15 January 1912).

25. *The Scotsman*, 9 October 1911.

26. *The Scotsman*, 15 January 1912.

27. *The Scotsman*, 26 February 1912.

28. *The Scotsman*, 29 February 1912.

29. *The Scotsman*, 15 June 1912.

30. *The Scotsman*, 30 November 1912.

31. *The Scotsman*, 20 February 1913.

32. *The Scotsman*, 5 March 1913.

33. *The Scotsman*, 4 December 1913.

34. Jane Ridley, 'The Unionist Social Reform Committee, 1911–1914: Wets before the Deluge', *Historical Journal* (1987), vol. 30, p. 403.

35. *The Scotsman*, 22 March 1913.

36. *The Scotsman*, 25 October 1913.

37. *The Scotsman*, 16 December 1913.

38. *The Scotsman*, 9 January 1914.

39. *The Scotsman*, 26 January 1914.

40. F. E. Smith, *'Unionist Policy' and Other Essays* (London: Williams & Norgate, 1913), p. 19.

41. World War I officer files WO 374/62742.

42. *The Scotsman*, 30 October 1918.

43. *The Scotsman*, 23 November 1935.

44. This new division, created following the 1918 Representation of the People Act, embraced the town of Perth as well as the old Eastern Division.

45. *The Scotsman*, 18 November 1918.

46. *The Scotsman*, 23 November 1935.

Chapter 2: 'A graceful and witty pen'

1. *The Scotsman*, 16 October 1922.

2. *The Scotsman*, 26 October 1922.

3. *The Scotsman*, 2 November 1922.

4. *The Scotsman*, 3 November 1922.

5. *The Scotsman*, 7 November 1922.

6. John Ramsden, *A History of the Conservative Party, vol. III: The Age of Balfour and Baldwin 1902–1940* (London: Longman, 1978), pp. 171–2.

7. *The Scotsman*, 20 November 1922.

8. *The Times*, 20 February 1923. Watson was later found a constituency in Carlisle.

9. Hansard, HC Deb, vol. 160, col. 1389.

10. Ibid., col. 1390.

11. *The Times*, 23 February 1923.

12. Hansard, HC Deb, vol. 160, cols 1391–2.

13. *The Times*, 23 February 1923.

14. Philip Williamson, 'Skelton, (Archibald) Noel (1880–1935)', in H. C. G. Matthew and Brian Harrison (eds), *Oxford Dictionary of National Biography* (Oxford: Oxford University Press, 2004); online ed., ed. Lawrence Goldman, January 2008, http://www.oxforddnb.com/view/article/40226.

15. D. R. Thorpe, *Eden: The Life and Times of Anthony Eden, First Earl of Avon, 1897–1977* (London: Chatto & Windus, 2003), p. 41.

16. *The Spectator*, 28 April 1923.

17. *The Spectator*, 5 May 1923.

18. Strachey papers, STR/19/5/11b.

19. Strachey papers, STR/19/5/11a. Strachey's 'Referendum book' appeared in

1924 as *The Referendum: A Handbook to the Poll of the People, Referendum, or Democratic Right of Veto on Legislation.*

20. *The Spectator*, 12 May 1923.

21. *The Spectator*, 19 May 1923. The Wyndham Land Act of 1903 had made it easier for Irish tenants to purchase land, eventually facilitating the transfer of around 9 million acres.

22. *The Spectator*, 19 May 1923.

23. Skelton was not always so serious. 'I was astonished when, on returning to Broadmeadows Cottage for supper, he completely dropped the manner of the earnest young politician and spent the remainder of the evening telling us Scots stories,' recalled Lady Tweedsmuir. 'I laughed a great deal, for Noel was the best of mimics and never over-stressed his points.' (Susan Tweedsmuir, *John Buchan, by His Wife and Friends* (London: Hodder & Stoughton, 1947), p. 204).

24. *The Spectator*, 26 May 1923.

25. Strachey papers, STR/2/13/1. Boothby later attempted his own definition of Conservative philosophy, with obvious Skelton influences. 'We can avoid the class war, and free the spirit of man,' he wrote, 'if we can create a property-owning democracy, on a foundation of social justice' (Robert Boothby, *I Fight to Live* (London: Victor Gollancz, 1947), p. 387).

26. Strachey papers, STR/2/3/1.

27. Strachey papers, STR/2/3/7.

28. Strachey papers, STR/2/3/8.

29. Strachey papers, STR/19/5/26a.

30. Strachey papers, STR/19/5/33a.

31. Ramsden, *A History of the Conservative Party, vol. III*, p. 178.

32. Ibid., p. 180.

33. *The Spectator*, 10 November 1923.

34. *The Scotsman*, 22 November 1923.

35. *The Spectator*, 24 November 1923.

36. *The Spectator*, 1 December 1923.

37. *The Scotsman*, 8 December 1923. Although Skelton lost Perth, the colourful Duchess of Atholl won West Perthshire for the Unionists, becoming Scotland's first female MP with a majority of just 150.

38. Ramsden, *A History of the Conservative Party, vol. III*, p. 183.

Chapter 3: 'A policy to inspire conviction'

1. Skelton even refused a presentation from the Perth Conservatives 'as he was not leaving them' (Conservative & Unionist Associations & Clubs, MS152 13/1/1).

2. John Ramsden, *A History of the Conservative Party, vol. III: The Age of Balfour and Baldwin 1902–1940* (London: Longman, 1978), p. 190.

3. Ibid., p. 187.

4. Skelton continued his work as an external examiner, also in history, at Edinburgh University for several years.

5. *The Spectator*, 12 January 1924.

6. Strachey papers, STR/19/6/3b.

7. Strachey papers, STR/19/6/6a.

8. Strachey papers, STR/19/6/6c. Younger was a former Unionist Party chairman.

9. Strachey papers, STR/19/6/6b.

10. *The Spectator*, 3 May 1924.

11. *The Times*, 26 March 1924.

12. *Ramsden, A History of the Conservative Party, vol. III*, p. 214.

13. Henry St John, 1st Viscount Bolingbroke (1678–1751), was an English politician and a leading spokesman for liberty and republicanism.

14. *The Spectator*, 12 July 1924.

15. *The Spectator*, 2 August 1924. As a result of this letter Loder was invited to stand for East Leicester, which he won at the 1924 general election.

16. *The Independent*, 6 September 1998.

17. Noel Skelton, *Constructive Conservatism* (Edinburgh: William Blackwood, 1924), p. 6, reproduced in Appendix B of this book on p. 227.

18. *The Spectator*, 1 December 1923. Lord Balfour of Burleigh had been secretary for Scotland from 1895 until 1903.

19. Andrew Roberts, *Salisbury: Victorian Titan* (London: Weidenfeld & Nicolson, 1999), p. 586.

20. Skelton, *Constructive Conservatism*, pp. 7–10, reproduced in Appendix B of this book on pp. 228–30.

21. *The Spectator*, 3 May 1924.

22. Strachey papers, STR/19/6/30c.

23. Strachey papers, STR/19/6/30b. Strachey wrote to Sir Robert Horne the same day: 'I am so glad you liked Noel Skelton's articles, I always thought them splendid; he is a first-rate man.' (STR/19/6/34a.)

24. Strachey papers, STR/19/6/30d.

25. Strachey papers, STR/19/3/30f.

26. *The Scotsman*, 29 October 1924.

27. *The Scotsman*, 31 October 1924.

28. Strachey papers, STR/19/6/30g.

Chapter 4: 'A great political teacher'

1. Interestingly, in a letter to Strachey dated 16 November 1924, Skelton wrote: 'I see you say good things of Churchill. No doubt these are right: but I feel that he is . . . of course, essentially a Die-Hard with a very distant strain of class prejudice in him.' (Strachey papers, STR/19/6/30e.)

2. Boothby wrote a regular column for *The Spectator* throughout the 1924 parliament, while Duff Cooper (under the pseudonym 'Watchman') wrote each week in the *Saturday Review* a column called 'The Comedy of Westminster'.

3. Captain Hon. John de Vere Loder (1895–1970) was the MP for East Leicester

from 1924 to 1929 and the Lewes Division of Sussex from 1931 to 1936. As Baron Wakehurst he was governor of New South Wales and later Northern Ireland. He married Margaret 'Peggy' Tennant – a daughter of the Liberal politician Sir Charles Tennant – in 1919, whose sisters later married two other former YMCAers, Thomas Dugdale (Nancy Tennant) in 1936 and Walter Elliot (Katharine Tennant) in 1934.

4. Oliver Harvey to John Loder, 7 November 1924, Wakehurst papers, WAK/4/2.

5. Harold Macmillan to John Loder, 5 November 1924, Wakehurst papers, WAK/4/2.

6. Oliver Frederick George Stanley (1896–1950), son of the 17th Earl of Derby, sat for Westmorland from 1924 to 1945 and Bristol West from 1945 until his death in 1950. He was PPS to the president of the Board of Education from 1924 to 1929.

7. Robert Spear Hudson (1886–1957) was a diplomat before becoming the MP for Whitehaven from 1924 to 1929 and Southport from 1931 to 1952.

8. Skelton had encouraged Boothby to apply for a seat, and soon after his election in East Aberdeenshire Skelton wrote admiringly: 'Right from the first he threw himself into the battle at Westminster, and he has developed a Lobby activity and House of Commons sense which some men take years to acquire.' (Robert Rhodes James, *Boothby: A Portrait* (London: Hodder & Stoughton, 1991), p. 65.) 'He put me into politics,' recalled Boothby in 1955. 'It took me a long time to forgive him for that.' (Hansard, HC Deb, 16 June 1955, vol. 542, col. 818.)

9. Sir Terence James O'Connor (1891–1940) sat for the Luton Division of Bedfordshire from 1924 to 1929 and later became solicitor-general.

10. Harold Macmillan, *Winds of Change 1914–1939* (London: Macmillan, 1966), p. 178.

11. Robert Boothby, *My Yesterday, Your Tomorrow* (London: Hutchinson, 1962), pp. 138–9.

12. Lord Wakehurst, 'A Look at the Century', pp. 26–7, Wakehurst papers, WAK/2/5.

13. Hansard, HC Deb, 26 March 1925, vol. 182, col. 773.

14. Harold Nicolson, *King George the Fifth: His Life and Reign* (London: Constable, 1952), p. 423.

15. *The Times* 5 December 1924.

16. *National Union Gleanings and Continuations* (1925), vol. 61, p. 88.

17. *The Spectator*, 13 December 1924.

18. Strachey papers, STR/19/6/34d.

19. Strachey papers, STR/2/13/9.

20. Strachey papers, STR/19/6/30h.

21. John Ramsden, *A History of the Conservative Party, vol. III: The Age of Balfour and Baldwin 1902–1940* (London: Longman, 1978), pp. 265–6.

22. *Quarterly Review* (1925), vol. 244, no. 483. On Labour's recent financial record, Skelton was more understanding. Lady Tweedsmuir recalled, 'An old lady timidly asked him if he did not think the Labour Government which had recently

relinquished power had been alarmingly extravagant? He replied, "No more than a Conservative or indeed any other kind – all Governments are hopeless about money." (Susan Tweedsmuir, *John Buchan, by His Wife and Friends* (London: Hodder & Stoughton, 1947), p. 205.)

23. *Quarterly Review* (1925), vol. 244, no. 483.

24. Frederick Alexander Macquisten (1870–1940) was, like Skelton, an advocate. He sat for the Springburn Division of Glasgow from 1918 to 1922 and Argyll from 1924 to 1940. The full name of his private member's bill was the Trade Union (Political Fund) Bill.

25. John Julius Norwich (ed.), *The Duff Cooper Diaries 1915–1951* (London: Weidenfeld & Nicolson, 2005), p. 208. Cooper continued: 'The Prime Minister replied that he regretted the division in the party but there it had to be faced. One side would be disappointed, and that was all he could say at present.'

26. Macmillan, *Winds of Change*, p. 171.

27. Hansard, HC Deb, 6 March 1925, vol. 181, cols 840–41. Baldwin was paraphrasing ('peace in our time') Disraeli on his return from the 1878 Congress of Berlin, as was Neville Chamberlain following his meeting with Hitler during the Munich crisis.

28. Macmillan, *Winds of Change*, p. 171.

29. Hansard, HC Deb, 31 March, vol. 193, col. 2281.

30. *The Times*, 3 August 1925.

31. Hansard, HC Deb, 26 March 1925, vol. 182, cols 775–6.

32. *Quarterly Review* (1925), vol. 245, no. 485.

33. Strachey papers, STR/20/1/13h.

34. The Referendum Bill of 1911; see p. 62.

35. Strachey papers, STR/20/1/5f.

36. Strachey papers, STR/20/1/13c.

37. Strachey papers, STR/20/1/13d.

38. Strachey papers, STR/20/1/13g.

39. John St Loe Strachey, *The Referendum: A Handbook to the Poll of the People, Referendum, or Democratic Right of Veto on Legislation* (London: T. Fisher Unwin, 1924).

40. *The Scotsman*, 13 May 1925.

41. Until the late 1950s Scottish peers elected sixteen of their number to sit in the House of Lords following 'general elections' held at Holyroodhouse at around the same time as UK general elections.

42. Sir William Bull papers, HC/LB/1/38/A/1g.

43. Robert Sanders, *Real Old Tory Politics: The Political Diaries of Sir Robert Sanders, Lord Bayford 1910–35* (London: Historians Press, 1984), entry for 14 July 1926.

44. *Quarterly Review* (1926), vol. 247, no. 490.

45. *The Scotsman*, 3 March 1926.

46. The retailer Debenhams later occupied this building.

47. *English Review* (1926), vol. 43.

48. Robert Self, ed., *The Neville Chamberlain Diary Letters, vol. II: The Reform Years 1921-27* (Aldershot: Ashgate, 2000), pp. 360–61.

49. Hansard, HC Deb, 3 May 1926, vol. 195, cols 149–52.

50. During the General Strike the YMCA's Oliver Stanley stood in as the stationmaster at Westminster Underground station, while John Loder worked at the booking office.

51. *The Times*, 22 May 1926.

52. Hansard, HC Deb, 29 June 1926, vol. 197, cols 1020–22.

53. Noel Skelton to Sidney Herbert, 31 October 1926, Baldwin papers, vol. 11, ff. 21–2.

54. *Quarterly Review* (1926), vol. 247, no. 490.

55. *The Times*, 7 December 1926.

56. Noel Skelton to Cuthbert Headlam, 18 December 1926, Sir Cuthbert Headlam papers. D/He/126/198.

57. Paul Gordon Gatland, 'The "YMCA" and the Search for a Constructive Conservatism in Britain, 1924–1929' (1990), PhD dissertation, University of London, p. 377.

58. Hansard, HC Deb, 14 February 1927, vol. 202, col. 669.

59. Robert Boothby et al., *Industry and the State* (London: Macmillan, 1927), 13.

60. Wakehurst, 'A Look at the Century', p. 28.

61. The 3rd Lord Tweedsmuir remembered Skelton staying at Elsfield from 8 to 11 June 1923, when he was seven years old. He said Skelton was always spoken of 'in tones of admiration' by his parents (Lord Tweedsmuir to the author, 8 January 2007).

62. Tweedsmuir, *John Buchan*, p. 52.

63. Hansard, HC Deb, 6 July 1927, vol. 208, col. 1316.

64. Hansard, HC Deb, 6 July 1927, vol. 208, col. 1334.

65. Tweedsmuir, *John Buchan*, p. 205.

66. Ibid., p. 63.

67. Ibid., pp. 205–6.

68. Hansard, HC Deb, 9 May 1927, vol. 206, cols 84–8.

69. John St Loe Strachey died in 1927, depriving Skelton of an important journalistic patron.

70. *Quarterly Review* (1927), vol. 248, no. 492. According to the minutes of Skelton's constituency association he also wrote and distributed a pamphlet on socialism during March 1927. This does not seem to have survived.

71. Hansard, HC Deb, 1928, vol. 213, col. 605.

72. Hansard, HC Deb, 5 March 1928, vol. 214, cols 863–71.

73. Hansard, HC Deb, 9 July 1928, vol. 219, cols 1975–9.

74. Hansard, HC Deb, 18 May 1928, vol. 217, col. 1462. This concern at the rising

level of 'Irish blood' in Scotland was, in the late 1920s, a commonly held view, not least among members of the Church of Scotland.

75. Hansard, HC Deb, 3 December 1928, vol. 223, col. 967.

76. Hansard, HC Deb, 20 February 1929, vol. 225, col. 1248.

77. Hansard, HC Deb, 23 May 1928, vol. 217, col. 2105.

78. Chamberlain had addressed a meeting of Skelton's constituents at Perth City Hall on 30 January 1928, suggesting the two knew each other reasonably well.

79. Johnston was elected a Conservative MP in 1931.

80. *The Scotsman*, 18 November 1989.

81. Colin Coote, *A Companion of Honour: The Story of Walter Elliot* (London: Collins, 1965), p. 148.

82. Noel Skelton to Katharine Tennant, 29 July 1928, Baroness Elliot of Harwood papers.

83. Skelton to Tennant, 3 August 1928.

84. Skelton to Tennant, 4 August 1928.

85. Skelton to Tennant, 5 August 1928.

86. Skelton to Tennant, 8 August 1928.

87. Skelton to Tennant, 19 August 1928.

88. Skelton to Tennant, 20 August 1928.

89. Skelton to Tennant, 23 August 1928.

90. Skelton to Tennant, 30 August 1928.

91. Skelton to Tennant, 4 September 1928.

92. Skelton to Tennant, undated but c. late 1928.

93. Skelton had earlier resided at 11 Castle Street, also in Edinburgh.

94. Skelton to Tennant, 4 October 1928.

95. Skelton to Tennant, 10 October 1928.

96. Skelton to Tennant, 17 October 1928.

97. Skelton to Tennant, 19 October 1928.

98. Skelton to Tennant, 19 October 1928 (second letter).

99. Skelton to Tennant, 21 October 1928.

100. Skelton to Tennant, 23 October 1928.

101. In fact, it was Macmillan who suggested a scheme for alleviating industry by de-rating (removing or reducing rates) to the Chancellor, Winston Churchill.

102. Stuart Ball (ed.), *Parliament and Politics in the Age of Baldwin and MacDonald: The Headlam Diaries 1923–1935* (London: Historians' Press, 1992), p. 169. Bob Boothby, on the other hand, was deemed 'youthful enough to go anywhere and follow anyone if the individual attracts him'.

103. Ramsden, *A History of the Conservative Party, vol. III*, p. 292.

104. *Perthshire Advertiser*, 8 May 1929.

105. *Perthshire Advertiser*, 15 May 1929.

106. D. R. Thorpe, *Eden: The Life and Times of Anthony Eden, First Earl of Avon 1897–1977* (London: Chatto & Windus, 2003), pp. 41–2.

107. *Perthshire Advertiser*, 22 May 1929.

108. *Perthshire Advertiser*, 29 May 1929.

109. The 1929 general election was the first in which women under the age of thirty had been allowed to vote.

110. *Perthshire Advertiser*, 31 May 1929.

Chapter 5: 'My political bolt is shot'

1. Terence O'Connor lost his seat, as did Harold Macmillan in Stockton.

2. John Ramsden, *A History of the Conservative Party, vol. III: The Age of Balfour and Baldwin 1902–1940* (London: Longman, 1978), p. 292.

3. Conservative & Unionist Associations & Clubs, MS152 13/1/1.

4. When Lord Scone succeeded to the peerage in early 1935 the Liberal Francis Norie-Miller finally secured the seat at the resulting by-election, only to lose it to the Unionists at the general election a few months later.

5. Gerald Warner, *The Scottish Tory Party: A History* (London: Weidenfeld & Nicolson, 1988), p. 192.

6. The 'Unionist' nomenclature remained until 1965, when Edward Heath changed it to the 'Scottish Conservative and Unionist Party'.

7. Hansard, HC Deb, 19 July 1927, vol. 209, cols 323–4.

8. Hansard, HC Deb, 26 July 1929, vol. 230, col. 1666.

9. Hansard, HC Deb, 1929, vol. 229, cols 949–50.

10. Noel Skelton to Katharine Tennant, 4 July 1929, Baroness Elliot of Harwood papers.

11. Skelton to Tennant, 8 July 1929.

12. Skelton to Tennant, 10 July 1929.

13. Skelton to Tennant, 15 July 1929.

14. Skelton to Tennant, 19 July 1929.

15. Skelton to Tennant, 24 July 1929.

16. Skelton to Tennant, 3 August 1929.

17. Skelton to Tennant, 8 August 1929.

18. Skelton to Tennant, 26 August 1929.

19. Skelton to Tennant, c. September 1929.

20. Skelton to Tennant, 4 September 1929.

21. Skelton to Tennant, 25 September 1929.

22. Skelton to Tennant, 29 October 1929.

23. Skelton to Tennant, 17 December 1929. Katharine eventually outlived Skelton by nearly sixty years.

24. Noel Skelton to Harold Macmillan, 16 October 1929, Macmillan dep, c. 862, ff. 311–12.

25. Harold Macmillan, *Winds of Change 1914–1939* (London: Macmillan, 1966), p. 256.

26. Skelton to Macmillan, 5 November 1929, ff. 314-15.

27. Macmillan, *Winds of Change*, p. 256.

28. Susan Tweedsmuir, *John Buchan, by His Wife and Friends* (London: Hodder & Stoughton, 1947), p. 207.

29. Hansard, HC Deb, 29 October 1929, vol. 231, col. 24.

30. Hansard, HC Deb, 7 November 1929, vol. 231, col. 1380.

31. Hansard, HC Deb, 18 December 1929, vol. 233, col. 1584.

32. William 'Billy' Ormsby-Gore (1885–1964) was the Conservative MP for Denbigh from 1910 to 1918 and Stafford from 1918 to 1938. He was twice under-secretary for the colonies between 1922 and 1929, and Postmaster-General and first commissioner of works in the National Government from 1931 to 1936.

33. Anthony Eden, *The Eden Memoirs, vol. I: Facing the Dictators* (London: Cassell, 1962), pp. 11–12. William Shepherd Morrison (1893–1961) was Conservative MP for Cirencester & Tewkesbury from 1929 to 1959 and acquired the nickname 'Shakes' through his habit of quoting Shakespeare. 'Equipped with dark and glowing eyes beneath a thatch of white hair and a vibrant Highland voice' (C. R. Coote, *Editorial: The Memoirs of Colin R. Coote* (London: Eyre & Spottiswoode, 1965), p. 161), he was parliamentary secretary to the Attorney-General from 1931 to 1935 and Speaker of the House of Commons from 1951 to 1959.

34. Eden, *The Eden Memoirs, vol. 1*, pp. 11–12.

35. Coote, *Editorial*, p. 151. John Strachey was a Labour MP and the son of Skelton's former editor, John St Loe Strachey.

36. Skelton to Tennant, 16 January 1930.

37. Tweedsmuir, *John Buchan*, p. 207.

38. *Yorkshire Post*, 21 January 1930.

39. Skelton to Tennant, 15 January 1930.

40. *Yorkshire Post*, 22 January 1930.

41. *Yorkshire Post*, 23 January 1930.

42. *Yorkshire Post*, 24 January 1930.

43. Eden, *The Eden Memoirs, vol. 1*, pp. 13–14.

44. *Quarterly Review* (1931), vol. 257, no. 509. John Gretton (1867–1947) was Conservative MP for Burton from 1918 to 1943. Britain had been forced to abandon its imperial concession at the port of Hankow following Chinese nationalist riots in 1927.

45. *The Times*, 30 October 1930.

46. This discovery was recorded in John Loder's 1935 book, *Colonsay and Oransay in the Isles of Argyll: Their History, Flora, Fauna and Topography* (Edinburgh and London: Oliver & Boyd).

47. Skelton to Tennant, 3 January 1930.

48. Skelton to Tennant, 31 August 1930.

49. Skelton to Tennant, 9 September 1930. Cyril John Radcliffe was a lawyer and fellow at All Souls. Ironically, in 1939 he married Antonia Mary Roby, the former wife of Katharine's brother, John Tennant.

50. Hansard, HC Deb, 13 November 1930, vol. 244, cols 1977–8.

51. Hansard, HC Deb, 20 November 1930, vol. 245, cols 760–61.

52. Ramsden, *A History of the Conservative Party, vol. 3*, p. 314. Baldwin was paraphrasing his cousin, the poet and writer Rudyard Kipling.

53. Skelton to Tennant, 23 April 1931, Walter and Katharine Elliot papers, Acc 12267 (28).

54. *Quarterly Review* (1931), vol. 257, no. 509. The Duchess of Atholl remembered Labour MPs being very sensitive about Russia. 'On one occasion, my friend Noel Skelton met with so much interruption every time he pronounced the word "Russia" that he ended by referring to it as "the country which cannot be named".' (Duchess of Atholl, *Working Partnership: Being the Lives of John George, 8th Duke of Atholl and of His Wife Katharine Marjory Ramsay* (London: Arthur Barker, 1958), p. 188.)

55. *Quarterly Review* (1931), vol 257., no. 509.

56. Skelton to Tennant, 23 January 1931.

57. Skelton to Tennant, 13 February 1931.

58. Skelton to Tennant, 16 February 1931.

59. Skelton to Tennant, 23 April 1931.

60. Skelton to Tennant, 25 April 1931.

61. Skelton to Tennant, 10 May 1931. This was a collection of Eden's foreign policy articles for the *Yorkshire Post*, which had been published by John Murray in 1926.

62. Skelton to Tennant, 12 May 1931.

63. Skelton to Tennant, 26 May 1931. This, unfortunately, could not be traced.

64. Skelton to Tennant, 11 July 1931.

65. Skelton to Tennant, 21 July 1931.

66. Skelton to Tennant, undated.

67. Skelton to Tennant, 25 July 1931.

68. Tweedsmuir, *John Buchan*, p. 204.

69. Skelton to Tennant, 31 July 1931.

70. Skelton to Tennant, 13 August 1931.

71. Skelton to Tennant, 11 August 1931.

72. Skelton to Tennant, 28 July 1931. The Nazi leader, Adolf Hitler, had recently formed a pact with the German National leader, Alfred Hugenberg, while the question of Anschluss, the union of Germany and Austria, had again become pertinent.

73. Skelton to Tennant, 14 August 1931.

74. Skelton to Tennant, 16 August 1931.

75. Skelton to Tennant, 17 August 1931.

76. Skelton to Tennant, 19 August 1931.

77. Skelton to Tennant, 17 August 1931.

78. According to Cuthbert Headlam, Skelton had 'a rooted objection' to Mosley, whom he had encountered while staying with Oliver Stanley (Stuart Ball (ed.),

Parliament and Politics in the Age of Baldwin and MacDonald: The Headlam Diaries 1923–1935 (London: Historians' Press, 1992), p. 193).

79. Skelton to Tennant, 23 August 1931.

80. Coote, *A Companion of Honour: The Story of Walter Elliot* (London: Collins, 1965), p. 123.

81. Skelton to Tennant, 24 August 1931.

82. Skelton to Tennant, 27 August 1931.

83. Skelton to Tennant, 28 August 1931.

84. Skelton to Tennant, 29 August 1931.

85. Skelton to Tennant, 3 September 1931. Skelton sent Katharine a telegram in France the same day. It read: 'Love from Archie's understudy – Noel.'

86. Skelton to Macmillan, 9 September 1931, Macmillan dep c. 862, f. 249.

Chapter 6: 'A short life and not a very merry one'

1. The Welsh Office was created in 1964, while the Northern Ireland Office followed in 1972.

2. It seems that Skelton's friend John Buchan had been offered the post, but declined.

3. The Marquis of Reading was Foreign Secretary, but since he was a member of the House of Lords, Eden became the de facto foreign minister in the House of Commons.

4. C. R. Coote, *Editorial: The Memoirs of Colin R. Coote* (London: Eyre & Spottiswoode, 1965), p. 160.

5. *The Times*, 19 September 1931.

6. The Combined Scottish Universities constituency elected three MPs by single transferable vote to represent graduates of the four ancient Scottish universities, Edinburgh, Glasgow, St Andrews and Aberdeen. The seat was abolished following the Second World War and ceased to exist at the 1950 election.

7. *The Scotsman*, 12 October 1931. 'With deep respect to Mr Noel Skelton,' someone wrote after his death, 'his transfer from the Perth Division to the University representation was, as is known to all of us, an arrangement of convenience carried out "through the usual channels".' (*The Times*, 28 November 1935.)

8. *Glasgow Herald*, 22 August 1931.

9. *The Scotsman*, 14 October 1931.

10. *The Scotsman*, 21 October 1931. This unfortunate trio represented the only Labour ministers to remain in the government. All three were expelled from the Labour Party as a result.

11. *The Scotsman*, 21 October 1931.

12. *Glasgow Evening Times*, 20 October 1931.

13. 27 October was a Tuesday, and was the last time a UK general election was held on a day other than Thursday.

14. George Pottinger, *The Secretaries of State for Scotland 1926–76: Fifty Years of the Scottish Office* (Edinburgh: Scottish Academic Press, 1979), p. 50.

15. When Skelton died in November 1935, Colville replaced him as under-secretary at the Scottish Office.

16. Coote, *Editorial*, p. 160.

17. Kenneth Young, *Sir Alec Douglas-Home* (London: J. M. Dent, 1970), p. 28.

18. Later Sir Charles, he remembered that Skelton was a 'very stimulating minister [who] had produced a lively book about Conservative policy before becoming an under-secretary of state. He had both an enquiring and critical mind and was very receptive to ideas.' (Scotland's Record Acc 7330 55–6.)

19. Skelton to Tennant, 14 January 1932, Baroness Elliot of Harwood papers.

20. Skelton to Tennant, 20 January 1932.

21. Skelton to Tennant, 8 April 1932.

22. Skelton to Tennant, 26 June 1932.

23. *The Scotsman*, 17 March 1932.

24. *The Scotsman*, 21 May 1932. Addison houses were thus named after Christopher Addison (1869–1951), who, as the first Minister of Health, pioneered the provision of state-built housing.

25. *The Scotsman*, 21 May 1932.

26. Hansard, HC Deb, 22 June 1932, vol. 267, col. 1124.

27. *The Scotsman*, 28 November 1932.

28. Collins was also, like Skelton, in increasingly poor health.

29. The Scottish Secretary gave Skelton, 'who, I may say, has been very helpful to me' (Hansard, HC Deb, 24 November 1932, vol. 272, col. 299), additional responsibilities for Scottish education, as well as housing and health.

30. *The Scotsman*, 5 November 1932.

31. Scottish Office papers, HH1/799.

32. Hansard, HC Deb, 24 November 1932, vol. 272, cols 250–51. 'The debate on the Address continued and was duller than ever as it was devoted to the discussion of Scottish Home Rule!' wrote Sir Cuthbert Headlam in his diary. 'Apparently this movement is becoming a serious one – what an age of absurdity we live in!' (Stuart Ball (ed.), *Parliament and Politics in the Age of Baldwin and MacDonald: The Headlam Diaries 1923–1935* (London: Historians' Press, 1992), entry for 28 September 1932).

33. Hansard, HC Deb, 24 November 1932, vol. 272, cols 294–8.

34. Hansard, HC Deb, 24 November 1932, vol. 272, cols 353–60.

35. *The Scotsman*, 2 July 1934.

36. *The Scotsman*, 1 December 1932.

37. *The Scotsman*, 30 December 1932.

38. *The Scotsman*, 10 July 1933.

39. *The Scotsman*, 6 May 1933.

40. Hansard, HC Deb, 26 July 1934, vol. 292, col. 2023.

41. *The Scotsman*, 22 February 1934.

42. *The Scotsman*, 27 January 1934.

43. *The Scotsman*, 10 February 1934.

44. *The Times*, 16 March 1934.

45. 'Mr Walter Elliot weds Miss Tennant', British Movietone News no. 252A (BFI National Library).

46. Katharine's nephew, the present Lord Crathorne, says his aunt never once mentioned Skelton to him, although she did confess the affair to the historian D. R. Thorpe when he mentioned having seen Skelton's letters in the library at her home, Harwood House. Walter Elliot died in 1958, and K in 1994; there were no children.

47. Hansard, HC Deb, 27 March 1934, vol. 287, col. 1843.

48. Ian Levitt (ed.), *The Scottish Office: Depression and Reconstruction 1919–1959* (Edinburgh: Scottish History Society, 1992), p. 90.

49. Ball, *Parliament and Politics in the Age of Baldwin and MacDonald*, p. 300.

50. Eden led the delegation, which also included the Foreign Secretary, John Simon, also leader of the National Liberals.

51. *The Scotsman*, 22 September 1934.

52. *The Scotsman*, 12 November 1934.

53. Following dinner with Skelton on 6 March 1935, Sir Cuthbert Headlam noted that he disapproved of a note 'chiding Germany' recently dispatched by the Prime Minister, Ramsay MacDonald (Ball, *Parliament and Politics in the Age of Baldwin and MacDonald*, p. 234).

54. *The Scotsman*, 9 January 1935.

55. *The Scotsman*, 2 February 1935.

56. *The Scotsman*, 18 February 1935.

57. Hansard, HC Deb, 21 February 1935, vol. 298, cols 666–8.

58. *The Scotsman*, 20 April 1935.

59. *The Scotsman*, 20 June 1935.

60. *The Scotsman*, 18 August 1935.

61. *The Scotsman*, 28 August 1935.

62. *The Scotsman*, 22 October 1935.

Chapter 7: 'A man of ideals, and a man of vision'

1. Hugh Fraser, *The Representation of the People Act 1918, with Explanatory Notes* (London: Sweet & Maxwell, 1918), p. 5.

2. *The Scotsman*, 23 November 1935. The situation, however, was not unprecedented. At the 1906 general election, Mr T. Higgins, an Irish Nationalist, won North Galway but died on polling day. And in 1929, Mr H. Yates, the Labour candidate for Rugby, died three days before polling day, and the election had to be postponed.

3. *The Times*, 23 November 1935.

4. *The Scotsman*, 23 November 1935.

5. *The Times*, 23 November 1935.

6. *The Scotsman*, 23 November 1935.

7. 'I think perhaps Noel's epitaph might be', Lady Tweedsmuir added, 'that he preferred, in a world of mass-production and mass-movements, quality in all things rather than quantity' (Susan Tweedsmuir, *John Buchan, by His Wife and Friends* (London: Hodder & Stoughton, 1947), pp. 202–4).

8. *The Times*, 25 November 1935.

9. *Perthshire Advertiser*, 27 November 1935.

10. *The Scotsman*, 26 November 1935.

11. Evelyn Skelton died aged seventy-six. In her will, she made allowance for unclaimed money from her estate to fund a trio of scholarships to commemorate her brother at Trinity College, Glenalmond, Christ Church College, Oxford, and the University of Edinburgh. These were never established.

12. *The Times*, 30 November 1935.

Chapter 8: 'A property-owning democracy is the aim'

1. Nick Lee, 'Creating a "Property-owning Democracy": the Conservative Party and Popular Capitalism 1918–1951' (2007), MA dissertation, University of Durham, p. 48.

2. Harold Macmillan, *Winds of Change 1914–1939* (London: Macmillan, 1966), p. 178.

3. D. R. Thorpe, *Eden: The Life and Times of Anthony Eden, First Earl of Avon 1897–1977* (London: Chatto & Windus, 2003), p. 81.

4. Anthony Eden, *The Eden Memoirs, vol. I: Facing the Dictators* (London: Cassell, 1962), p. 12.

5. Thorpe, *Eden*, pp. 613–17.

6. John Ramsden, *The Age of Churchill and Eden* (London: Longman, 1995), p. 141.

7. *The Times*, 7 October 1948.

8. *The Times*, 9 March 1949.

9. *The Times*, 19 March 1949.

10. *The Times*, 28 January 1952.

11. *The Scotsman*, 15 February 1950. Churchill's phraseology was reminiscent of Skelton's, who wrote: 'We have yet to hear of a man who, in the Great War, rushed to arms to preserve his share in the London County Council Tramways or in Battersea Park' (*The Spectator*, 12 May 1923).

12. Macmillan dep c13/1 f89.

13. *The Times*, 29 November 1951.

14. Harold Macmillan, *Tides of Fortune 1945–1955* (London: Macmillan, 1969), p. 373.

15. Anthony Crosland, *The Future of Socialism*, new ed. (London: Constable, 2006), p. 306.

16. *The Times*, 13 November 1958.

17. Alistair Horne, *Harold Macmillan, vol. II: 1957–1986* (London: Macmillan, 1988), p. 554.

18. Lord Home, *The Way the Wind Blows: An Autobiography* (London: Collins, 1976), p. 59.

19. Lord Avon to Douglas-Home, 28 September 1964, Avon papers, AP 23/27/35.

20. David Dutton, *Anthony Eden: A Life and Reputation* (London: Hodder Arnold, 1996), p. 260. Clarissa Eden urged Eden's second authorised biographer, D. R. Thorpe, to emphasise Skelton's influence upon her late husband.

21. www.margaretthatcher.org/speeches/displaydocument.asp?docid=102777.

22. *Crossbow*, 29 August 1975.

23. www.margaretthatcher.org/speeches/displaydocument.asp?docid=102801.

24. www.margaretthatcher.org/speeches/displaydocument.asp?docid=103029.

25. Hansard, HC Deb, 15 May 1979, vol. 967, cols 73–87.

26. *The Times*, 4 August 1982.

27. Hansard, HL Deb, 5 June 1985, vol. 464, col. 785.

28. *The Guardian*, 30 January 2006, www.guardian.co.uk/politics/2006/jan/30/conservatives.davidcameron. Cameron was still using the phrase more than a year later. 'Disraeli . . . cleared the slums, legalised trade unions,' he enthused. 'Macmillan and Butler continued that tradition by emphasising housing and a share-owning, property-owning democracy' (*Sunday Times*, 22 April 2007).

29. Hansard, HC Deb, 9 April 2003, vol. 403, col. 286.

30. *The Herald*, 14 May 2007.

31. *The Guardian*, 4 September 2007.

32. Cabinet Office press release, CAB 120-09, 15 December 2009.

33. *The Guardian*, 15 February 2010.

34. www.respublica.org.uk/articles/ownership-state.

35. *The Guardian*, 11 February 2009.

36. www.historyandpolicy.org/opinion/opinion_25.html.

37. John Ramsden, *A History of the Conservative Party, vol. III: The Age of Balfour and Baldwin 1902–1940* (London: Longman, 1978), p. 207.

INDEX